Growing Up Fast

Transitions to Early Adulthood
of Inner-City Adolescent Mothers

Research Monographs in Adolescence
Nancy L. Galambos/Nancy A. Busch-Rossnagel, Editors

Growing Up Fast

Transitions to Early Adulthood
of Inner-City Adolescent Mothers

Bonnie J. Ross Leadbeater
University of Victoria, Canada

Niobe Way
New York University

LAWRENCE ERLBAUM ASSOCIATES, PUBLISHERS
Mahwah, New Jersey   London

Lawrence Erlbaum Associates, Inc., Publishers
10 Industrial Avenue
Mahwah, NJ 07430

Cover design by Kathryn Houghtaling Lacey

Library of Congress Cataloging-in-Publication Data

Leadbeater, Bonnie J. Ross, 1950–
Growing up fast : transitions to early adulthood of inner-city
    adolescent mothers / by Bonnie J. Ross Leadbeater and
    Niobe Way.
        p. cm.
Includes bibliographical references and index.
ISBN 0-8058-3736-1 (cloth : alk. paper)
    1. Teenage mothers—United States.   I. Way, Niobe,
    1963–   II. Title.

HQ759.4 .L43   2000
306.874'3'0973—dc21   00-037638
                                                      CIP

Books published by Lawrence Erlbaum Associates are printed on
acid-free paper, and their bindings are chosen for strength and
durability.

Printed in the United States of America
10 9 8 7 6 5 4 3 2 1

To Emilie
and
to all children
who inspire their parents
to become better people

Contents

Series Editors' Foreword

Nancy L. Galambos
University of Victoria, Canada

Nancy A. Busch-Rossnagel
Fordham University

It is with great pleasure that we introduce *Growing Up Fast: Transitions to Early Adulthood of Inner-City Adolescent Mothers* by Bonnie Leadbeater and Niobe Way. This book marks a transition in the Research Monographs in Adolescence series. The aim of this series is, as it has been since the first monograph appeared in 1994, to present the finest in scholarly thinking and research on adolescent development. With this volume, a new look to the series can been seen—a look that increases the accessibility of these books to a wider audience, including not only scholars and upper level undergraduate and graduate students, but also professionals and members of the public.

First, a new format for this series aims to attract those who wish to learn more about the adolescent experience without getting lost in the detail of the methods and analyses. To this end, the main body of the text presents general methods and results. Scholarly details of the work are placed in appendixes to which the interested reader can refer. A second highlight of this new look is the inclusion of impressionistic material, such as quotes from the adolescent mothers who were participants in this research. Such material brings to life the real issues of very real adolescents—their triumphs and struggles, their riches and poverty, their strengths and weaknesses.

This volume serves as an excellent example of the new format in our series. More than that, it serves as an ideal model of the important uses of qualitative research for understanding the adolescent experience. In this book, the authors draw on their in-depth examination of inner-city adolescent mothers to make constructive suggestions for social welfare policies and reforms. This book stands out among others by its social policy perspective and its focus on encouraging adolescent mothers to reach their potentials. We congratulate the authors for their valuable contribution to research on adolescence.

Preface

In 1987, when the research described in this book was just getting started, teenage parenting was generally thought of as a social problem of epidemic proportions that served to reproduce cycles of intergenerational poverty. Teenage parenting was considered to be a marker of a general problem-behavior syndrome for girls that might also include promiscuity, school dropout, and alcohol abuse. What we overlooked in our focus on risk statistics and pathology, particularly for minority group, poor, inner-city mothers, was that the majority of them do not demonstrate long-term negative outcomes. Ground breaking, longitudinal research by Furstenberg and his colleagues in Baltimore focused attention on subgroup differences in outcomes for women who became mothers as teenagers in the 1950s and began to reveal a very different picture of their development. Becoming an adolescent parent can compound multiple, preexisting adversities (e.g., inner-city poverty, minority status, learning disabilities, school failure, housing instability, etc.) or can contribute to reduced problems among young women who are inspired to make something of themselves on behalf of their child. Life-span outcomes are not static. They are affected positively or negatively by turning points (like dropping out of school), but these outcomes are based on past adversities and resources of individuals, their families, and their communities, and they anticipate the future opportunities that are available. There is a need for researchers and policymakers to increase attention to the variations in individuals and families' responses to adversities, the nature of the actual adversities that young mothers face, and the developmental pathways and processes that support strengths and positive changes for these young women and their children.

This book is among the first to report on the strengths of poor adolescent mothers whose children were born in the last decade and to clarify the nature of the current obstacles to acquiring the capacity for independent living that is now normative for young women in Western cultures. It not only presents data from a 6-year longitudinal study of young mothers, but also allows these women to tell their own stories in their own words. This book directs attention to intervention points where small investments in supporting women's strengths would yield large gains over time in advancing their abilities to permanently exit poverty. This book bridges gaps between researchers, program developers, and policymakers with a new approach to understanding the nature of this pressing social problem. We hope that our readers will include not only academic researchers, but also students, educators, program developers, young mothers themselves, and—perhaps most importantly—the policymakers who have the power to make a real difference inspired by the lives of these young women.

ACKNOWLEDGMENTS

This research was funded by grants from the Smith Richardson, Spencer, and Spring Foundations. It was also supported by a William T. Grant Faculty Scholars Grant to Bonnie Leadbeater and a National Institute of Mental Health Postdoctoral Fellowship to Niobe Way. We also appreciate the assistance of Leslie Jaffee, Angela Diaz, Linda Levin, Oriana Linares, and the staff of the Mount Sinai Hospital, Adolescent Health Center in developing this research and supporting our presence in the center during this work. A number of energetic graduate students at Yale University also contributed to the thinking and data analyses for this project, including Cybelle Raver, Sandra Bishop, Adena Bargad, Tony Raden, and Jean Turner. Research assistants contributing greatly to this project were Jane Christman, Ginny Knight, and Tricia Harmon. Several undergraduates also made this project work and contributed to our thinking, including Sara Buchdahl, J'Ingrid Clemons, Maryanne Ludwig, Sascha Meinrath, and Mialisa Villafane. Susan Doyle provided valued editorial assistance. The imagination, knowledge, and encouragement of several mentors and colleagues are also gratefully acknowledged, including Larry Aber, Joseph Allen, Betty Hamburg, and Gabe Kuperminc. Finally, we thank the young mothers who participated in this work for their efforts to educate us and for the inspiration that their ability to succeed in adverse circumstances gives to our own struggles with life's adversities.

—Bonnie J. Ross Leadbeater
—Niobe Way

CHAPTER

1

Introduction:
Beyond the Stereotypes:
What Kind of Problem
Is Teenage Parenting?

Ample research has demonstrated the long- and short-term consequences and social costs of teenage parenting (see Furstenberg, Brooks-Gunn, & Morgan, 1987; Harris, 1997; Hayes, 1987; Lawson & Rhodes, 1993; Musick, 1993; Nathanson, 1991). Recent volumes have also presented statistical trends in adolescent childbearing (e.g., Hayes, 1987), addressed the psychology of teenage mothers who have been sexually abused (Musick, 1993), and presented historical and political issues related to adolescent childbirth and parenting (e.g., Lawson & Rhodes, 1993; Luker, 1996; Nathanson, 1991). This research paints a clear, consistent picture of the enduring difficulties that accompany too early parenting, as well as the clear economic advantages of postponing parenthood in favor of advanced education. However, risk statistics comparing outcomes for adolescent mothers with those who delay childbearing until after age 20 and models that identify predictors of negative outcomes for adolescent mothers and their children can give the misleading impression that such risks, even when small, are certainties for adolescent mothers.

Indeed the stereotypical adolescent mother persists. She is a poor, often African-American or Hispanic female school dropout who is a victim of disadvantaged social circumstances, male sexual advances, and the inability to "just say no" to her own sexual urges. Her adolescence and education interrupted prematurely, she is haplessly thrust into a life course of welfare dependence as the single parent of a succession of out-of-wedlock children. She has also become the symbol of an array of interrelated social problems including increases in teenage sexual activity, the number of female-headed households, young children living in poverty, and welfare costs. It is these images with which adolescent mothers struggle, which they resist, and, in some cases, become in their rapid transition to young adulthood.

Although nationally only 30% of teen mothers fail to graduate from high school and only 3% have more than three children (Alan Guttmacher Institute, 1994), teenage mothers who become responsible, productive young parents are mistakenly seen as the resilient exceptions to the norm. Newspaper anecdotes occasionally outline the harried life of this exceptional adolescent mother who struggles against great odds to stay in school or find work. The lack of under-standing of the within-group differences in adolescent mothers' transitions into early adulthood fuels myths and misconceptions of their inevitable doom. Not knowing who does well, despite high-risk circumstances, and why, renders a uni-form picture of social and personal failure that discourages policy analysts, pro-gram developers, potential employers, and the adolescent mothers from envisioning more positive futures.

Policy development continues to address the needs of the stereotypical teen mother. Failure to witness the successes as well as the hardships of young mothers undermines intervention efforts. Focusing solely on the insurmountable needs of the mythical adolescent mother of three or more children who has a ninth-grade education and lives on welfare in substandard housing means less attention is given to the obstacles that threaten to derail working adolescent mothers. By ig-noring the majority who succeed, we fail to capitalize on the motivations and sup-ports that propel these adolescent mothers to strive to improve their own and their children's futures. As our expectations for these young families are limited, so too is the search for cost-effective, targeted interventions that can address the specific needs of those mothers who can benefit from them.

FOCUSING ON DIVERSITY

This book seeks to broaden knowledge of the life options open to and sought by African-American and Hispanic poor adolescent mothers from New York City. When pictured among a collage of negative stereotypes of teenage mothers, the young women from the Harlem and Bronx districts who were participants in what we refer to as the "New York study" of adolescent mothers are among those least expected to succeed. Yet we focus precisely on this group because their lives illu-minate the diverse pathways to young adulthood that these young women continu-ously construct and reconstruct. Becoming a parent was a turning point in all their lives, but they responded to this event as individuals with differing abilities, aspira-tions, and supports. They surprise us most with the diversity of their solutions to living in poverty and with the intensity of their desire to make their children's lives better. They also surprise us with the height of their youthful ambition when they succeed and the depth of their pain when they fail. We argue that adolescent moth-ers who enter young adulthood with the skills and desires to care for themselves and their children are not the resilient few. Rather, we examine the multidimen-sional processes that characterize the resilience in some areas of their lives of the majority of these young women.

Our progress in dealing with the problems of teenage parents has been blocked by sharp divisions over the causes of teenage parenting (poverty, sexual promiscuity, limited access to contraception or abortions, poor educational opportunities). Little agreement exists on how adolescent childbearing should be dealt with (prevention, punishment, or intervention) or by whom (individual, family, or state controls).

Embedded in the controversy are fragments of past social, health, and moral debates that fail to accommodate changing roles for women. Those who would respond to increased adolescent sexual activity with education about responsible contraception use still square off against those who advocate abstinence to end teenage promiscuity. Advocates of costly comprehensive services to improve the education and employability of teenage mothers are opposed by those who believe these services do nothing to deter poor teens from delivering out-of-wedlock babies. There is a clear need to move beyond statistical portrayals of adolescent mothers' lives to examine the processes that support (or thwart) their successful transitions to young adulthood. More streamlined, targeted, and flexible solutions are needed to adjust to reductions in welfare spending, but cost-effective solutions must be informed by a clear understanding of the varied needs of adolescent mothers in the 1990s.

THE PATHWAYS TO ADULTHOOD
FOR ADOLESCENT MOTHERS

Although only applying to girls in the last quarter of the 20th century, there is considerable consensus that the major developmental tasks of adolescence should involve gaining the means, through education or job experience, to become independent, both economically and in residence. We are accustomed to thinking that children and adolescents follow a linear path of incremental progress toward these outcomes in early adulthood.

Children's physical development clearly follows an upward growth trajectory punctuated by periods of relative acceleration (e.g., in beginning to walk and talk or entering puberty). These changes monumentally affect the ways that children interact with, and are seen by, their families and community. We believe that children show a similar path in their mental, social, and emotional development as they become progressively more educated, more responsible, more independent, more mature, more able to solve problems, and, eventually, more independent of their parents. These changes are accelerated by societally timed events like entering kindergarten or graduating from high school, which progressively demand children's increased interactions with widening social worlds. We argue that the diversity in the pathways to adulthood for young women reflects dramatic changes in normative views about women's relationship to work, marriage, and children. Beliefs about what is natural or predictable about adolescents' growth also carry with them societal hopes and, indeed, requirements for their social and economic progress.

However, events that disrupt this progression are seen as challenging or potentially derailing a child's natural course of development. Bearing a child as a teenager is one such disruption. From a societal perspective, this event represents a decisive and negative turning point in an adolescent's development—one that essentially renames teenage girls "teenage mothers," thus abruptly and prematurely ending their adolescence. Yet, ironically, there is considerable stability in developmental transitions even as dramatic as this one. Rutter and Rutter (1993) cogently described the connection between discontinuity and continuity in development across the life span:

> It is one thing to accept the crucial nature of the transformation and it is quite another to suppose that it has no connection with what has gone before and that it wipes clean the tape of past skills and experiences. (p. 68)

There is no doubt that having a baby as a teenager can be a critical transforming event, but this event alone neither erases the tape of past experiences nor determines future ones. The internal and external resources that determine all adolescents' responses to the challenges and demands of early adult development (be they parenting, work, or college) build up over their lives. Statistical snapshots focusing on the birth of a child to a teenager can wipe clean past hardships and successes, as well as variations among the resources and abilities that minimize the effects of having a child at a young age.

WHAT DOES IT MEAN TO BE GROWN?

There is considerable ambivalence and debate about the developmental status of adolescent mothers and the standards against which adulthood should be assessed for these women. The majority of adolescent mothers are 18 years or older and, as such, are eligible for many of the privileges of adulthood. Nevertheless, researchers, programmers, and the public alike frequently refer to them as *kids having kids* (Maynard, 1997). However, policymakers insist that these children-come-mothers should be expected to finish high school and get jobs to support their offspring. Is a sexually experienced woman of 18 who has given birth to a child an adult? As one doctor told a young mother at the delivery of her child: "You are a woman now." When is a woman still a child?

What growing up means for adolescent mothers reflects not only their personal goals, abilities, and talents, but also social prescriptions and opportunities for their adult behavior. In any society, being recognized as an adult is conditional on meeting certain culturally specific requirements, such as graduating from high school or college, demonstrating financial independence, or getting married. We might wonder how these adolescent mothers would define successful early adult transitions.

It has frequently been argued that in poor cultures with few opportunities for employment, becoming a mother may confer on young girls adult status and a modicum of respect that otherwise might not seem accessible. Although none of the women in the New York study of adolescent mothers described themselves as "children," their responses when asked what it means to be a woman clearly suggest that adulthood is also more than motherhood for many of them. In her reply, one young mother clearly recognized the difference:

Young girls, where I live, they have kids. And they have the attitude, oh, you know, I'm grown now. I've got my own baby. Wake up! You're not grown, you only have a child, you're only a mother.... Grown people, quote unquote, have responsibilities such as paying their own rent, living in their own apartment, fending for their own selves, not depending on welfare. When you start doing those things for yourself, then you're grown.[1]

Many of the young mothers in the New York study agreed on these markers of adulthood. Financial independence and being able to support one's children were central to feeling grown up, but so too was having an apartment—being in one's own place. A working mother of two children described it this way: "In one sense I do [consider myself really a woman], but the only thing I think is holding me up right now from really putting myself as the title, as a woman, is me still being with my mother."

One third of the mothers in the New York study were working mothers—store clerks, dental assistants, bank tellers, nurse's aides, computer operators, janitors. We describe their ambitions and strategies for coping with the stresses of work and family. Like the stereotype, many mothers in the New York study (69%) were on welfare 6 years after delivery, but even these young women did not comprise a single group. Many of the mothers on welfare were able to use the financial help they received to advance their skills and education. For a few mothers, welfare dependence seemed their life plan. For others, it was a default position—a last resort in the face of serious illnesses, learning disabilities, or traumas.

CHAPTER OUTLINES AND PREVIEW OF KEY FINDINGS

This chapter outlines far-reaching changes in the historical and social contexts that have framed adolescent parenting as a social problem over the past half century. Current debates reflect long-standing disagreements about the nature of this problem. Is it a moral problem rising from the counterculture values of youth that began in the 1960s? Is it a medical problem related to inadequate knowledge about, or lack of access to, heath education, health care, or contraception? Is it rooted in poverty, joblessness, or educational disadvantage? How are changing roles for women and men implicated? In 1950, a majority of women in their early 20s were engaged in full-time childrearing; only 11% of women with children under age 6 were in the labor force; by 1994, this number was 61.7% (Children's Defense Fund, 1995). Is teenage parenting a social problem fueled by increased demands for a more educated and skilled labor force? Is it a function of changing marriage patterns or a decline in marriageable men—especially in poor communities? Is teenage parenting a manifestation of intergenerational values passed from teenage mothers to their daughters?

---

[1] Pseudonyms were assigned to all mothers participating in the study, and identifying information has been changed for the protection of their privacy.

We address each of these questions briefly in an effort to set the stage for understanding the historical and social context of this problem. We argue that the combined effects of increasing adolescent sexual activity, rising contraceptive use by teens, declining adolescent pregnancies, increasing demands for women to be educated and work, higher costs of childrearing, and declines in marriage and marriageable males create the context in which parenting has become clearly off-time for adolescent women in the 1990s. Indeed, in the current context, parenting as an adolescent can spuriously reflect both socially deviant and morally (or sexually) irresponsible individual choices. However, this view fuels the stereotype of adolescent mothers that undermines efforts to create real understanding of the problem in the 1990s and real solutions. Data from the New York study suggest that having a child as an adolescent is more than an individual choice—embedded as it is in this complex and changing social context.

Chapter 2 ends with a detailed description of the participants in the New York study—a 6-year study of inner-city, poor, minority group adolescent mothers and their children. They were aged 14 to 18 when their children were born and were recruited from a community-based health center where they brought their children for well baby care at least once in the first month of the children' life. All came from Manhattan or Bronx counties—communities with extreme density, poverty, minority group concentration, unemployment, single-parent families, school dropout, and crime. The 1991 census data (Kids Count, New York State, 1994) indicate that 33% of children in New York City were living below the poverty line. Bronx county had the highest rate of any county: Half of the children were poor.

Chapter 3 discusses the concept of resilience as it informs our understanding of the within-group differences in adolescent mothers' transitions to early adulthood. Beyond identifying resilient individuals as the exceptional success story, we highlight the constellation of individual strengths as well as the contextual circumstances that allowed a majority of mothers in the New York study to successfully adapt to early adulthood at least in some domains of their lives. We begin with a qualitative review of the interview data of a group of 15 mothers who, by the 6-year follow-up, had graduated from high school, went on to college or work, and reported good physical and mental health (low levels of depressive symptoms). Themes identified in these young women's descriptions of their experiences as inner-city teenage mothers demonstrate the interrelated processes of resilience that facilitated their adaptive transitions to early adulthood. These themes recur throughout this book as predictors of positive outcomes for the majority of the adolescent mothers, and their absence often marks the stories of mothers who do not enter early adulthood on an equal footing to their peers.

Using a quantitative approach to data analyses, chapter 4 reports on the predictors of school and employment outcomes for these adolescent mothers. By the 6-year follow-up, 52% of the New York sample of mothers had graduated from high school, 14% had some college, and 37% were employed full or part time. Better school and work outcomes depended largely on the mothers' pre pregnancy school achievement, but within-group differences in depressive symptoms, repeat pregnancies, and stressful life events were found for mothers who (a) consistently attended school following the pregnancy and birth, (b) dropped out after the pregnancy or birth but subsequently returned to school, (c) dropped out after the pregnancy or birth and did not return, or (d) dropped out before the birth but did not return. These subgroups were highly stable over the 6 years of the New York study. About one third of the adolescent mothers were working by the 6-year follow-up. Surprisingly, compared nonworking mothers, working mothers were less likely to have lived with their own mothers at delivery. They also reported fewer depressive symptoms and stressful life events, although the stresses of work clearly emerge as salient for this group. Chapter 4 concludes with an analysis of the mothers' decisions to have additional children and the effects of these choices for their school and work outcomes.

Chapter 5 presents case histories of two working mothers, Teressa and Charise. Teressa is on maternity leave from her job and lives with the father of her second child. She would like to go back to school to guarantee her promotion to manager in the mortgage department of a bank where she works as a computer operator, but they cannot afford to lose her salary. Charise has returned to live with her mother after her boyfriend is jailed. She works as a nurse's aide and wants to become a registered nurse. These young women's pride in their stable jobs is clear. Their aspirations for the future have grown in proportion to the guarantees and securities these jobs hold for them and their children. Both focus on the future and worry about being too dependent on a man's support. However, the extraordinary stresses in their lives do not disappear as they juggle child and extended family responsibilities, day care, and work demands.

Chapter 6 addresses within-group differences in patterns of welfare use for the adolescent mothers in the New York study. Like the mothers in the Baltimore study (Harris, 1997), who had their children as adolescents, persistent users differed along many dimensions (including health problems, repeat pregnancies, living with a male partner, and high school graduation) from mothers who had one or two episodes of welfare dependence. We focus on both the stability and changes in the mothers' life experiences concerning welfare—from before the delivery of their first child as a teenager to the 6-year follow-up. We also use interview data to examine the decisions of the adolescent mothers who were not on welfare during the first year postpartum to go on to welfare. Wanting to care for their own children, struggling with illnesses, surviving family violence, and experiencing periods of homelessness were among the reasons that these mothers reported using welfare.

Chapter 7 details three case studies to illuminate differences in the patterns of welfare use by mothers in the New York study. At the 6-year follow-up, each of these mothers was on welfare, but they revealed remarkably different strategies in their use of welfare as they moved toward the attainment of residential and financial independence. Melissa was among the mothers who were successfully using welfare to complete educational or job training programs. Helen represented the largest group of welfare users. Her initial school successes were overwhelmed by recurrent obstacles and stressful life events. By the 6-year follow-up, she was no longer in charge of her future; she was waiting for her life to change. Vivian represents mothers who set aside their own educational and work goals to take on the responsibility of caring for their children. Fearing abuse of their preschoolers by strangers, these mothers saw themselves as accepting the struggle with a meager welfare income to be with their children and waited to return to their goals when their children were in school.

Chapter 8 examines the mothers' romantic relationships with their male partners. As many have argued, adolescent parenting as a social problem stems less directly from concerns about the age of the mothers than from their marital status. In this chapter, we investigate the course of the mothers' relationships with their children's biological fathers up to 6 years postpartum. The majority of these relationships end as the fathers get involved in other relationships, abuse drugs, go to prison, or become abusive or excessively controlling of the mothers. The involvement of the biological father was related to more child problem behaviors at the 3-year follow-up and was unrelated to the child outcomes by the 6-year follow-up. We analyzed the interview material to identify resilient processes in the 12 relationships that lasted. Although almost all of these couples had a period of separation, the women's ability to become self-supporting and the men's abilities to take on more gender equitable roles allowed the couple to reunite on a stronger footing.

Chapter 9 focuses on domestic violence. Of the 93 mothers interviewed at the 6-year follow-up, 41% had experienced abuse by a male partner. The majority of the mothers left these abusive relationships. Those who left were dramatically less depressed and less self-critical, less likely to have experienced abuse as a child, and more likely to be working than the 12 mothers who stayed in abusive relationships. We use interview data at the 3- and 6-year follow-ups to chart the processes that helped these young women leave violent relationships. Findings that the downward spiral of depression and self-criticism within the relationship was halted by the mother's realizations that it is she who is economically self-sufficient, that she and her children need protection to survive the abuse, and that supportive others were available to help them get out of the abusive situation. The abuse experience, however, leaves scars. The hard-won, fiercely held self-sufficiency of these young women often leaves them angry and unable to trust relationships with new male partners, eliminating a source of potential help that many of these mothers would need to pull themselves out of poverty.

Chapter 10 focuses on the adolescent mothers as parents or, more accurately, as co-parents. In fact, only a few of these mothers parented their children alone. For most, extended family are also involved (57% of the grandmothers provided some day care), and a majority of the children spent time in out-of-home care, averaging 14 months in the first 5 years of their lives. Levels of maternal depressive symptoms, parenting warmth, and involvement in child's school activities predicted differences in child behavior problems at 3 and 6 years of age and in their school-based competence at 6 years of age. Beyond these maternal factors, however, differences in the parenting support afforded by extended family (usually the grandmothers) and the availability of stable housing were also related to the children's problem behaviors and to these children's competence for entering school. Given that the majority of adolescent mothers had initially lived with and had support from their own mothers, we also illuminate the circumstances in which this does not occur. Our findings suggest that legislating co-residence will not improve the numbers of adolescent mothers who live with an adult, given that such problems as illness, addictions, abuse, conflict, overcrowded housing, or even the grandmothers' employment were obstacles to the grandmothers' participation. Center-based child-care experiences were related to aspects of greater competence for school entry. Forty-seven percent of the children attended a child-care center or preschool (an average of 8.34 months).

Chapter 11 addresses the program and policy implications of our data. Knowledge of the within- group differences in adolescent mothers' transitions to young adulthood allows for a reconceptualization of the kinds of public assistance needed to aid optimal transitions. Even poor, inner-city mothers must be seen to comprise diverse groups of young women with diverse needs. Costly comprehensive programs are not needed for all. Many mothers need little more than day-care and tuition assistance to stay on track. Flexible assistance targeting educational, work experience, housing stability, financial, or child-care problems is needed. Uniform policies, like requiring residence with and financial dependence on the teen's family of origin, can serve some teens while undermining the efforts of others.

A variety of targets and approaches are conceptualized to aid adolescent mothers and their children's fathers in the transition to early adulthood. To prevent long-term welfare dependence, innovative approaches to public assistance are suggested that reflect and support the developmental tasks of this age group. Work has become normative for women. Most women seek to become self-supporting. Policies that influence adolescent mothers need to address girls' and women's development at several critical points (e.g., focusing on educational success and career development for inner-city girls before a pregnancy occurs and addressing child-care needs of all working women with infants, toddlers, or school-age children). Targeting resources and obstacles to women's development would also reduce the negative consequences of adolescent parenting. For example, policies that curb family and partner abuse are needed to create more positive outcomes for adolescent mothers. Policies are needed that enhance gender equity in relationships and the means (rather than just the requirement) whereby young biological fathers can provide a visible contribution to their children's support.

Policies directed specifically at teenage mothers must also reflect an understanding of the resilience processes that facilitate young women's transition to early adulthood. Investments in these young women's success, at the point in their lives when they are motivated by the birth of their child and when acquiring the means to become self-supporting is normative, could reduce long-term welfare dependence. Moreover, the social institutions (college, job apprenticeships) are in place to accept the challenge of assisting young people to meet the challenges of late adolescence; all adolescents must have access to these resources to ensure their success. The mental health needs of adolescent girls' clearly need to be addressed. There is little doubt that depressive symptoms in young women with children increase the likelihood of negative outcomes for both these women and their children.

The American Context: Sex, Marriage, Work, and Poverty

᪲

Since at least 1950, the United States has had the highest rates of teenage birth and abortion of any developed country (Alan Guttmacher Institute, 1994; Jones et al., 1986; Nathanson, 1991). In 1988, the U.S. birth rate for teens was twice as high and the abortion rate for teens almost three times as high as those in Canada, despite similar levels of adolescent sexual activity in the two countries (Alan Guttmacher Institute, 1994). Several reasons have been suggested for the higher U.S. rates, including a wider gap between rich and poor; limited access to and motivation for education, jobs, health care, contraception, or abortions; less openness about sexuality on the part of parents and educators (but not peers or the media); lack of media reinforcement of responsible contraception; and lack of societal consensus about the morality (or immorality) of premarital sexuality.

Yet teenage childbearing is hardly new in the United States or elsewhere, nor has it ever been uncommon. However, the view of teen parenting as a social problem is relatively recent and coincides with wide-reaching social and demographic changes that have diminished expectations that childbearing will occur only within marriage. As adolescent sexual activity increases and marriage grows less likely for young parents, moral outcries against welfare dependency, sexual promiscuity, and out-of-wedlock births focus on teenagers.

THE GROWTH OF TEENAGE PARENTING
AS A MORAL PROBLEM

Concerns about the morality of youth as a separate group grew between 1960 and 1970 as adolescents increased in both number and visibility. As hippies, political protesters, and social activists, youth became a potentially rebellious social force in need of control. As the number of babies born to adolescent mothers was inflated by births to teenage baby boomers, the perception of adolescent parenting as a problem grew. The birth rate per 1,000 adolescents actually declined. The visibility of teen parenthood expanded as well. Fewer and fewer adolescent pregnancies led to marriage or adoption, and adolescent motherhood came to be viewed as an epidemic (Alan Guttmacher Institute, 1976). Concern over out-of-wedlock births gradually came to focus on the morality of adolescents. Nathanson (1991) summarized these historical changes:

> Diffuse anxiety about the morality of youth, generated by the countercultural ferment of the late 1960's created a climate receptive to the 1970's explosion of "knowledge" describing and cataloging in intimate detail the sexual and reproductive behavior of white [as well as black] teenage women.... "Adolescent pregnancy" could readily be accepted as a public problem because it fed on as well as fueled preexisting moral concerns. (p. 58)

In her book *Dangerous Passage,* Nathanson (1991) charted the rapid evolution in policy debates on out-of-wedlock births. In 1960, use of the birth control pill was approved for adult women in the United States under the supervision of a doctor. Throughout the 1960s and well into the 1970s, controversies about access to birth control remained focused on adult women. Although opponents believed allowing unwed women access to birth control meant condoning immoral sex without consequences, supporters (represented in particular by Planned Parenthood) hoped access to birth control would limit the negative social consequences of out-of-wedlock births and reduce welfare dependency by poor adult women.

As evidence of high levels of teenage premarital sexuality became available from surveys conducted in the early 1970s and as the number of out-of-wedlock births to teenagers began to soar, concern refocused on the consequences of childbearing for the health and economic success of teenagers and their children. Improving access to contraception among sexually active teenagers was seen as a means to prevent sexually transmitted diseases and unwanted pregnancies. One of the first steps taken to address adolescent pregnancy as a public problem was a 1972 amendment to the Social Security Act requiring states to provide family planning services to sexually active minors. The problem of adolescent pregnancy was also addressed in the 1978 Adolescent Health, Services, and Pregnancy Prevention and Care Act, which was designed to provide comprehensive services to pregnant and parenting adolescents. Also passed in 1978 was an amendment to the Family Planning Services Act mandating federally funded family planning projects to provide services for adolescents (Nathanson, 1991).

Dissenters to this legislation questioned the desirability of providing adolescents with the means to disguise their sexual activity (birth control) or avoid the natural consequences of sexually promiscuous behavior. Having to deliver and rear a child, it seems, was to act as the punishment that would deter girls' sexual activity. At the same time, comprehensive services or welfare benefits to adolescent mothers, they argued, offered an economic incentive to immoral teenage sexuality and irresponsible parenting.

Neither side of the debate saw its predictions realized. Adolescent sexual activity continued to rise despite both the potentially punishing effects of having an out-of-wedlock child and increased access to birth control, carefully regulated by the medical profession. Despite legislation in the 1970s approving the use of birth control by unmarried teens, the dire biological, personal, and social consequences of early childbearing were not halted by medical professionals and health educators. Birth rates to teenagers did not fall dramatically; instead they gradually rose from 1988 to 1991. Hopes of stemming the tide of teenage pregnancies gradually gave way to outrage concerning the epidemic of out-of-wedlock teenage mothers (Alan Guttmacher Institute, 1976).

Accessible birth control has not guaranteed pregnancies will be planned for American women of any age; between 1990 and 1995, 18.7% of births to women over 30 were unintended (Abma, Chandra, Mosher, Peterson, & Piccinino, 1997). Further, the alarming rise in illegitimacy and explosion of welfare rolls is not due only to adolescent mothers; in 1990, teenage out-of-wedlock births comprised only 31% of nonmarital births (Alan Guttmacher Institute, 1994).

Nevertheless, with the legalization of birth control first and abortions for unmarried women later, adolescent girls could be held morally responsible for choosing to have an out-of-wedlock child or failing to prevent a pregnancy. Similarly, the decision to raise a child alone could be seen as the deliberate choice of the sexually liberated or promiscuous girl, rather than as the result of male joblessness, infidelity, or irresponsibility. Although pregnant unwed girls were once the unfortunate victims of an accident or mistake that could be set straight by marriage, these girls are now held accountable for their deliberate choices to have intercourse or abstain, to continue or abort a pregnancy, and to marry or remain single. The perceived moral gulf between responsible adolescent girls who keep their choices open and irresponsible girls who choose to give birth to illegitimate children has greatly widened, especially when each is held up against the ideal, college-educated, economically independent woman of the 1990s. The intense controversy and extreme positions that have emerged over the problem of teenage childbearing continue to shape and limit political solutions.

Nowhere has the controversy over the morality of solutions to the rising rate of adolescent births been more passionate than in realm of welfare policy (Handler, 1995). Since at least 1988, families formed by a teenage birth have received more than 50% of the payments distributed by Aid to Families with Dependent Children (AFDC; Alan Guttmacher Institute, 1994). Recent policies suggest reducing the economic incentives for teenage parenting by limiting how long poor families can receive AFDC, denying welfare benefits to teenagers, refusing additional support to children born to families on welfare, and requiring welfare mothers to work or attend school. Yet copious research (reviewed by Wilson & Aponte, 1987) has shown that levels of AFDC benefits had essentially no effect on adolescent fertility patterns. Rates of births to adolescents actually rose between 1980 and 1992, a period during which benefits declined an average of 22.8%. Moreover, states with higher benefits do not have higher teenage fertility rates. Nonetheless, the visibility of adolescent mothers as welfare recipients continues to overwhelm this evidence relating welfare benefits and the teenage birth rate. The tension between teenage pregnancy and parenting as moral or as social problems continues, but the social context of this debate has changed dramatically.

CHANGING SOCIAL NORMS: SEXUAL ACTIVITY AND THE CHOICES OF AMERICAN ADOLESCENTS

Declining Birth Rates to Teens

Estimates of how many adolescents became sexually active before their 18th birthday were largely unavailable prior to the 1978 publication of Zelnick and Kanter's surveys of sexual activity, contraceptive use, and pregnancy among teenagers. Researchers collecting these data even today face censoring by schools, parents, and funding agencies. Many believe that asking teens questions about their sexual activity may suggest approval of it, invade their privacy, or yield untruthful responses. Nevertheless, detailed surveys of teenage sexual activity continue to be published in newspapers and scholarly journals, increasing the visibility of and concerns about adolescent sexual activity.

The Alan Guttmacher Institute (1994) report, *Sex and American's Teenagers,* as well as statistics from the 1995 National Survey of Family Growth (Abma et al., 1997), document increases in recent rates of teenage sexual activity, sexually transmitted diseases, and use of contraceptives, as well as declines in rates of teen pregnancy, abortion, and childbearing. In 1970, slightly more than half of men and one third of women had had intercourse by age 18. By 1995, almost twice the percentage (63%) of women reported having intercourse by this age (see Fig. 2.1). Sexual activity in girls under age 15 remained low and is often associated with coercive sex (Moore, Nord, & Peterson, 1989). These statistics are similar across race or ethnicity, religious group, family income, and urban or rural residence. Moreover, by 1990, most teens (more than 70%) initiated sex before marriage.

For all teens, pregnancy rates increased 7% from 1980 to 1990 and then dropped 5% by 1992 (Henshaw, 1997). The pregnancy rate for sexually experienced teens declined between 1972 and 1990 (from a high of 254 per 1,000 in 1972 to 207 per 1,000 in 1990). Birth rates per 1,000 teens dropped from 62 in 1972 to a low of 50 in 1986 and then rebounded to 62 in 1991 (see Fig. 2.2). As with the pregnancy rate, however, since 1991, births to teens have dropped each year. In 1998, the latest year for which statistics are available, 51 in 1,000 teens had births (Child Trends, 1999).

Abortion rates per 1,000 women ages 15 to 19 increased from 19 in 1972 to a peak of 44 in 1985 and dropped off to 36 by 1992 (Alan Guttmacher Institute, 1994; Henshaw, 1997). Adoption has almost ceased to be an option for young women. The majority of teens who give birth now keep their babies. Between 1982 and 1988, only 3% of White and 1% of African-American babies born to never-married women were placed for adoption, compared with 19% and 2%, respectively, between 1965 and 1972 (Moore, Miller, Glei, & Morrison, 1995).

In 1995, more than 50% of teenage girls reported using some method of contraception, although this varied by race/ethnicity (see Fig. 2.3). Moreover, as education to prevent AIDS continues to reach teenagers, already notable increases in

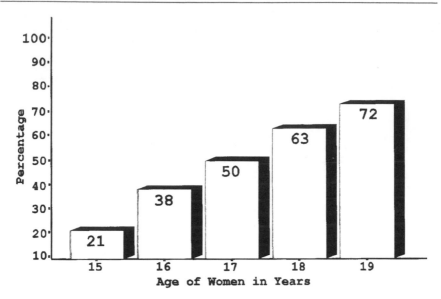

FIG. 2.1.   Percent of unmarried 15- to 19-year-old women who had ever had intercourse, 1995.

teens' use of condoms (54% of sexually active students reported using condoms at last intercourse in 1995 vs. 48% in 1988) may further reduce births to teens (National Center for Chronic Disease Prevention and Health Promotion [CDC], 1995). Still, for many teenage girls, the willingness to use birth control continues to compete with their fears about and experiences of the negative side effects and their worry about the risk to their reputation if they are too prepared for or too assertive about sexual activity (Fine, 1988).

Many factors are potential contributors to the changing statistics for teenage sexual activity and childbearing. The earlier physical maturation of teenagers that has accompanied improved nutrition and health over the last century (known as the *secular trend* in sexual maturation) may play a role. At the turn of the 20th century, the average American woman began menstruating at 15 years of age, compared with the current average age of about 12.5 years (Alan Guttmacher Institute, 1994).

The levels of adolescent premarital sexual activity may also be less surprising given that the average age of first marriages has risen dramatically since the 1970s—from 20 years of age for women and 23 for men in 1970 to 24 for women and 26 for men in 1990. Given that the average girl reaches puberty around 12.5 years of age and the average boy around 13.5, the interval between puberty and marriage is about 12 years for women and 12.5 years for men (Alan Guttmacher Institute, 1994).

Descriptions and displays of adult and teenage sexuality in music, movies, television programs, magazines, and advertising are no longer taboo. Even the bodies of female child figures in animated films like Disney's *The Little Mermaid* and *Pocohontas* are

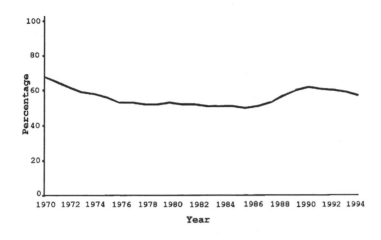

FIG. 2.2.   Live births per 1,000 women ages 15 to 19 years.

overtly sexualized (Leadbeater & Wilson, 1993). Main characters deliberate the pros and cons of sexual activity in their own minds and with their partners and peers in television programs specifically directed at young teens (e.g., *My So Called Life, Blossom, Boy Meets World*). Teens appearing on programs like *Full House,* which are targeted at even younger audiences, are shown discussing similar dilemmas with their parents. Music videos also provide an ongoing stream of sexually explicit and exciting images. For children living in overcrowded housing in poor communities, overt displays of sexuality are the norm (Vera, Reese, Paikoff, & Jarrett, 1996).

Changes in the norms for teenage sexual behaviors have coincided with changes for adults in the structure of marriage, employment patterns and opportunities, valuing of children, and costs of childrearing. Together these changes have dramatically reconfigured family life in the United States. These changes have also increased the social cost of adolescent parenthood and have a particularly onerous impact on adolescent mothers and their children.

Parenthood Without a Husband: The Disappearance of Marriageable Men

As many authors have pointed out, adolescent pregnancies, intended or mistimed, were previously covered up by marriage (Furstenberg et al., 1987; Lawson & Rhodes, 1993; Luker, 1996). In 1955, only 15% of births to teens occurred outside of marriage, compared with 72% in 1992 (Moore et al., 1995). From 1960 to 1964, only 33% of first births to 15- to 17-year-olds occurred outside of marriage compared with 81% between 1985 and 1989 (Moore et al.).

Marriage continues to diminish as an option for adolescent mothers, although many of the fathers of children born to adolescent mothers are not teenagers. Indeed,

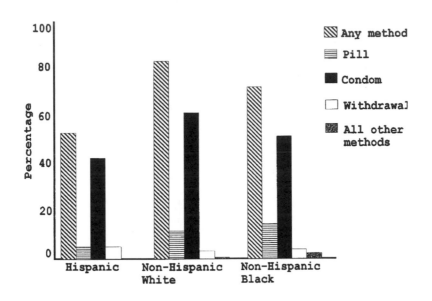

FIG. 2.3   Women under 20 years of age who reported using the specified method of contraception at first intercourse, 1990–1995.

two thirds are over 20 and 19% are as much as 6 years older than the adolescent mother at the time of a first birth (Alan Guttmacher Institute, 1994). According to the William T. Grant Foundation (1988) report: *The Forgotten Half, Pathways to Success for America's Youth and Young Families,* marriage rates for all 20- to 24-year-old males declined by 17.8% between 1974 and 1986 (see Table 2.1) and were lower for African Americans than for Whites and Hispanics at each point (see Table 2.1).

The drop in the marriage rate parallels a decrease in earnings for this age group of men over the same time period. Although 58% of 20- to 24-year-old males earned higher than the three-person poverty level in 1973, only 44% were able to do so by 1986. The mean annual income (in 1986 dollars) of 20- to 24-year-old males who were not in school dropped an average of 26% from 1973 to 1986. For African Americans, declines were more severe (61% for those without a high school diploma, 44% for those with a high school diploma, and 43% for those with some college) than they were for White and Hispanic men.

Basic educational requirements for entry-level jobs have simultaneously risen. Few jobs are available to unskilled men or those with only a high school diploma (William T. Grant Foundation, 1988). The William T. Grant Foundation report concluded unequivocally, "The more years of education completed, the higher one's earnings, the greater likelihood that young men will marry" (p. 27). Without employment opportunities that allow young men to provide a family with an income above the poverty level, these men are less desirable marriage partners. They may

TABLE 2.1

Marriage Rates of 20- to 24-Year-Old Males (in Percentages)

Ethnicity	1974	1980	1986
All	39	28	21
White, non-Hispanic	40	29	23
African American, non-Hispanic	29	17	11
Hispanic	44	36	24

even be an economic liability if they must be economically supported or if their limited, often irregular, income or child support is subtracted from the more stable public assistance benefits or employment incomes of mothers of their children.

Rising Expectations for Women's Work

Roles for women have changed. At the turn of the century, women were legally unable to own property and, in the event of marital disruption, husbands were typically awarded sole custody. Even when women gained legal rights to vote and hold property in 1920, the socially appropriate role for White mothers in nuclear families was seen primarily as the emotional and moral guardians of their children and home. As more people moved to cities and out-of-home work, fathers increasingly became the single wage earner for the nuclear family (Fasick, 1994). In this context, it is not surprising that welfare was first popularly known as *mothers' pensions,* supporting the belief that deserving poor mothers (e.g., those who were widowed but not those whose children were illegitimate) would be supported by society in taking care of their children (Handler, 1995). By the 1960s, the medical profession and child-care experts were uniformly concerned about the negative effects of disrupting mother–child bonding or attachments. Indeed, postwar opposition to working women and out-of-home child care focused on the dangers of disrupting mother–child bonds for children's later social, emotional, and intellectual development. Simultaneously, fathers came to be seen as less relevant to the emotional health of their children.

Throughout the 1970s, research on girls' identity development found that career choice was not a discriminating concern (Schenkel & Marcia, 1972). Girls' attitudes toward premarital sex and concerns about intimacy were considered more significant domains for girls' conflicts about who they would become. Today, a woman is no longer expected to find her identity in her choice of an intimate partner, nor can she depend on a partner's income for economic support. She is expected to be her own woman with her own career (Ludtke, 1997), and she is expected to support her children by working. A woman's ability to economically support her children moves to center stage. Coupled with a labor market that demands higher levels of education for jobs that yield sufficient wages to live above the poverty line, early childbearing can only be seen as an impediment to women's economic survival.

Nevertheless, most positions for women continue to pay substantially less than for men with similar levels of education (Bonvillain, 1995). This has a significant impact on woman-headed households. Among women ages 18 to 34, 48% were paid wages too low to lift a family of four out of poverty ($12,195 in 1990; Strawn, 1992). A mother who worked 40 hours a week for 52 weeks a year at the 1994 minimum wage of $4.25 would have earned $8,840. This figure is over $600 less than the poverty level for a single-parent family with one child (Zill & Nord, 1994). Yet having sole responsibility for their children's economic support has also become commonplace for women who choose to have them.

The Cost of Choosing Children

Having a child has become an expensive choice—a luxury not all can afford. Childbearing, once the natural expectation of young married couples, is now sanctioned only for those who are economically secure. Yet each year, fewer and fewer families of young children meet this standard.

In contrast to earlier times, when children's labor added to household income, today children have increasingly become an economic burden to parents (Fasick, 1994; William T. Grant Foundation, 1988; Zelizer, 1985). Compulsory education, laws against child labor, and increasing demands for higher levels of education have extended the period in which the young are not in the workforce and are instead dependent on their parents' income. As Fasick (1994) pointed out: "The removal of children from most paid work and their forced attendance at school changed them from a potential asset to a clear liability" (p. 15).

Today, day-care expenses are weighed against the value of women's (although rarely men's) work. A majority of families continue to rely on relatives for day-care assistance, but extended family members are often working or living far away from today's mobile, working families. Child care provided by relatives most often requires balancing work shifts for two-parent families (mother–grandmother or mother–father; Presser, 1989). Educational costs of children also add to their status as a financial liability. Costs of a college degree now rival costs of mortgages. Tuition, even at small community or state colleges, is out of reach for many families. Youth in low-income families and those who are African American or Hispanic are much less likely to remain in school than those with higher income levels and who are White or Asian (Children's Defense Fund, 1995).

Although many youth work part time in minimum-wage, short-term jobs, frequently in the retail or fast-food industries, their income is rarely added to their families' income. With the growth of a commercial market directly targeted at teens, much of their income goes to purchase the clothes, music, activities, and other products that permit them access to adolescent culture.

There is considerable social consensus about the appropriate roles for both male and female adolescents and young adults. Adolescents are expected to be out of the workforce pursuing an education. With little access to income that will allow them to support themselves or a child, they are not expected to live independently or marry. For teenage girls, beginning a family—once the central task of their late adolescence—has become a strongly sanctioned mistake that can derail them, economically, for a lifetime. Adolescent mothers clearly violate norms for adolescents when they fail to stay on a course that will increase their earning potential. They also violate the norms for adult women by not acquiring the skills needed for employment. Childbearing, as a teenager, becomes increasingly "off-time."

ADOLESCENT PARENTING AND PREEXISTING POVERTY

Although rates of teenage sexual activity differ little by family income or racial or ethnic groups, rates of teenage childbearing do (Mathews & Ventura, 1997; see Fig. 2.4). Early childbearing is clearly concentrated among the poor: 56% of births to 15- to 19-year-olds are to poor teens and 27% are to low-income teens. Birth rates for African Americans and Hispanics are one and a half to three and a half times that of Whites. Overall, more babies are highly represented among those who cannot support the costs of childbearing.

Adolescents living in areas of concentrated poverty are born subject to the changed expectations that accompany current roles for women, but they lack the resources to achieve these new expectations. Poor girls make their life choices in the face of different possibilities than do girls from higher income families (Leadbeater & Way, 1996). Children from poor communities often receive substandard education and are exposed to high rates of dropout; they are members of jobless communities with few employed men; they live in (and often care for) families with poverty-related illnesses (e.g., asthma, obesity, diabetes, hypertension, alcoholism); their families are unable to find or afford trustworthy day care; and they are unable to pay for or save for postsecondary education. Even the security deposit for an apartment is beyond the reach of most poor young adults, and the occupational options open to them are in low-wage jobs.

The negative social conditions that serve to maintain poverty (joblessness, school dropout, early male mortality and incarceration, female heads of households, disabilities) all disproportionately affect those who are already poor (Wilson, 1995), those from minority groups (Donovan, 1995), and those from the inner cities of metropolitan areas (National Center for Children in Poverty, 1990). Poverty rates for children under age 6 rose dramatically between 1970 and 1993, from about 17% to 26% (Children's Defense Fund, 1995). Minority children were nearly one and a half times as likely as White children to experience poverty in 1987 (National Center for Children in Poverty, 1990). Children in female-headed households are especially likely to live in poverty. Poverty rates for children living with single mothers (never married, separated, divorced, or widowed) were 61% in 1987 and 54% in 1992. These children are at highest risk for long-term poverty.

Do teenage births cause intergenerational poverty? As noted earlier, births to teenagers made up only one third of the 1,165,000 out-of-wedlock births in 1990 (Alan Guttmacher Institute, 1994). Poor adult women encounter similar difficul-

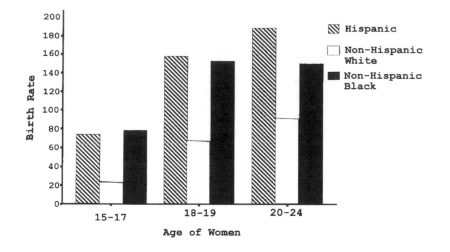

FIG. 2.4.   Birth rates per 1,000 women by race ages 15 to 24, 1994.

ties pulling their families out of poverty (National Center for Children in Poverty, 1990). Despite the public consensus about the negative consequences of early childbearing for the economic and educational futures of poor teens, there is no simple correlation between early childbearing and later poverty. Indeed, understanding the causal relations between early childbearing and later socioeconomic status (SES) requires distinguishing the effects of early childbearing from those of family background, socioeconomic, or educational status prior to the adolescent pregnancy (Astone, 1993; Leadbeater, 1996). It is unlikely that interventions that address teenage promiscuity or teenage childbearing alone can stem the compounding negative contributions of substandard education, inner-city joblessness, discrimination, and family background in perpetuating intergenerational poverty.

Several studies have demonstrated that the effects of early childbearing on mothers' incomes and/or educational attainments are often dramatically reduced when family background or pre-pregnancy socioeconomic, marital, or educational status is taken into account (see reviews by Moore et al., 1993, 1995). In recent research involving a nationally representative sample of women who had reached age 27 when surveyed, Moore et al. (1993) found that young age of childbearing alone did not lead to poverty; the effects of childbearing age differed by race or ethnicity. African-American women, who were older at the first child's birth, had a slightly smaller chance of being poor at age 27, but this depended on the number of subsequent children born. In other words, African-American women who delayed childbearing had slightly fewer children by age 27 and thus had lower income needs. In contrast, for Hispanics, delaying childbearing had a more substantial effect on the likelihood of being in poverty at age 27, but this depended on a number of factors including highest grade completed, age at first marriage, work experience, the respondent's own earnings, and other family income. For Whites, the effect of waiting to bear children was similar to that for Hispanics, and the likelihood of being in poverty at age 27 depended on number of subsequent children born, decreased earnings, and later marriage. Focus on age at first birth as a predictor of poverty can lead and has led to misguided and ineffective policies and interventions.

Are Adolescent Mothers Choosing Poverty?

Recent research (Bane, 1986; Harris, 1997) on the contribution of changes in family structure (out-of-wedlock births, divorce, separation, or widowhood) to the growth in poverty has also created questions about how much poverty occurs subsequent to such changes (event-driven poverty) and how much existed before the change in family structure occurred (reshuffled poverty).

Typically, when poor women establish new female-headed households, poverty rates increase. Bane (1986) explained that society tends not to support an individual's choice to live alone in these circumstances:

> To the extent that poverty is "chosen," to the extent that people accept poverty to achieve privacy by moving from a non-poor joint household to a poor independent household, society in the aggregate is less willing to assume the responsibility for supporting the person who has made or suffered from the decision. (p. 230)

Do teen mothers choose or accept poverty as a trade-off for freedom or independence? A majority of adolescent mothers live with a parent or parents when they give birth and for at least a year after. Changes in the income needs of their family of origin are initially responsible for greater poverty and residential overcrowding in these families. Consistent with this view, using 1959 to 1983 census data, Banc (1986) found that poverty spells for African-American adults were more frequently initiated by changes in income needs (46.3% experienced an increase in need or a drop in income) than from transition into a female-headed household (initiating 23.2% of spells), although the reverse was true for Whites (21.6% and 50.5%, respectively).

Although the ability to establish an independent household is seen as a marker of development for most young adults in this society, it is not within the reach of most poor adolescent mothers. Their success in making the transition to independent households is limited by an overall lack of affordable housing, the unwillingness of landlords to rent to teenagers, the teen's inability to save the necessary security deposit, and long waiting lists for subsidized housing. Given that a majority of 15- to 19-year-old mothers are already from poor or low-income families at the birth of their first child, we should ask not how teenage childbearing causes poverty, but rather how it is that many of these young mothers escape poverty?

Increases in out-of-wedlock births to adolescent mothers in the past decades underscore societal views of teenage parenting as both a social and moral problem. Changing socioeconomic situations during the past four decades have disproportionately affected mother-headed families subsisting in poverty. Declining marriage rates, increasing educational requirements for employment, decreasing earnings, gender gaps for earning potentials, and increasing societal pressures for self-sufficiency among women have all confounded the economics of childbearing, particularly adolescent childbearing. Many of the effects of early childbearing on maternal outcomes are also confounded by pre-pregnancy family and educational status. The following chapters are dedicated to detailing the continuities and discontinuities and within-group differences in the lives of 120 African-American and Hispanic inner-city adolescent mothers and their first-born children living in poverty.

There is an acute need to understand the varied transitions to adulthood among poor young mothers. How do some escape poverty? What holds others back? It is clear that changing expectations of women clash with declining economic conditions for women from poor communities. It has become commonplace for policymakers to say that poor teens need better alternatives to adolescent childbearing and parenting to be motivated to avoid pregnancy (e.g., Freeman & Rickels, 1993). However, many young women are more motivated to make their own lives better after their child's birth than before. Policymakers hoping to reduce poverty need to know more about the real beliefs, goals, and circumstances of adolescent mothers' day-to-day existence. This will help them capitalize on the energy that these young women bring to their struggle in early adulthood to escape, rather than choose, poverty on behalf of their children.

THE NEW YORK STUDY OF ADOLESCENT MOTHERS

Participating in this 6-year study, which began in 1987, were 126 adolescent mothers and their children. Participants were recruited from among the adolescent mothers who brought their 3- to 4-week-old infants for well-baby care to an urban adolescent health center affiliated with a large teaching hospital where most of these children were born. This strategy allowed us to make initial contact with first-time adolescent mothers of generally healthy children who lived in the inner-city communities surrounding the health center. It also restricted the participants to those mothers and babies who had been able to leave the hospital before the infant was 1 month old (thus excluding seriously ill or premature babies and seriously ill mothers), retained custody of the child (thus excluding drug-addicted mothers), and had the motivation, ability, or assistance to get a newborn by taxi or subway to their first well-baby appointment. Many of the mothers had previously used the clinic for their own health care and birth control services, and their infants were also seen by their primary doctors. Participants represented approximately 89% of the adolescent mothers who enrolled at the clinic over an 18-month period.

Who the Mothers Were: The Social and Demographic Context

At the time of the first interview, the mothers participating in the study were 14 to 19 years old (M =17.1, SD = 1.2). They were primarily African American (53%) or Puerto Rican (43%). Most (99%) had given birth for the first time, lived with their own mothers (72%), and came from families on welfare (65%). On average, they had completed 9.5 (SD = 1.3) years of school; 45% remained in school and 10%

had already graduated from high school. The majority of the children were from full-term deliveries and were of normal birthweight.

The adolescent mothers all came from Manhattan or Bronx counties. These counties have extremely dense populations and high levels of poverty, minority group concentration, unemployment, single-parent families, school dropout, and crime. Data from the 1991 census (Kids Count Data Book: New York State, 1994) indicate that 33% of the children in Manhattan and half the children in the Bronx were living below the poverty line. Hispanic and African-American children were more likely to be poor than those from other ethnic or racial groups. Almost half (46%) of children in Manhattan and 55% of children in Bronx counties lived with one parent. Thirty-two percent of Manhattan mothers with children under the age of 18 and 37% of those from Bronx county were not high school graduates. Birth rates to 15- to 19-year-olds were 83 in 1,000 in Bronx county and 57 in 1,000 in Manhattan. Rates of arrests for violent crimes numbered 57 in 1,000 for 13- to 18-year-olds in Bronx county and 86 in 1,000 in Manhattan.

The Interview Points

The mothers were seen in individual interviews six times. Interviews were conducted by research assistants with at least a master's degree in social work, counseling, or developmental psychology. The initial questionnaire at 3 to 4 weeks postpartum (Time 1) collected data on the mothers' education level, family welfare status, levels of stress and depressive symptoms, quality of relationships with their own mothers, and access to other social supports. All measures are described in Appendix A. Similar data were collected again when the children were 6 months (Time 2), 12 months (Time 3), 28 to 36 months (Time 5), and 6 to 7 years (Time 6). The wider gap at Time 5 ($M = 32$ months postpartum, $SD = 4$ months) reflected increased difficulties in finding the mothers within the window provided for by the study's funding. Data collected at 20 to 24 months (Time 4) consisted of child language assessments and videotapes of mother–child interactions. Time 6 data were collected from June to October 1994 to capitalize on the warmer weather and reduce the expense of maintaining an active field research site over a year-long period.

Assessments of the children's problem behaviors were collected from the mothers when the children were 3 and 6 years of age and from the children's kindergarten or first-grade teachers at about 6 years of age. Maternal reports of child behavior problems were obtained at the 3-year follow-up using the Child Behavior Checklist/2-3 (CBCL/2-3; Achenbach, 1992) and at the 6-year follow-up using the Child Behavior Checklist/4-18 (CBCL/4-18; Achenbach, 1991). These measures yield scores for internalizing and externalizing behaviors as well as total problems. Teachers' reports of child behavior problems were obtained using the Teacher Report Form (TRF) of the CBCL (Achenbach, 1991). Teachers' assessments of the children's competence at 6 years of age were also collected using the Vineland Adaptive Behaviors Scales, Classroom Edition (Sparrow, Balla, & Cicchetti, 1984).

At Times 5 and 6 (referred to throughout the text as the 3-year and 6-year follow-up points), qualitative data were also collected in audiotaped, semistructured interviews (see Appendix B) designed to elicit the mothers' descriptions of their daily lives since the birth of their children, their aspirations for themselves and their children, their plans to accomplish these goals, their views of themselves as women and mothers, and the stability and quality of their social support networks. All interviews were transcribed and subjected to content coding and case study analyses as described next. These data were available for 79 of the 84 mothers who completed questionnaires at the 3-year follow-up (2 mothers left before completing the interview, and three audiotapes were inaudible) and for all of the 93 mothers who completed questionnaires at the 6-year follow-up.

The number of participants varied somewhat at each interview point due to difficulties in locating the mothers or scheduling the interviews in the short time frames between assessments. Data were complete for:

- 113 (94%) mothers at the 12-month follow-up
- 82 (68%) mothers at the 20-month follow-up
- 84 (70%) mothers at the 3-year follow-up
- 93 (78%) mothers at the 6-year follow-up

The mothers who were not in the sample at the 6-year follow-up did not differ systematically from the remaining participants on any of the initial demographic or predictor variables except race. All mothers who described their race as *other* and 84% of the African-American mothers were retained at the 6-year follow-up, compared with 67% of Hispanics [$\chi^2(2) = 6.6, p = .04$]. Given that few differences related to race have been found in previous research with this sample, the differential attrition was not expected to influence current findings.

Continuities and Discontinuities in the Mothers' Lives

The data collected at six time points allowed us to identify how key aspects of these young women's lives had changed or stayed the same during the first 6 years after they became mothers, especially their welfare status, further education, subsequent childbearing, and success in finding housing.

Among the mothers who remained in the sample at the 6-year follow-up, we found that at the end of the 6-year period:

- a similar number were on welfare at the start of the study (63% at the 12-month follow-up, compared with 69% at the 6-year follow-up)
- the average gain in educational level was 1.76 years (on average, the mother had completed 11.47 grades (*SD* = 1.92) at the 6-year follow-up, compared with 9.71 grades (*SD* = 1.37) at the 12-month follow-up)
- the majority had moved out of their mothers' households (22% lived with their mother at the 6-year follow-up, compared with 76% initially)
- sixteen (17%) were married, compared with two initially
- most (61%) had more than one child

However, this statistical picture of overall gains and losses obscures important subgroup differences among the mothers, as well as differences in the continuity and discontinuities they experienced along the way. Although researchers often have predicted negative outcomes that on average appear highly stable across time for teens who become mothers, we attempt to present a more accurate picture of the stability (and, indeed, instability) of both positive and negative events (welfare, high school graduation, subsequent births, finding housing) in the early adult lives of these young women. Risks for negative outcomes may be higher for adolescent mothers than for women who delay childbearing until their 20s, but negative outcomes are not the norm.

For adolescent mothers, experiences after the delivery of their first child are thought to be key in determining their economic futures. In a 17-year follow-up of adolescent mothers who delivered their first child in Baltimore in the 1950s, Furstenberg and his colleagues (1987) reported that mothers who had more positive postdelivery experiences in education and who had limited subsequent fertility had better economic outcomes.

Obtaining a high school diploma and gaining significant employment experiences are the major developmental tasks of all adolescents in the later teenage years. Although parenting a child as a teenager can be an obstacle to development, on average, 70% of women who become mothers as adolescents do graduate from high school (Alan Guttmacher Institute, 1994). A majority leave welfare for work, and long-term welfare dependence is an exception (Handler, 1995).

Being on welfare, dropping out of school, having their own apartment, moving out of their mothers' homes, and even getting pregnant are not singular or static events in the lives of young mothers. Many go on and off welfare, some continuously attend school, some drop out and return, some move out of their own mothers' homes and then move back in, some have their own mothers move in with them, half of their subsequent pregnancies end in abortions or miscarriages, most marriages end, but some have long-term supportive relationships. Their periods of welfare dependence reflect the transitions in their economic status as they cope with the changes in work or school attendance, day-care arrangements, housing, child and personal illness, and relationships with their mothers and male partners. These transitions also build on the adolescent's life experiences before she became a mother.

The outcomes for young mothers at any single point can only be seen as snapshots of the obstacles and successes in their developmental trajectories. Individual variability in the transitions to young adulthood of the women in the New York study was seen in many aspects of their lives, including their needs for and uses of welfare, the determinants of their educational and employment success, their reasons for limiting or not limiting subsequent births, their experiences in obtaining their own housing, their relationships, and parenting successes. We address this diversity in the following chapters. We attempt to show the links of these differences with their past experiences, as well as how having a child as a teenager marked a turning point for their futures.

3

Resilient Processes: Gaining Strength From Challenge and Support

We begin our investigation of the diversity in outcomes for the mothers in the New York study by focusing on the stories of success. Parenting at a young age did not derail these young women. Indeed, some were motivated to improve their own lives because their children added meaning and purpose to their young lives. By looking specifically at the group of adolescent mothers who, 6 years after the birth of their first child, were working or in school, physically healthy, and showed no signs of psychological distress, we can highlight the sources of their resilience. How did they succeed in adverse contexts of inner-city poverty? What supported their success?

Since the late 1970s, researchers have been investigating the mechanisms and processes that lead some individuals to thrive despite adverse life circumstances (Baldwin et al., 1993; Cicchetti & Garmezy, 1993; Masten & Coatsworth, 1998; National Institute of Mental Health, 1996; Rutter, 1979; Werner & Smith, 1982). As a result of this large body of research, we know much about the predictors of resilient outcomes and the dynamic processes of resiliency among a wide range of high-risk populations (see Cicchetti & Garmezy, 1993; Cicchetti, Rogosch, Lynch, & Holt, 1993; Luthar, 1991; Luthar, Dorenberger, & Zigler, 1993; Masten, 1994; Masten & Coatsworth, 1998). Strikingly, however, resiliency among adolescent mothers has rarely been studied.

Although research indicates that the majority of adolescent mothers experience positive outcomes (e.g., high school graduation, employment; Alan Guttmacher Institute, 1994; Brooks-Gunn & Furstenberg, 1986; Horwitz, Klerman, Kuo, & Jekel, 1991; Leadbeater, 1996; Way & Leadbeater, 1999), most research on this population has focused on the predictors of, the risk factors associated with, or the negative outcomes resulting from teenage parenthood. Even research that has examined the pathways toward diverse outcomes for adolescent mothers (e.g., Furstenberg et al., 1987; Horwitz et al., 1991; Leadbeater, 1996; Way & Leadbeater, 1999) has not examined resilient processes in particular.

Early resilience research emphasized individual capacities that compensated for or resisted risk processes. Werner's (1993) formative research focused on children and youths "who pulled themselves up by their own bootstraps, with informal support from kith and kin" (p. 513). However, this emphasis on personal bootstrapping has preempted needed research investigating the family, cultural, and societal contexts that support resilience. Continuing to emphasize individual strengths, Masten and Coatsworth (1998) defined *resilience* as "manifested competence in the context of significant challenges to adaptation or development" (p. 205). However, they went on to define *competence* as a

> pattern of effective adaptation in the environment either broadly defined in terms of reasonable success with major developmental tasks expected for a given age and gender in the context of his or her culture, society and time or more narrowly defined in terms of specific domains of achievement such as academics, peer acceptance, or athletics. (p. 206)

Given the dramatic sociocultural changes in response to adolescent parenting over the past decades as well as the changes in roles for young women, it is clear that *reasonable success* for adolescent mothers cannot be understood outside of this context. Moreover, the young mothers in the New York study succeeded in contexts not only of adversity, but of supports that in many ways determined the success of their personal efforts.

Resilience cannot be understood as a static outcome achieved once and for all despite all future challenges (Pianta & Walsh, 1998). Resilience also does not reside within the individual as a personality trait. Rather, dynamic, multidimensional processes characterize resilience (Cicchetti & Garmezy, 1993; Masten & Coatsworth, 1998). Protective processes can promote resilience. These processes include experiences, events, and relationships that interrupt or reverse downward developmental trajectories, diminish the impact of stressful situations, reduce the negative chain reactions that characterize pathogenic family and school situations, promote the development and maintenance of self-efficacy, and provide opportunities for positive education, vocational, and personal growth (Gore & Eckenrode, 1996; Rutter & Rutter, 1993).

Children develop new vulnerabilities and strengths as they grow older, and these influence their ability to cope with the stresses they undergo subsequently. For example, an adolescent may have an understanding of the importance of planning for the future that a young child may not have. This new understanding may enhance the adolescent's ability to resist negative behaviors when he or she is confronted with obstacles. The ways young people develop, maintain, and express strength in the midst of adversity vary depending on their developmental stage, external expectations, and life circumstances (Masten & Coatsworth, 1998). In this chapter, we begin to map these resilient processes among a small group of adolescent mothers in the New York study.

Resiliency researchers have particularly underscored the importance of conceptualizing resiliency as multidimensional (Cicchetti & Garmezy, 1993; Luthar, 1991; Luthar et al., 1993; Masten & Coatsworth, 1998; Yoshikawa, Seidman, Allen, Aber, & Friedman, 1997). Although early research operationalized resiliency based on singular outcomes for individuals (e.g., educational achievement or social competence), Luthar's (1991) research with inner-city adolescents suggests that some students who reported having good grades and social competence also reported high levels of psychological distress. Other researchers have also found that an individual's success in one or two areas of life may be accompanied by internal struggles with depression or continued exposure to stressful circumstance such as poverty (Masten & Coatsworth, 1998; Wright, Masten, Northwood, & Hubbard, 1997).

As a consequence of such findings, researchers have recently emphasized the importance of examining the psychological, behavioral, and physical dimensions of individual resilience, or competence, as well as the contextual factors that allow such dimensions to flourish (Masten & Coatsworth, 1998). Researchers have also argued that the domains included in a definition of *adaptation* should be relevant and appropriate for the population under investigation (Cicchetti & Garmezy, 1993; Luthar, 1993; Yoshikawa & Seidman, 1999).

In the New York study, we based our definition of *adaptation* on domains previously examined by researchers of inner-city adolescents (Luthar, 1991, 1993; Yoshikawa et al., 1997) as well as those that are appropriate markers of success for adolescent mothers in particular (Horwitz et al., 1991). The four domains we included were educational attainment, employment, mental health, and physical health. Although each of these dimensions taken separately captures only a small part of what it means to thrive, taken together they provide a broad benchmark of successful adaptation (Luthar, 1993).

We selected all of the young mothers from our sample who at the 6-year follow-up scored well in all four dimensions. These 15 mothers had graduated from high school, were working or in school, reported positive physical health (above the mean on the physical health scale), and reported few depressive symptoms over the previous 3 years, according to the Beck Depression Inventory (BDI).

These young mothers were determined to accomplish and, indeed, were accomplishing their highly ambitious goals. They included Marie, a Puerto Rican young woman from the South Bronx who had her first child when she was 17. Marie had suffered through years of rejection by her mother and her child's father, was kicked out of the house when her child was born, and reported receiving little emotional support from her family members as she was growing up. Six years after the birth of her child, Marie was completing college at a prestigious university, was a member of her college dance troupe, worked at two jobs to support herself and her son, and was in a loving and supportive relationship with a man.

Although our resilient mothers told many stories of hurt, vulnerability, and suffering, they were not overwhelmed or incapacitated by their difficult experiences. They were able to move forward in their lives despite and occasionally because of their difficulties. These young mothers had become parents at a young age and were growing up in a poor urban environment. However, by their early 20s they were accomplishing what many of their middle-class peers in the suburbs who had not become mothers were not.

Intrigued by these 15 young women—women who clearly did not fit any stereotypes of adolescent mothers or urban young women in general—we sought to understand the patterns and textures of their lives. We chose not to compare those who appeared to be coping well in early adulthood with those who appeared to be coping less well, but to listen closely and carefully to the stories told by this small group of mothers who appeared to be doing well in many areas of their lives. We were interested in the processes and fluctuations of their strengths and coping rather than identifying particular individual characteristics as resilient.

A content analysis was conducted by two data analysts to determine differences and similarities among the interviews of the young mothers (see Strauss, 1987). A content analysis first involves detailed readings of each interview. Following these readings, the interview data are partitioned into content domains for the comparison of themes across individual cases. In our study, themes that were detected independently by both data analysts were considered common themes in the interview data.

RESILIENT PROCESSES

At the 6-year follow-up, the 15 young mothers who were doing well were between 21 and 25 years old. Most were raised by their own mothers ($N = 12$). However, one woman was raised by her grandmother, one was raised by her father and grandmother, and one was raised mainly by her father (although at age 14, she moved in with her mother). Nine of the young mothers had gone on to college, and six had begun working directly after high school. Most of the mothers worked full time or were in school. Three of the mothers were going to school and working at least part time, one was going to school and did not work, and two worked more than 40 hours a week (one of the latter two women was also in school). These mothers had typically worked full time or had been in school consistently over the previous 3 to 4 years, although many of them had not worked during the first year after their child was born.

At the 6-year follow-up, 12 of the young mothers had one child and three had two children; 12 did not receive public assistance and 3 did (these three also worked). Four of the women were married, and all but one of the women were in an intimate relationship with a man (four were still involved with their child's father). We discuss these resilient relationships in chapter 8.

These women had extremely active lives that typically involved splitting their time between their job or jobs, going to school, spending time with their boyfriend or husband and their respective families, and spending quality time with their child or children.

The family context of these 15 young mothers varied along the dimension of support provided by their immediate family members. Four mothers had positive and supportive relationships with their immediate family members, particularly with their own mothers. Their mothers were typically available to help them with child care so they could continue their education or find a job. Although these four women had struggled through difficult times (one was abused by her boyfriend, and another, as a child, witnessed her father beat her mother on a regular basis), they were generally surrounded by supportive immediate and extended family members and friends. What led to their resiliency and strength was readily apparent as they spoke about how their mothers, friends, aunts, uncles, grandmothers, grandfathers, boyfriends, and sometimes fathers had "been there" for them on a continual basis.

In contrast, the 11 other women had dealt with extraordinary difficulties involving their immediate families. Nine had experienced rejecting, hostile, abusive, or neglectful relationships with their own mothers, and two experienced the death of their own mothers when they were children. Three of the grandmothers were drug addicted while six were physically or verbally abusive or neglectful. Only two of the nine mothers who reported rejecting, hostile, and abusive relationships with their own mothers as children and adolescents had close relationships with their mothers at the 6-year interview. Unlike the women with family support, these young women had to cope with extremely difficult and stressful circumstances at home. The sources of their resiliency were less apparent.

Despite the dramatic differences in the supports provided by immediate family members, common themes could be detected in the 6-year interviews of these 15 women, including:

- being raised in a strict and disciplined home environment,
- receiving conditional rather than unconditional support from family members (i.e., support provided within the context of clear expectations and demands by the person providing it),
- having family members, friends, and boyfriend or husbands who strongly valued education and who were often in school themselves or had seemingly satisfying careers,
- having positive role models and supportive relationships with siblings, extended members of the family, best friends, or current boyfriends,
- wanting to disprove their families' doubts about their potential for success,
- having an optimistic attitude or a confidence that obstacles could be surmounted,
- having a strong desire, a will, "a want," or a passion to succeed, and
- having access to and support for postsecondary education.

These common themes were not independent of each other, but rather woven together, creating processes of strength and resiliency in contexts where they could be maintained and developed. For example, those mothers who reported receiving conditional support from their own mothers also reported having a positive attitude and a determination to succeed. Marie, for example, said she became independent precisely because the support provided by her mother was contingent on Marie "doing something with herself." She knew she had to pursue certain goals, such as getting her own apartment, if she was going to receive child care help from her mother. Having a positive attitude or a determination to succeed may not have been possible without her mother's conditional support.

The remainder of this chapter presents case studies that highlight how these common themes were experienced within individual lives. Although listing the common themes detected in the interviews may be informative, the nuances, shapes, and details of these processes are revealed in the narratives of the young mothers. As we begin to understand the meanings of these themes for the young mothers, it becomes possible to understand how these interdependent themes foster positive outcomes.

Marie: Having Strength, Determination, and Optimism

Marie, a Puerto Rican woman, coped with extraordinarily difficult situations in her young life, but she had come through with an inspirational sense of optimism and determination. Marie was 17 when she had her son. Her child's father used to beat her and, at one point, raped her. She struggled to get out of this relationship for many years (see chap. 9), becoming bulemic at one point and also contemplating suicide. Finally, when her child was 2 years old, she found the strength to leave him. She said she had "finally had enough."

At the 6-year follow-up, Marie was completing her fourth year in an electrical engineering degree program. She also held two jobs and worked 49 hours a week. She was the leader of a college dance troupe and was heavily involved in her sorority. Marie was also in a deeply committed relationship with a man whom she had been seeing for a year and a half.

Marie was raised by her mother, who was extremely strict and abusive with Marie. Marie reported that when she was a child, she was often beaten by her mother when she behaved poorly or, as she said, "for unknown reasons":

> My mother disciplined me very, ummm, she disciplined me very well, ha … in a sense like, uh, physically … I think my mother, uh, I don't know because she had a lot of anger in her or she was suffering so much in her own way. But she, I think she sometimes disciplined me very … you know I didn't like that way she did it. I … I still remember some of the things she's done to me and you know, but … my mother, she never even give me a chance to think about what [I] did. My mother was like okay [and I was like] beat me up now so therefore I can stop being punished you know, ha … that wasn't my idea of, I don't even know why she even hit me sometimes.

Although Marie struggled to understand, she was still angry with her mother's behavior:

> My mother was so strict about so many things and I don't know, it's just, oh it just so weird, I couldn't even have a conversation with my mother, because she always made me feel awkward or she always seemed to me I was always wrong or something.

However, Marie was greatly appreciative of how much her mother pushed her to continue her education:

[My mother said] you have that fire in your eyes and I know you want to go to school, you know. I want to make sure that you finish. But she always told me that if I never went back to school, she was never gonna help me with my son. But she saw that I've tried, so she tried.

Like the mothers of her peers, Marie's mother was only willing to help her if she was willing to help herself. The support provided by her mother was conditional.

Marie attributed her success to her mother's encouragement of her education and her mother's strict and demanding behavior:

I think it's my mother ... see my mother never realized what she's done to me. I give a lot of credit to my mother, my mother used to always push schooling to me. It's very important to do this, it's very important, it's like she has all these things, and it's like my mother's strict ways and everything really made me realize I really need to do certain things, I have to live this life, I need to make sure that I succeed ... And I think because of that, and because of my mother ingrained that in my head.

Marie also resisted becoming the negative stereotype her mother expected. She said her mother was disappointed in her pregnancy:

... all the promises I used to tell my mother, she thought it went down the drain when I had my son. She didn't think I was even gonna get my diploma from high school. But I [did]. And, umm, so that whole year when I had my son I had a year off, she didn't think I was gonna go back to school and I just told her, yes I'm going back, I'm going back. And she ... didn't believe me. She's like, sure, right ... be the typical Puerto Rican around the neighborhood or something. And I didn't like that 'cause it was like she didn't even have faith in me ... but I proved her ... wrong.

Like Marie, many of the resilient young women, especially those who went on to college, spoke of people in their lives who strongly valued education and pushed them to continue their education. Taylor, who was raised by her grandmother, said that it was her grandmother's influence that led her to pursue a higher education:

'Cause my grandmother, like, always that was the one thing. No matter what, get an education. So when I was being pregnant with him I still went to school. Everyday, got up and went to school, graduated, two days later started college ... no matter what, rain, sleet or snow, I was up going to school. So it was like a pattern ... That's all I knew was school. Getting up, going to school ... I'm just built on education, cause that's all I've been ... my family instilled it in me.

At the 6-year point, Marie loved her relationship with her mother. She said that ever since her mother saw Marie successfully pursue her educational goals, she had been helping and supporting Marie. In fact, Marie's mother had been taking care of Marie's son since he was born. Many of the resilient women stated that their mothers or grandmothers were willing to take care of their children while they were working or in school. Even Melinda's mother, who was drug addicted, helped Melinda take care of her daughter during the first few years, often getting up at one in the morning to feed her granddaughter when Melinda was too exhausted to feed her.

At the 6-year interview, Marie had a relationship with a man whom she met in college. They were living and attending college together. Marie pushed her boyfriend to take his education seriously and said with pride in her voice that now she and her boyfriend were "really into [their] books." She enthusiastically described how happy they were together and how committed they were to each other and to raising her son. Her boyfriend had been a clear source of support over the previous 2 years.

Of the 15 resilient women, 11 spoke about having positive and supportive relationships with their boyfriends or husbands (3 spoke about not receiving enough support from their boyfriends, and 1 did not have a boyfriend). They stated that their boyfriends or husbands were not only supportive of them but also of their children. Being a good father or caregiver of their children was, in fact, a common expectation and requirement in their relationships with men.

Rosalyn: Stable, Strict Family Support

A great deal of research has demonstrated how warm authoritative maternal relationships are protective of children in adverse circumstances (Masten & Coatsworth, 1998; McLoyd, 1998). The adolescent mothers in the New York study who succeeded were no exception. Rosalyn, a young, Puerto Rican mother, was 18 when she had her first child and 20 when she had her second. She married the father of her children because her mother felt it was the "right thing for her to do" when she got pregnant:

> We wanted to live with each other. And my mother was like, no, you know, you gotta get married, it's not right ... she's like, get married, it's better that way ... You're more sure of your family like that. So I said okay, and he said, alright, and you know, we got married.

Rosalyn's father, who had not been very active in her life, did not approve of the marriage because her husband was Dominican and she was Puerto Rican. However, she married and the relationship has lasted for 11 years. Her husband was extremely supportive: "I'm happy I have him. He's really good to me, and I know he loves me. He shows it ... so I'm happy." Throughout the interview, Rosalyn spoke positively about her husband: "We talk about anything, we have the same likes ... I trust him ... He trusts me."

At the time of the interview, Rosalyn was working full time as a bank teller and her husband worked as a salesperson for a major manufacturing company. She received her GED soon after having her first child and had been working at a full-time job ever since. Rosalyn said she would like to go to college but, at that point, she and her husband needed the money from her job, so she was continuing to work.

Rosalyn was raised by her mother in a religious Pentecostal household that Rosalyn described as *very strict* and *overprotective*. Descriptions of strict parents were one of the most pervasive themes among the resilient young women. More than half of the women stated that the persons who raised them had clear and rigid rules that they were forced to abide by as they were growing up or else suffer the, occasionally, physical consequences.[1] For example, Taylor, a young African-American woman who recently graduated from a four-year college with a bachelor of science degree in nursing said that, like Rosalyn, she was raised in her grandmother's strict household. Taylor said she was glad her grandmother had been so strict because "she gave me all the values that I have ... I don't think that if I lived with my mother I would be who I am now.... I don't think so. Because [my mother] is so lenient."

Yet Rosalyn said she had always been and still was very close with her mother:

I always had a good relationship with my mother ... I can tell her anything ... anything even if it's like sexual stuff with my husband. I'm not embarrassed to tell her.... My mother's there when I need something. I call her up and I say, you know, I don't know, Mom, you know. This is not working out for me, and you know, mostly my job and stuff, or maybe if I have a problem, even with my husband, anything! You know? I could call her and she's always there for me. You know? Anything I need.

Rosalyn said she and her mother had been particularly close since she had her son. Having a child brought her and her mother closer together. When asked why, she said, "I think I grew up, and I was a mother just like her. And, it was different, I wasn't a little girl anymore. I was married with a kid. I understood things better." Rosalyn also had a best friend named Sonia to whom she could "tell anything." Rosalyn and Sonia regularly spent time together with their children who were about the same age. Rosalyn said she had always had best friends in her life.

The sources of Rosalyn's resilience seemed instantly apparent in her interview. Despite early childbearing and growing up in a poor urban environment, Rosalyn had been surrounded by supportive people who provided her with both emotional and material support. She was in a stable and supportive relationship with the child's father, her mother, her grandmother, and her best friend, and these relation-

---

[1]Werner (1993) also found in her longitudinal study of resiliency among a Hawaiian, low-income sample, that many of the more resilient young adults spoke about having had to adhere to strict rules as a child. These rules seemed to set clear guidelines concerning appropriate behavior.

ships had clearly helped her to thrive. The stability of her relationships made it easier for her to attain her goals, and her trust and ambitions may have, in turn, enhanced her relationships with her husband and her best friend, who also appeared to have high ambitions for themselves. Rosalyn's story was typical of the four women who had family support for their successful adaptations. The interviews also show that the protective processes of support go beyond warmth, material support, and strictness. The mothers or extended family of the mothers who succeeded believed that they could and demanded that the adolescent mother stay *on track* despite having a child.

SUPPORT THAT CHALLENGES AND BELIEVES IN YOU

Like Rosalyn, Glenda said it was the support from her mother, father, sister, aunts, uncles, and best friends that helped her maintain her strength in the midst of multiple obstacles. Glenda had her child when she was 18 and worked as a word-processing secretary at the 6-year follow-up. She still lived with her mother but was actively trying to get her own apartment. When asked what had helped her so far, she said:

Definitely the support of my mother and my family. Definitely, I mean because I already had in my mind that I had [my child], I wasn't going to let her stop me. If my family wasn't there I'm pretty sure maybe I might not have been where I am now.... There has always been somebody there to help me. Even my friends, for that matter ... My mother and my father and my sister and my family was there for me, I mean I didn't really go through anything harsh.

Like Rosalyn, Glenda was raised by her mother and had a close relationship with her. Her mother believed she could make something of herself. As Glenda put it:

If I had a problem, I would talk with her. And as far as helping mentally, physically, and financially, she's just been there ... I mean she told me, she always drilled into my head, I mean don't let having a baby stop you. They slow you down, yes, but you can go out there and make something of yourself and be something. That does not stop you. Because you have one, that does not mean you, let's say fall into a little bottle where you can't get out. I mean the jar has lifted. It's just that my mother gave me the opportunities and I took them and I did something for myself.

Stories of family members repeatedly emphasizing the belief that having children should not stop a young mother from accomplishing her goals were common among all of the women who succeeded. Their family members not only encouraged them to pursue their goals, but stated that they would only help them if they "helped themselves." Glenda said her mother told her, " 'As long as I see you doing something for yourself, I'll always be there to help you.' So she sort of gave me the push."

Beebe, an African-American young mother of two children who was in a master's program in criminal law and worked as a legal aid at the 6-year follow-up, also said that her aunt (her mother died when she was 12) told her that she would help her "as long as I'm on the right track, you know. As long as I do what I've got to do.... "

Belinda, a half African-American and half Puerto Rican young woman, also talked about the conditional support provided by her mother. When asked where she got her push to achieve, she answered, "from my mother, 'cause my mother wasn't having any, I could not stay home and not do anything." Her mother had not allowed her to stay home, she said:

> She didn't allow me. And my mother wasn't the type to babysit while I go and do whatever. I had to be actually doing something worthwhile for her to watch him.... So it started off as my mother, but it continued because it's something that I wanted to do.

These families' expectations and demands embedded in the context of their support pushed these young women toward successful outcomes. The child-care and material support provided by their mothers was clearly important to their success, but so too were conditions attached to this support. These grandmothers were ready to recognize success and believed their daughters could achieve it. When their daughters took advantage of opportunities and were on track, they offered more. The effort was bidirectional, not just giving.

Glenda's boyfriend, a policeman, had also been extremely helpful throughout their 3-year relationship. When asked what she particularly liked about this relationship, she said, "we both want the same things. We both want the better things out of life. We don't want to just sit there and expect them to get handed to us. We find ... we're capable and able to go out there and do something and make something of ourselves." Typical of many of these adaptive women, Glenda surrounded herself with people who shared her ambitious goals. She was attracted to and by other strong people who supported the resiliency she showed.

Johanna: Disproving Doubts

Like Marie, Johanna suggested that it was her family's doubts and disappointment, in part, that motivated her to accomplish her goals. Burdened by their families' rejection and doubt, these mothers encountered extremely stressful periods immediately after the birth of their first child. However, their families' doubts eventually came to be seen as the negative identities that these mothers were determined to avoid.

Johanna, a young African-American women, had recently been promoted to assistant supervisor at her job at the 6-year follow-up. She had her first child when she was 15 years old and her second child when she was 18. In contrast to the mothers with a supportive context of family, she had been on her own since the age of 15. Johanna always had a "bitter" relationship with her abusive mother:

Everything that I did, my mother hit me … I used to think that my mother abused me when I was a child, because everything, she would hit me. Everything. It was never, could you explain to me why you did that but just whack, you know. Just always hit me. So and I, I hated her for that, you know. And, I'm still bitter for those things.

Johanna said she could never speak with her mother about her concerns or problems and had never felt close to her. However, like many of the other more successful mothers, Johanna reported that her mother was strict with her as she was growing up: "My mother was always on my back, maybe if I'm out at 5, I had to be upstairs by 7:30. Most of my friends were just coming out at 7:30." At the age of 15, Johanna left her mother's home because of her mother's abuse. She moved into a home for girls that was run by nuns and then into a home for young mothers. At that point in her life, she had no one in her family who had been willing "to back her up" and she had nowhere to turn: "I know what it's like to not know where am I gonna sleep tonight or what am I gonna feed them, or you know? This one needs a coat, that one needs shoes, how you gonna do it?" A nun taught her to:

take [difficult experiences] as a learning experience, and see what you can get from it, you know? … she got my life back on track. She got me back in school, you know. The kids were going to a babysitter, she gave me stability.

The nuns at the young mothers' home provided enough material and emotional support that Johanna was eventually able to leave and live independently when she was 18.

At the 6-year point, Johanna had grown. She still rarely spoke to her mother, but she began to actively resist being like her. She said: "I've learned that I can't make my mother happy.… Our relationship has left me really bitter.… I do everything in my power not to be like her." Johanna said she had gone through a long period after her child was born when her primary activity each day was watching many hours of television. Perhaps no longer needing to try to make her mother happy, and with the nun's support, Johanna said she decided to "change [her] life around" and joined a back-to-work program that placed her in an agency where she worked as a clerk. She eventually moved up the hierarchy to become an assistant supervisor. In her interview, she proudly showed her interviewer a copy of a *New York Times* article about her and her peers in the work program as an example of a successful young woman who had overcome many odds in her life.

Johanna said one of the reasons she chose to "turn her life around" and pursue her goals was that she wanted to prove her family wrong:

I did something with myself after my … family said, she's not gonna do that, she's gonna have six kids, seven kids, and so on, so on, she'll never amount to anything. I have two children, I have an apartment, I'm an assistant supervisor, you know?

Johanna also attributed her success to her support group. When asked if she felt confident that she would do what she wanted to do, she said she felt she could with the help of the people that supported her:

> … my support group … the people that I'm able to let it out to, you know. Just sometimes, you know, it can be six months into the year, and I haven't cried, you know? Which is not healthy, I don't think. If you have two children. So, um, their being there for me, just to let it out.

Her support group included her current boyfriend (she had been with this boyfriend, who was not the father of her children, off and on since the seventh grade), her aunt who had "always made me feel special," her "spiritual godmother," her cousin who had "always been there for me," her bosses at work who were "like my three mothers," and the nun with whom she lived at the residential home.

Although Johanna had had a particularly difficult relationship with her mother, the consistent support that she had received from many other people in her life sustained her as she struggled toward success with her children. The positive effects of support, believers, and positive role models—a stable context of others on the transition to young adulthood—is clear.

Melinda

Similar themes emerge from Melinda's story. At the 6-year follow-up, Melinda, a young African-American woman, worked full time at a hardware store and was in her second year in college studying communication arts. She was married and had been with her husband, her child's father, for 10 years. He worked in a stable job as a mail carrier and had an associate's degree. Melinda had her only child when she was 16. She was raised by her father after her mother became addicted to drugs. She chose, however, to move in with her mother at age 14 to live near her new boyfriend (and soon-to-be husband). Like Taylor, Melinda blamed her mother's lenience for her temporarily irresponsible behavior:

> I met my husband at 14 years old, I mean, you think you are grown at that age … especially when you have nobody really on you like disciplining you … there was no discipline in my house when I was 14. But the early years before 14, my father was very strict. He was very upset when I got pregnant. He was very upset at my mother, not me, because she was on drugs and he didn't know about it … and she wasn't watching over me like she should have, she wasn't keeping me in the house. I was roaming the street, 4 or 5 in the morning at 14 years old, that's too young to be out.…

In a barely audible voice, Melinda explained to her interviewer that the reason her mother became addicted to drugs was because her mother was molested by her own father and then separated from her siblings, who were put into different foster homes. Melinda seemed protective of her mother while angry that she had to assume a caregiver role at a young age:

> I had kids at a very young age, it was then that she was on drugs … I had two brothers and a sister, so I was taking care of all three of them. When my husband met me at 14, I was with them, everywhere we went the kids were with us.

Her early experience as a caregiver, however, may have strengthened her belief that she could take care of herself and a child despite the neglect of her mother.[2]

Throughout her interview, Melinda said that she had never felt fully accepted by her mother, but she cannot give up the longing she feels for her own acceptance and love for her mother to be reciprocated:

> I want my mother to accept me. I want her, if she disagrees with me, then let me know about it but still be on my side and that's not where she is. She's not by my side. I don't think I could depend on her, you know, she's not really there for me. I want her to love me unconditionally, maybe she do, I don't know that. That's why she should show me, you know … maybe she looks at me as though I don't need that love.… But, I need my mother's love, I need for her to accept me … it hurts me.… My mother is the only one in this world that can hurt me.… My mother, it's like it's straight to the bone, you know because I always loved my mother. When she was on drugs I never disowned her. I was always by her side. Always claimed her as a mother, you know what I'm saying? Never was ashamed because that was my mother and today I still claim her, you know, she's my mother. She wasn't there for me, so what, I love her. That's the way I feel and I wish she could love me the same, you know.

Melinda's desire for acceptance and approval from her mother led her to try repeatedly to prove her worth to her. Like Glenda and Marie, Melinda was hurt by her mother's behavior, but motivated by her mother's doubts and lack of acceptance. She was determined to prove to her mother that she was capable of great things.

Melinda said that not only had her mother not been there for her, but her father has not been able to provide what she needed either: "Sometimes, even as an adult, I'm afraid to talk about certain things with him because I really don't know how he'll react." She believed that she would not have become pregnant if her father had been able to believe in her. She said:

> All I needed was someone there for me saying, Melinda I want you to be better. You don't need a relationship with a boy at such a young age, we love you, that

---

[2] Werner (1993) reported that many of the resilient adults she interviewed spoke of having to care for their younger siblings as adolescents because their own parents were not able or were not around to provide such support.

type of thing. I think it would have been different if he was there, you know, emotionally, you know, just being there.

Melinda was not alone, however. Her support came from outside of her immediate family. Her large network included her husband, best friends, grandmother, uncles, and cousin. She described her husband as a "nice, loving, and giving" man who was "a wonderful person.... He's just been great. He helped me deal with a lot of my family problems.... He was always there for me." Although she said that recently she did not feel appreciated enough by her husband, she was firm in her belief that he had helped her cope with her family difficulties. Her best friend, Diane, had also helped her. She had been close friends with Diane for about 4 years and spoke to her regularly. Diane and her husband babysat for Melinda's child when Melinda and her husband wanted to go out, and Melinda returned the favor.

Melinda said her support network included not only her husband and best friend Diane, but also her cousin. She described her cousin as a "very positive picture. She's what I want to be. She's where I want to be. She has a beautiful home. She's almost 40 years old with one child that's 3 years old. She has like the perfect life, I think." Melinda said that her cousin, a teacher, was like a sister to her, providing support, advice, and guidance. Melinda's support network appeared to work as a buffer against the stress of her mother's drug addiction and her father's lack of emotional support:

> When I got pregnant at 16, I was ashamed because that wasn't something I really wanted. I had higher expectations for myself. I was embarrassed, you know, it was just terrible for me, you know the feeling, being pregnant at 16, but I got over it because I knew I had people that was going to stick behind me.... I guess if I was a single parent things would be hard, but because I have a spouse and I have people that care about me, they have made life easy for me.

The mothers who worked or went to school and were married or in long-term romantic relationships were frequently close friends with other mothers who provided positive role models and who shared their desires to make something of themselves. In fact, several of the young mothers made a point of distinguishing themselves from their peers who did not work or go to school. They spoke with irritation about their peers who didn't "do anything with themselves." Charise, who had her child at 16 and worked as a nurse's aide, mentioned that she and her close friends all had good jobs: "We all work in a hospital and we all have had jobs for a long time so everybody else [around me] is either on welfare, you know ... they think of us as a different group because we work." Beebe said:

> I choose my friends carefully, you know, people I'm going to be around. I know a lot of people around my sister's block where I used to live that I grew up with and knew me since I was in kindergarten.... We'll talk or whatever ... but as far as exchanging numbers, you know, I just ... I try to associate myself around positive

people, people that can help me or teach me something or people that want to do something.... People that's similar [to me] ... they are trying, they are doing something, I try to associate with them so we push each other and maybe one day they may be tired and I say, come on you can finish that paper, or I may be tired. You know, it works both ways.

The more successful mothers also often had family members who were actively pursuing their own academic and career goals. When Beebe was asked where she got her strength from, she said: "My family. I have a very productive family. They've done well for themselves and I just want to follow." Sabine had a grandmother who went back to college and got her master's degree and also took some doctoral classes at a prestigious university. "She was an inspiration," said Sabine, who was then in her third year of college.

Building on a foundation of supportive others and staying focused on the positive also helped Melinda stay on track. Her positive attitude had been critical in her path to success (which, in turn, likely encouraged her positive attitude): "Even the bad things, I mean, like I say, everything has a reason, there always turns out to be some good behind it." When she discussed some of the difficulties she had been having with her husband, she said, "If he thinks something is not working out right, [we] sit down and he will tell me, my feelings might be hurt but I look at it in a positive way, you know, well this is something I can work on to make things better." Melinda firmly believed that the obstacles or difficulties in her life could be overcome.

Sabine, an African-American young woman who had been unemployed but was in college at the 6-year follow-up, said she too had seen the benefits of being optimistic:

> I just might not have money for my rent and then in the mail a letter comes saying we owe you some more money and I get $99 and that's a contribution toward my rent ... my grandmother always told me that if I took care of myself and my children the way I was supposed to that good things would happen and it just has been happening.

A hopeful, optimistic, or positive outlook helped these mothers maintain their determination and persistence. They discussed their positive attitudes or belief that barriers could be overcome with an urgency in their voices. This suggested that this belief was not simply a cliché, but a fundamental part of their survival strategy. They needed to believe that they could and would do well in their lives to continue trying to succeed.

These more successful women had clear goals and saw themselves as strong and determined. They had a passionate desire to learn from their experiences and pursue their goals. Marie said: "I like to do my best. I'm a workaholic, like I said, I'm a perfectionist, I wanna do, I wanna do the best I can at something." When Taylor was asked what might help her accomplish her goals, she said:

me ... my willingness to want, you know, what I want ... my demand of myself. That's what always helped me accomplish my goals. As long as I believe that I can do what I want to do, and don't let nothing stand in my way, and it's up to me to make my life. There is no one else that's gonna do it but me. So that's what's gonna help me accomplish my goals.

Beebe said, "I know what I want to do, I know what I have to do to do it and I don't try to side-track to this, I try to stay one way and go forward." When asked to describe herself, Johanna recognized she needed someone to back her up (especially her mother), but she was able to draw strength from her ability to cope with the stresses in her life. She said:

You ever go through something in your life and you don't have anyone to back you up? And you need that really, and that's when you really need someone to back you and they are not there. And you make it anyway.... That's what I am, I'll do it anyway ... I'm stubborn. I think that, um, I'm very determined, I'm a very determined person, I have a determined will about myself. Um, if I put my mind to it, it's gonna be done ... I think that I'm a very strong person ... the things that I went through in my life, I was very young. Um, I think most people might have went crazy, dealing with that sort of thing. Those things, out of each situation in my life, I took something from it. It took a lot out of me, but I took something back ... from this situation I had, I got strength, from this situation there's tolerance, from that situation ... you know different things came out of a lot of different things that make me up as a person, I've gotten from what I went through in my life.... It'll come when it comes. And if it don't come, move on.

The young mothers who showed resilience in the face of life' adversities saw themselves as resilient as well. They knew that they persisted in ways that many of their peers were not able to. They were proud of themselves and clearly wanted others, including their interviewers, to recognize their accomplishments and successes.

UNDERSTANDING THE SOURCES OF RESILIENCY

The case studies of Marie, Rosalyn, Glenda, Johanna, and Melinda reveal how the processes or themes of resilience detected among of the 15 women were woven together to create adaptive outcomes within individual lives. Many of these processes have been noted in other studies of resiliency or competency among high-risk populations. For example, authoritative parenting that involves warmth, structure, and high expectations has consistently been associated with positive outcomes among high-risk populations (Masten & Coatsworth, 1998; Werner & Smith, 1982, 1992). Extended family support networks and close ties to prosocial adults outside the family are also commonly considered protective factors for individuals in high-risk environments. In addition, a sense of self-efficacy, determination, and a positive outlook have also frequently been associated with resilient outcomes (Masten & Coatsworth, 1998; National Institute of Mental Health, 1996; Werner & Smith, 1982, 1992). However, our investigation of a subsample of our young mothers suggests that, beyond independent predictors of success, these protective factors are interdependent processes that jointly support positive outcomes.

The processes that we detected that have not been regularly addressed in the previous research on high-risk populations are those related to challenges and constraints. The young mothers spoke of the importance of receiving conditional rather than unconditional support from their families and of being motivated because they wanted to disprove their families' doubts about their abilities. The mothers suggested that it was not simply support that helped them move forward, but also the experience of challenge, constraint, and doubt.

Moderate levels of stress in supportive contexts may produce challenges, which, when handled successfully, strengthen an individual's sense of competence (Cicchetti & Garmezy, 1993). The young mothers in our sample suggested that their families' doubts about their potential, as well as the *conditional* support provided by their mothers or guardians, not only motivated them to accomplish their goals but ultimately heightened their sense of accomplishment.

These challenges, however, did not have positive consequences when the mothers did not have the support of extended family members, friends, boyfriends, or role models who valued education and had satisfying careers or high levels of self-confidence. However, the support they received from their families and the inspiration they drew from associating with positive role models and resisting negative models may not have had such positive consequences without their accompanying challenges. The themes detected in the young mothers' interviews wove together with no single process evident without the presence of the others. Understanding how these influences work together is crucial to understanding the development of coping skills, resilience, and strength.

It is also important to understand how the coping strategies and resilience of adolescent mothers changed (Cicchetti & Garmezy, 1993). If we had focused on Marie at the 1-year follow-up (when she was still involved with her abusive boyfriend), she would not have appeared as resilient as she did in her 6-year follow-up interview. Her ability to thrive fluctuated over time as she confronted new challenges, obstacles, and opportunities.

Furthermore, had we defined successful adaptations differently, we would have considered a different subgroup of young mothers as resilient. The 15 mothers were identified as resilient because they were doing well along four dimensions (education, employment, mental health, and physical health). Had our resilient dimensions focused on social competence, parenting skills, and mental health, for example, an undoubtedly larger group of young mothers within our sample would have been identified as resilient. Although it is likely that the women we described in this chapter would still have been categorized as resilient given their strengths in many areas of their lives, many more women would also have been included. Understanding the processes that lead some mothers to thrive in particular areas of their lives and not in others should be an additional goal for future studies of adolescent mothers.

We have known for more than a decade that the majority of adolescent mothers eventually graduate from high school, find stable employment, move into their own apartments, and raise children who do not have children as adolescents (see Brooks-Gunn & Furstenberg, 1986; Horwitz et al., 1991; Leadbeater, 1996). However, we are only beginning to understand the factors that help mothers attain these goals (see Way & Leadbeater, 1999). Future qualitative and quantitative research should examine the goals of young mothers, the strategies they use to accomplish their goals, and the reasons for and contexts of these strategies and goals. We need to move beyond negative stereotyping of this population to explore the ways in which supports and challenges produce strength, resistance, and healthy adaptation among many young mothers.

Pathways to Adulthood: School and Work

❧

Perhaps the most dramatic change since the 1970s in U.S. society is the rise in participation of women, many of them mothers, in the labor market. Between 1970 and 1994, the number of mothers with children under the age of 6 who were in the labor force more than doubled from 30% to 62% (Children's Defense Fund, 1996). However, most positions for women, and thus for mothers, continue to pay substantially less than those for men with similar levels of education. The average family income in mother-only families in 1993 was $12,073, compared with $23,305 in father-only families (Zill & Nord, 1994). The net value of a mother's working is also often substantially reduced by the costs of child care, transportation, and clothing. At the same time, increasing numbers of out-of-wedlock births and high divorce rates mean that mothers are likely to be responsible for their families' income. In 1993, 23% of children under 18 lived in mother-only families and 3% in father-only families (Zill & Nord, 1994).

For all young women in the 1990s, the normative transition from adolescence to adulthood is one from school to work. For adolescent mothers with young children, the expectation that they work has escalated as the norm of working mothers infuses the middle class. As Zill, Moore, Nord, and Steif (1991) concluded in their report on welfare mothers as potential workers: "demanding that welfare mothers with young children get a job or take part in vocational training can in some sense be viewed as moving them into the mainstream" (p. 17). Moreover, a majority of these young women want to work and to be able to make a living wage (Spalter-Roth, Burr, Hartmann, & Shaw, 1995). The question is no longer how can welfare support women and their children, but how can welfare support mothers so they can work?

DESIGNING POLICIES THAT HELP

To design policy reforms that would address this question requires an analysis of the stresses that work places on poor mothers and the resources that are most valuable in reducing these stresses. Can mothers really manage to work full or part time, advance their careers through education, and provide adequate care for their children? Can employers afford to offer mothers personal leave days for child illness and school holidays, and flex time for children's medical appointments and school conferences? The demands of caring for children can easily threaten the job stability of mothers in low-paying jobs. It is clear, as described in chapter 5, that young mothers who make the transition from welfare to work have more education and more family support—that is, they have more of the resources that enable them to work. How can these resources be supplemented for adolescent mothers who are making this transition?

Legislation that mandates what a majority of working mothers are already accomplishing on their own gives the appearance that something is being done to change welfare as we know it, but such legislation does not address the problems of adolescent mothers who are falling behind. The reasons some teenage mothers do not keep up with the majority of mothers—those who exit welfare within 2 years—are varied (see chaps. 6 and 7; Harris, 1997). Poor school performance, learning problems, depression, health problems, abuse, and lack of family support are all factors that, in part, determine the outcomes for these young women, often well in advance of the delivery of their first child or first welfare episode (Hao & Brinton, 1997; Leadbeater, 1996; Upchurch, 1993; Zill, Moore, Smith, Steif, & Coiro, 1997).

Many recent studies have assessed young single mothers' transition to work using economic and sociological models with large national data sets. These studies have assessed the relative advantages, over and above a mother's family background characteristics, of post-pregnancy resources such as residence with a grandmother or mother, child-care assistance, presence of role models who are working, limiting subsequent births, and neighborhood level of income (e.g., Hao & Brinton, 1997; Upchurch, 1993; Wilson, 1987). Survey research often illuminates the factors that helped those young mothers who succeeded on their own; the factors that could aid young mothers who are having difficulty making a successful transition to work may be very different. For example, although grandmother support may predict more positive outcomes, it cannot be mandated for teen mothers who do not have it when these grandmothers are ill, abusive, or even working.

The processes through which these factors influence school achievement and employment outcomes for adolescent mothers are complex. For example, Hao and Brinton (1997), using data from the Youth Survey section of the 1979 to 1992 National Longitudinal Survey of Labor Market Experience, found that for young single mothers, kin co-residence was related to job entry but not job maintenance in the labor market. (The data were for women between the ages of 14 and 21 in January 1979 who were single mothers as a result of either out-of-wedlock births or divorce.) Hao and Brinton (1997) suggested that living with family members may improve a young mother's entry into the workforce as a result of family expectations that mothers be engaged in productive activities, help with child care by family members, and exposure to the normal work routine of adults. However, in low-income, high-unemployment neighborhoods, families that insist on continued education and productive activities, and provide models of working parents, may be rare (Wilson, 1995). However, working family members often cannot provide child care so their teenage daughters can attend school.

This chapter focuses on the mothers in the New York study who were not on welfare at the 6-year follow-up. In many ways, they are similar to the mothers on welfare who were also in school or working (see chaps. 6 and 7). Indeed, many had had welfare episodes. Many were dealing with extraordinary stress. Moreover, their employment status was continuously challenged by the stresses of work.

THE TRANSITIONS TO WORK AMONG THE NEW YORK SAMPLE

Most of the young mothers in the New York study wanted to graduate from high school and find work. By the 6-year follow-up, 52% had graduated from high school, 14% had attended some college, and 37% were employed full or part time. At the initial interviews and even 3 years later, however, many of the mothers had life plans that did not include feeling pressure to work or stay in school. Many aspired to low-income jobs that seemed to be within easy reach; others anticipated continued support from their child's father. Some of the young mothers aspired to be accountants, but in fact talked about training programs for bookkeeping jobs. One said she wanted to become a physician's assistant, but talked about going to a 6-week program to be a doctor's receptionist. Many had no idea what income to expect from different jobs or what high school credits or what post-high school training were needed to gain entry into the profession they wanted.

By the 6-year follow-up, the reality of supporting a child or children alone and the desire for their children's life to be better than their own pushed many mothers into new attitudes toward work and welfare. These women became ever more aware during their early adult years that work was the only way out of their day-to-day struggle with welfare and poverty. Anticipating and changing their futures became paramount. Charise, whose story is detailed in the next chapter, contrasted becoming independent with living day-to-day:

> I'm not helpless and ... in order to go somewhere you have to come from somewhere and you have to make a rock for yourself to stand on. Basically, I feel I've done that.... Like, if you're not independent, you have no worries, no plans for tomorrow, nothing to look forward to, like, you're just living on a day-to-day basis. And basically, I'm not. I know what the future holds and I know what every-

day life is and basically I can see that this is for today, but I know I'm going to need this for tomorrow. Basically I think that's independent.

Sherry, who finished an associate's degree in accounting when her child's father left her, contrasted her life on welfare with her life as a working mother, saying for her it was about:

> wanting to be the best, not wanting to have a difficult life, to be a burden on anybody. I mean I was a teen parent, and I had my son very young. But I still saw girls that were my age or younger or older who did not know, who had no idea. They would just be welfare recipients for the rest of their lives. They had no idea of how to get out. So I didn't want that. I didn't want to have to go to an appointment to see a social worker and have to give her my whole life history, and be dependent on a check that comes each month.... I wanted to get an income tax return. I want to get my paycheck, I want to go somewhere and just work and have good things, I want to have a bank account, travel, and do things that I wanted to do, have a house, that's all.

Considerable research has addressed predictors of successful school outcomes for adolescent mothers, and we review it briefly here. Less research has focused on the successful work outcomes of adolescent mothers. Even in this study, given the young age of many of these mothers, our investigation of work outcomes is limited. However, the interview data elicit the nature of the day-to-day lives of mothers who did work, offering clear suggestions for policies that could address the stresses of work and make their job experiences more stable.

Getting Through School With a Baby

Although school-age parenting is typically disruptive to optimal school achievement, past research has extensively demonstrated the considerable diversity in educational outcomes for adolescent mothers (Alan Guttmacher Institute, 1994; Furstenburg et al., 1987; Haggstrom, Kanouse, & Morrison, 1986; Harris, 1997; Henshaw, Kenney, Somberg, & Van Vort, 1989; Leadbeater, 1996; Linares, Leadbeater, Kato, & Jaffe, 1991; Moore et al., 1993; Mott & Marsiglio, 1985; Scott-Jones, 1991; Scott-Jones & Turner, 1990; Upchurch, 1993). Predictors of high school graduation for adolescent mothers include antecedent factors (i.e., poverty, ethnicity/race, and parents' educational, employment, and marital status), as well as events that occur subsequent to the first birth (i.e., stressful life events and repeat pregnancies).

National statistics indicate that a majority of adolescent mothers (71%) eventually do complete high school. However, few (20%) pursue a college education (Alan Guttmacher Institute, 1994). Although a few adolescent mothers are able to get financial aid and an even smaller number receive scholarships to attend college, actually saving for a college education or receiving and repaying student loans is not possible for poor families that live from month to month on limited income from welfare or work. Some teen mothers struggle with loans for short-term job training programs in word processing and other basic skills that promise, but often cannot deliver, placement in jobs that offer sufficient income to repay the costs of the training. Mothers who only graduate from high school face staggering competition in a job market that demands increasing levels of education (Strawn, 1992). Some adolescent mothers plan to return to school or job-training programs as their own children enter school. However, Scott-Jones and Turner (1990) found no cohort differences in educational outcomes for nationally representative samples of African Americans (ages 20–24, 25–34, or 35–44) who had all become mothers as adolescents, suggesting change in their status after the early 20s is unlikely.

Adolescents from disadvantaged family backgrounds who become mothers before the age of 18 are at particular risk for negative outcomes. Upchurch (1993) prospectively assessed relations between early schooling and childbearing experiences in a sample of women who were ages 14 to 18 in the initial interviews in 1979. Using data from the National Longitudinal Survey of Youth (NLSY) collected annually for 7 years, she reported that 53.1% of White, 59.5% of African-American, and 36.7% of Hispanic women who became mothers before the age of 18 had graduated from high school or received a GED by the time of the 7-year follow-up (i.e., by ages 21–25). Those who had dropped out of school before they became pregnant came from the least-educated family backgrounds and were more likely to be White or Hispanic than African American. African Americans were more likely to drop out of school after becoming pregnant than were Whites or Hispanics.

Despite the concentration of inner-city, disadvantaged mothers in the New York study (which might result in lower graduation rates), the overall percentage of women in the New York study who had graduated or received a GED by the 6-year follow-up was similar to the NLSY statistics for African Americans and Hispanics. By that point, 52% of the mothers remaining in the sample (35% of Puerto Ricans and 59% of African-Americans) had graduated. Sample attrition was unrelated to school status at 12 months postpartum; however, more Hispanic mothers (33%) than African-Americans mothers (16%) [χ^2 (2, $N = 120) = 6.6, p = .04$] were lost to follow-up, perhaps exaggerating the differences between these groups at Time 6.

Educational attainment is higher for African-American than for Puerto Rican teenagers in the communities represented by this sample (New York's Dropouts-to-Be, 1989), thus it is not surprising that the adolescent mothers in our sample reflected the same pattern. Those who dropped out before they became pregnant were more likely to be Hispanic (57%), whereas those who dropped out after the pregnancy were equally likely to be Hispanic (52%) or African American (45%; Linares et al., 1991). The African-American adolescent mothers also had somewhat higher work commitment scores than the Puerto Ricans.

Women's positive identities as mothers remain strong in traditional Hispanic cultures, offering resistance to the middle-class, Euro-American norm of working mothers (De Leon, 1996; Garcia-Coll, Escobar, Cebollero, & Valcarcel, 1989).

The subculture's valuing of motherhood reduces social pressures to simultaneously pursue work and child-care goals. The mothers of the African-American adolescents were more educated than those of the Puerto Ricans and may have modeled and emphasized the importance of their daughters' education and independence more than the Puerto Rican mothers (De Leon, 1996; McLoyd & Hernandez-Josefowicz, 1996).

The New York sample of mothers who had not graduated by the 6-year point were, at delivery, slightly younger (17.0 years, $SD = 1.7$) than mothers who had graduated (17.4 years, $SD = 1$). Even taking this into account, nongraduates were more likely to be more delayed in their grade placement (ideal age for grade minus last grade completed) at delivery (1.7 years, $SD = 1.0$) than those who graduated (1 year, $SD = .94$). However, comparisons of graduates and nongraduates obscure the dramatic within-group differences in educational success among these mothers. Indeed, we found considerable group differences in educational achievement among the New York sample. Subgroups differences were already apparent at the 12-month and 36-month follow-ups.

At the end of the first year, the mothers were categorized into school outcome groups determined from their responses to questions about the type of school they were enrolled in, when they last attended, their last grade completed, and their current grade level assessed by self-report three times in the first year. The criterion for in-school status was defined as current school attendance (not merely school enrollment) or attendance in the last marking period for interviews during the summer months.

The sample was divided into four groups:

- *Continuous attenders/graduates* (41%) were mothers who attended school through the pregnancy and the first year postpartum (Times 1, 2, and 3) or had graduated from high school or a GED program.
- *School returners* (21%) were mothers who were not in school during the pregnancy or at Times 1 or 2, but had returned by Time 3.
- *Before-pregnancy dropouts* (12%) were mothers who had dropped out before the pregnancy and were not attending school at Times 1, 2, or 3.
- *After-pregnancy dropouts* (26%) were mothers who had dropped out of school during the pregnancy or by Times 1, 2, or 3.

At 3 years postpartum, there was considerable stability in these groupings: 78% of the mothers remained in the group they had been in at 12-months postpartum (Leadbeater, 1996). None who had dropped out before the pregnancy had returned to school, few (6%) of the after-pregnancy dropouts returned later, and more mothers (15%) had dropped out by the 3-year follow-up. Mothers who were in the before-pregnancy dropout group reported the highest levels of depressive symptoms at delivery of all groups (Linares et al., 1991). Those who had returned to school by 3 years postpartum were experiencing fewer depressive symptoms and had higher occupational commitments than mothers in persistent dropout groups (Leadbeater, 1996).

Again using the school group categorization at 1 year postpartum, substantially more mothers who were consistent attenders (71%) or returners (59%) had graduated by the 6-year follow-up than had those in the before-delivery (17%) or after-delivery (29%) dropout groups [χ^2 (3, $N = 92$) = 17.4, $p < .001$]. However, not being in school in the early postpartum period did not make it impossible to return, nor did being in school guarantee success. One quarter of the mothers who had dropped out by 1 year postpartum graduated by the 6-year follow-up, whereas a fifth of those who were in school at 1 year postpartum did not complete high school.

The effects of several variables shown in previous studies to influence school outcomes were examined longitudinally at 1, 3, and 6 years in multiple regression analyses (Leadbeater, 1996; Linares et al., 1991; Way & Leadbeater, 1999). These variables included whether the teen lived with her mother, the quality of their relationship, the presence of support from friends and boyfriends, levels of self-reported stress and depressive symptoms, number of repeat pregnancies, and occupational aspirations or commitment. However, when the teen's grade placement before the delivery (ideal grade for age minus last grade completed; i.e., an assessment of prior school performance) was entered into this equation, it was found to be the **only** independent predictor of the mothers' delayed grade placement at 1 and 3 years postpartum (Leadbeater, 1996; Linares et al., 1991). Delayed grade placement at delivery also remained a strong predictor of educational achievement at the 6-year follow-up, although number of repeat pregnancies and more emotional support from the grandmothers also predicted fewer grades completed (see Table 4.1; Way & Leadbeater, 1999).

Although there is some evidence that early intervention programs can impact school outcomes for adolescent mothers (Klerman & Horwitz, 1992; Seitz, Apfel, & Rosenbaum, 1991), the educational success of minority group adolescent mothers clearly depends on the attention given to reducing school failure in adolescent girls *before* they become parents. It is possible that some of the mothers in our sample may still return to school or job training programs as their own children enter school. However, the stability in the school status of this sample and national samples (Scott-Jones & Turner, 1990), as well as difficulties in paying for post-high school education and caring for subsequent children, suggest that further changes in school outcomes with age are unlikely.

Becoming a Working Mother

In one of the few studies to look at within-group differences in adolescent mothers, Harris (1997) distinguished predictors for three groups of adolescent mothers: those who left welfare as they entered a new job, those who "worked their way off of welfare" by combining part-time or low-paying jobs with welfare income, and those who never worked. Her findings leave little doubt that adolescent mothers who were older and more educated at the birth of their first child and who had more background family resources (e.g., more educated parents) were more likely to leave welfare completely when they began to work. Mothers who abandoned their education for early job entry fared less well over time, suggesting that the effects of educational attainment exceed those of experience even in low-paying jobs.

TABLE 4.1

Standardized Final Beta Weight for Predictors of Last Grade Completed at 1, 3, and 6 Years Postpartum

Variable	Delivery	3 Years	6 Years
Time 1 delayed grade		−.48**	−.27*
African American	.16[t]	.1	.02
On welfare	−.20*	.02	.01
Life stress[a]	−.01	−.08	−.1
Repeat pregnancy	—	−.14	−.22*
Depressive symptoms[a]	−.12	−.14	−.22[t]
Lives with mother[a]	−.01	−.01	−.06
Family support[a]	−.12	−.24[t]	−.32*
Number in analyses[b]	120	72	79
Multiple R	.32	.62	.55
Overall F statistic	2.19*	4.65**	3.70**

[a]Assessed as concurrent variables at delivery and as averages of three assessments done in Year 1 (Time 1, 2, and 3) for the follow-ups at Time 3 and 6.
[b]Numbers used in the follow-up analyses vary due to listwise deletion of missing variables.
[t]$p < .10$.
*$p < .05$.
**$p < .01$.

Mothers who married or cohabited with a partner were also much less likely to work. However, work was less normative for married women in the period studied (the 1960s and 1970s) than it is at the beginning of the 21st century.

Our comparisons of working and nonworking mothers in the New York study at the 6-year follow-up are qualified by the small sample size (only 34 mothers worked) and by the relative youth of these young women. Also, the mothers who were enrolled in college programs had the greatest income potential, but by and large were still in school and worked only part time. Nevertheless, some early trends were already apparent. The 34 mothers who worked earned on average $8.65 an hour ($SD = 2.65$, with a range between $5 and $13 an hour). Comparing the mothers' incomes in categories of no income, less than $6 an hour, and more than $7 an hour, earnings were related to high school graduation ($\chi^2 = 16.3$, $df = 2$, $p < .001$), but not college attainment at that point. Thirty-six percent ($n = 8$) of those with higher wages were married, compared with only 12% of the nonworking mothers, ($\chi^2 = 8.9$, $df = 2$, $p = .01$), suggesting that these women may be either more attractive marriage partners or feel more prepared for marriage.

Earnings and educational attainment at the 6-year follow-up were moderately correlated ($r = .34, p < .001$) as expected, although this correlation was inflated by the large numbers of mothers with no income. This correlation was smaller ($r = .19$) and nonsignificant for working mothers alone, but these results were also driven by the small cell numbers and lack of variance created by the young age of these working mothers. Nevertheless, 86% ($n = 19$) of the highest income earners had graduated from high school, compared with 37% ($n = 22$) of the no-income group ($\chi^2 = 16.3, df = 2, p < .001$).

Twenty-nine percent of the African-American mothers worked, compared with 48% of Puerto Ricans. Both working and nonworking mothers were similar in age at delivery ($M = 17.3, SD = 1.2$ and $M = 17.1, SD = .96$ years, respectively). Compared with nonworking mothers, working mothers at the 6-year follow-up reported significantly fewer concurrent stressful life events and fewer depressive symptoms (concurrently and at the 3-year follow-up; see Table 4.2). Overall levels of social support were similar for working and nonworking mothers at each assessment point, but working mothers were less likely to live with their own mothers at delivery or at the 3-year follow-up. Somewhat fewer children were born to women who worked, although differences were not significant. Although the economic disadvantages of multiple births to teens seem so apparent as to be common sense, many factors go into the decision to deliver a second or third child for all women, and these are equally complicated decisions for teenage mothers.

Avoiding Pregnancies, Abortions, and Having More Children

The rate of repeat pregnancies among adolescent mothers is extremely high, and few of these are planned. A study of minority inner-city women found that one third of adolescent mothers had become pregnant within a year of the birth of their first child (Koenig & Zelnik, 1982). In the New York study, 22% had repeat pregnancies by the end of the first year, 68% by 3 years postpartum, and almost all of the young women (89%) by the 6-year follow-up.

The view that a lack of career opportunities for poor young women makes their choice of limiting childbearing less costly for these young women has been widely held (e.g., Hayes, 1987). Indeed, giving up a low-paying job may not be so difficult for a young mother when the high levels of stress encountered by poor working mothers are weighed against the pleasures of caring for a young child. However, whether early childbearing causes poor educational and work outcomes or whether initially poor educational outcomes cause early childbearing has been the subject of a debate that also applies to subsequent pregnancies for adolescent mothers (East & Felice, 1996; Leadbeater, 1996; Upchurch & McCarthy, 1990). The answer is most likely yes to both causal directions.

In the New York study, being in school was a protective factor against subsequent pregnancies. At the 1-year follow-up, fewer of the mothers (18%) who at-

TABLE 4.2

Means (and Standard Deviations) of Predictors for Mothers Who Worked or Did Not Work at the 6-Year Follow-up

Variable	At Delivery		3-Year Follow-up		6-Year Follow-Up	
	Works	No Work	Works	No Work	Works	No Work
Grade achieved	10.1	9.7[t]	11.6	10.8*	12.2	11.10*
	(1.4)	(1.3)	(2.0)	(1.2)	(2.0)	(1.7)
Life stress	13.6	12.4	N/A		9.3	13.9*
	(7.6)	(7.5)			(6.2)	(6.6)
Number of children	N/A		.56	.73	1.5	1.9
			(0.51)	(0.45)	(0.70)	(0.72)
Depressive symptoms	12.1	14.4	6.3	12.1**	7.1	12.3**
	(6.3)	(7.4)	(4.5)	(9.4)	(6.6)	(9.8)
Lives with mother	.64	.83*	.40	.63[t]	.18	.22
			(0.50)	(0.49)	(0.34)	(0.42)
Social support	11.6	13.1	N/A		33.2	32.6
	(6.1)	(6.0)			(10.3)	(10.0)
Multivariate F df	2.1[t]		4.47**		3.30**	
	(5, 86)		(4, 67)		(6, 84)	

Note. N/A = variable not assessed; age is a covariate.
[t]$p < .10$.
*$p < .05$.
**$p < .01$.

tended school continuously during the first year postpartum had repeat pregnancies than those who returned after a brief period of dropout (32%), dropped out after the pregnancy (63%), or dropped out before the pregnancy (69%). Repeat pregnancies were also significantly related to school status at the 3-year follow-up: By that time, 39% of the consistent attenders had had one or more pregnancies, compared with 68% of the returners, 93% of the after-pregnancy dropouts, and 70% of the before-pregnancy dropouts. In addition, by 3 years postpartum, only 7% of attenders had a full-term delivery, compared with

18.8% of returners, 46.7% of the after-pregnancy dropouts, and 30% of the before-pregnancy dropouts.

Not surprisingly, by the 6-year follow-up, mothers who had only one child were more likely to have graduated from high school (69%) and to be working (52%) than those who had two children (52% graduated, 27% worked). Mothers with one child were six times more likely to have graduated and twice as likely to be working than mothers with three or more children (11% graduated, 23% worked). All of the mothers who had some college courses by the 6-year follow-up had only one or two children.

However, decisions about rearing another child are not only economic. Accessibility to and the cost of abortion, timing of the pregnancy, age of the father, quality of the mother's relationship with the child's father and her own mother, mother's and child's health, and availability of day care influence a young mother's fertility decisions (Alan Guttmacher Institute, 1994). Having a repeat pregnancy soon after the first delivery may make it more likely that the young mother will continue the pregnancy if she intends to be home when her children are young. Unintended pregnancies as well as decisions about abortion figure into fertility decisions of these mothers. These decisions also depend on the mothers' and their partners' and families' beliefs about abortion and the cost (averaging about $250 in an outpatient clinic; Henshaw, 1997). The majority of the New York mothers had subsequent pregnancies that were terminated by abortions (there were also a few miscarriages): 61% of mothers with one child, 80% of those with two, and 76% of those with more than two children had abortions.

One mother, Deanna, talked about her decision not to have an abortion initially:

> When I first got pregnant, right, I was so scared because I didn't know what to do. I was only 16 years old. I was like, I want to get an abortion. And my mother, she was a no abortion person. You know, she just kept having babies after babies. She was like, no way, no way, you are not going to go killing my first grandchild.

Before this child was a year old, however, the grandmother, a drug addict, refused to help and forced her daughter and grandchild to move out. Deanna had no subsequent children, but reported being pregnant two other times.

In the New York study, there were few prospective markers to suggest which of the mothers would go on to have additional children. We classified the 93 mothers who participated in the 6-year follow-up as having one (39%, $n = 36$), two (43%, $n = 40$), or three or more children (18%, $n = 17$). There were no differences in these groups at delivery in the mothers' ages, grades of school completed, family welfare status, or support from the child's father. They also did not differ in the perceived quality of relationships with their own mothers or in the levels of stress or depressive symptoms they experienced. As we report in chapter 6, mothers with three or more children also did not have more welfare episodes than mothers with only one child (over the 6-year follow-up period).

Mothers who had more than one child by the 6-year follow-up were more likely to have been living with their own mothers at delivery [(58%, compared with 87%

and 88% for mothers with 2 or with 3 or more children, respectively) χ^2 (2, $N = 93$) = 10.5, $p = .005$]. The availability of child-care assistance may make second births possible for some of these mothers (East & Felice, 1996). Mothers with three or more children were more likely to be on welfare at the 6-year point (more than 80%, compared with 50% of those with only one child), raising questions about their long-term prospects for staying off welfare.

Repeat pregnancies do add exponentially to the obstacles an adolescent mother faces in returning to school, finding child care, working, or supporting her family on welfare—a fact these mothers also recognized, given that a majority of them chose to have abortions rather than subsequent births. The question of why the rate of unwanted repeat pregnancies is so high among these mothers remains disturbingly open even in this intensive study. East and Felice (1996) found that adolescent mothers who had a repeat pregnancy within 6 months postpartum were more likely to not have returned to or dropped out of school, live with a male partner, receive welfare, and have child-care assistance from the grandmother at 6 months postpartum. In the New York study, only ongoing attendance in or returning to school appeared to have an effect on limiting repeat pregnancies in the early postpartum years, and the mechanisms through which this is achieved are obscure. School-based programs for young mothers may permit greater access to birth control. It is also possible that the personal competence, self-respect, and optimism gained from winning the struggle to stay in school motivates young women (or gives them the authority) to avoid sexual activity or take responsibility for birth control use.

However, cultural prohibitions against open discussion of sexuality, the absence of a discourse on women's sexual desires, and emphasis on women's victimization by men's desire undermine women's agency in effectively using birth control (Fine, 1988). The belief that men's sexuality is innately more difficult to control (both in terms of being able to postpone intercourse and loyalty to a single partner) abounded among the women in the New York study. Women frequently believed they were giving the man something he wanted (sex or children) without a clear vision of their own desires. Concerns about being subject to overcontrolling relationships were mentioned frequently by the young mothers who were in relationships with men (see chap. 8). Indeed, 30% of the women in the New York study reported an experience of abuse (hitting or excessive control) by their child's father or another male partner.

Birth control has come to be seen as women's responsibility. However, young women frequently defer to the *wisdom* and desires of their more experienced, generally older partners. The partners and potential partners of young women need to be brought into dialogues about preventing unintended pregnancies. From a policy perspective, incentives (punitive and positive) directed against teenage mothers who have more children while on welfare need to take into account the role of men. At present, men who father second or third children who end up in welfare-supported households are rarely targeted by prevention or intervention efforts. Education about and assistance in providing male birth control may help decrease subsequent births and abortions in adolescent mothers. In addition, financial, educational, or job training incentives for young men who become fathers (e.g., more rapid service or reduced costs for birth control or abortions for couples that attend educational programs to discuss birth control attitudes and options) may help prevent multiple pregnancies in adolescent women. Child-care assistance may also mediate the effects of subsequent children on outcomes for adolescent mothers, but it also adds to the stress of work (see chaps. 5 and 10).

CHAPTER

5

Life as a Working Mother: Teressa and Charise

Twenty-two of the mothers in the New York sample were working and received no income from welfare by the 6-year follow-up. Most of these young women (*n* = 18) also lived apart from their own mothers, but only three lived alone. The others lived with husbands or boyfriends who contributed to their income or provided child care, possibly suggesting that even with full-time work they could not support their children alone. However, a variety of factors likely co-occurred to contribute to their relative success in both relationships with male partners and work: With incomes, these women are more desirable partners. As we have seen, working mothers also tended to be less depressed and less stressed than nonworking mothers. Living with the grandmothers was not an option for many of these working women. The grandmothers were unavailable due to illness, moves, drug addictions, or histories of abuse or neglect. For the three mothers who lived alone at the 6-year follow-up, their situations reflected recent life transitions, including a separation from a boyfriend, an unintended pregnancy that had occurred in a new relationship, and family (who the mother was living with) moving away.

Overall, the young working mothers who lived in their own apartments had considerable stability in their lives by early adulthood. They saw themselves as having grown. They were busy with adult activities. As Sibylle said of herself and her husband, the baby's father:

> We're growing old. We're young but we say we're growing old. We're old people to everyone else, and it's just the basic routine where it's working, and bringing enough money to pay the bills, and take care of our necessities and that's basically it. And then, you know, if we do it right, we do enough so that we can have one or two days, you know out of a month that we go or whatever, to enjoy ourselves and do something special with her [our daughter].

Another mother, Anne, described her transition from an uncertain teenager to a woman:

I've passed teenage life, teenage crises…. When you are a woman, you are more mature. You carry yourself more mature. You basically need to have someone though, but when you are a teenager you are still experimenting, you're unsure where you want to be, who you want to be, what you want to look like, how you want to look … what image you would like to portray. And when you become a woman, it fits into place.

Six years after the delivery of their first child, these young mothers had the goals and aspirations of most young working women. Most of these adolescent mothers were involved in a new relationship, had just delivered or were considering having another child, and were in stable jobs with possibilities for advancement. For the women with their own apartments, young adulthood seemed like a period of settling in and looking forward. The working mothers who still lived with their own mothers were more unsettled.

At the 6-year follow-up, seven of the mothers who were working continued to share a residence with their own mothers. As a group, these working mothers were in flux, dissatisfied with their current lives, looking for their own apartments, and struggling with school and with what they referred to as their careers, not jobs. Like the working mothers who lived alone, most had broken off their relationship with their child's father and were determined to care for themselves and their children without a man. They saw their early pregnancy as delaying their progress and regretted having started to have children soon, but now they were taking charge. Each woman expressed the feeling that she was different from other young mothers—she was not going to be just a teen mother on welfare. Three of these mothers shared apartments they had found on their own with their mother, who, due to illnesses, had moved in with them. For the other six, moving out of their mother's apartment remained a major goal.

In this chapter, we describe the transitions of two of the working mothers in some detail. Each elaborates the stresses of her work but also its rewards. Teressa, on maternity leave from her job, lived with the father of her second child. Her worries about the future are familiar to all working women: how to pay for her children's education, save money, advance in her job, arrange day care for her three children, move to a better neighborhood, and maintain her relationship. Despite uncertainties, she was generally optimistic about her ability to encounter stress and deal with it. Charise is also a working mother. She had her own apartment but now lived with her mother. She recently broke up with her child's father who was in jail. Her life remains more unsettled than the mothers who no longer lived with their own mothers as she struggles to find suitable housing. For her, early adulthood is a period of reawakening, of getting her own life back on track. Disillusioned about relationships with men, Charise focused on self-reliance, financial security, and independence—on "building herself a rock to stand on."

TERESSA: STRIVING UNDER STRESS, SAFEGUARDING THE FUTURE

Teressa was 18 and in her last year of high school when her daughter, Julia, was born. Three years later, she had finished high school and was happy with her job as a secretary. She was hoping to work her way up to becoming an administrative assistant. Teressa's own mother, who at age 22 was left unable to walk without a cane as the result of a car accident, supported herself on welfare and cared for Julia when Teressa was at work. Teressa appreciated her mother's help and, although wanting to be independent and have her own apartment, had no plans to move out of her mother's house. She had tried welfare for a short time but preferred to work. She explained:

> I guess I like to have my own things. Welfare just pays you for what you need, they just give you food and if you have an apartment it's just for shelter.... If you don't work, how are you going to pay that rent? So I mean I was on it for a while because I had to. I was in high school and had a part time job and I wasn't able to support myself with a part-time job.

At the 3-year interview, Teressa thought she would eventually marry Julia's father, whom she had been with for 6 years, but she hesitated: "He wants to get married ... he bought me a band. My mother is really happy that he wants to marry me. I'll marry him, but not now." While acknowledging that he loved her and was providing for her, Teressa saw him as troubled and frequently depressed:

> Ever since I met him he's just been a serious person. I guess he had a really bad father.... His father was really cruel and would punish ... really bad punishment ... wouldn't let the boys go outside when they were boys.... He would abuse his mother, his daughter, his children, so I guess he still has that in his mind and I think he's still really depressed about that.... If I were to leave him I don't think that he would make it on his own. I've been everything for him.

She wondered if he, or any man, would be able to help her have money to "be independent, buy a house, and get out of here"—the goals that she had set for herself as an adolescent. She says:

> If I was to break up with Julia's father and I meet someone else, I definitely would think if he was to have something for me and, you know, I definitely want a whole house in the future, but if I meet someone who doesn't think about his future then I wouldn't be interested in that person.

At the 3-year interview, Teressa was secure in her mother's ability to care for Julia, but she worried about Julia's future. Would she be able to take care of her in a neighborhood where drugs were everywhere? How would Julia do at school? She says having a child makes her want to live:

I keep thinking of when she starts school, you know, if they going to take good care of her? You hear so many things that happen in day care, I just want to make sure nothing happens to my daughter. My daughter is everything. I don't want to die because I have a baby.... If I have to leave my boyfriend for her, everything now is just Julia, that's my main concern.

By the 6-year follow-up, many things had changed for Teressa and Julia. Teressa no longer lived with her mother, she was in a new relationship, and she had a 6-month-old daughter. Her unpaid maternity leave from her bank job was ending in 2 weeks. Teressa and her second child's father, Juan, were trying to decide whether she should return to her job operating a computer in the mortgage department of a bank. They did not know how they would juggle child-care options for Julia, who was then 7, Juan's 6-year-old who lived with them, and their new baby. All three children had different needs and different people willing to care for them. Teressa's mother would care for Julia only, Juan's mother would take his daughter, and a friend could sit with the new baby. As Teressa said: "Well, I have three people, basically. It's just that they're all charging me different, like for a week." Teressa described her dilemma about returning to work without having her mother care for the new baby:

We want to do right for the baby, but now that she's here, I mean, we both have great jobs. If I work full-time and he works full-time, we could basically get by, but right now I just know how fun it is for the baby to have me and with Julia I went right back to school and I worked full-time 'cause my mother had her, I was so comfortable. She was the best babysitter, but now it's just basically a friend. I've known her for years, but it's just not the same, so I feel very uncomfortable leaving her full-time with someone else. I'd like to just stay with her and Julia also 'Cause she needs me also, right now.

But staying home was not really an option, Teressa said:

We need both incomes now, not just one ... I wanted to be able to go back to school so that maybe I can stay home for a couple of years and then he can pay everything. But we realized during the time that I was home [on maternity leave] that there's no way to pay everything.

Teressa's work was also important to her self-esteem. Before the new baby, she had been in line for a promotion to assistant manager and was thinking about going back to school to become eligible for further promotions. However:

Then I became pregnant, so [since the baby was born] I've been away from work for 6 months, so there's no way that they can even promote me to assistant manager, so that's been on my mind. So I know I have to go back to school. It's not now, it's maybe when my daughter is 2 years old. It seems like forever, but I'm sure that I'm going back, because I know that I have to go back 'cause my job is important to me right now … when [my supervisor] told me that I lost the chance of becoming assistant manager, and I spoke to her about it, she said not to worry about it. If I go back full time and continue my education, then they would promote me.

Teressa's concerns about her job were also laden with concerns about the stability of her current relationship and her future ability to support her two girls, possibly alone. Teressa was again refusing to marry her new child's father, against her parents' wishes and despite his proposal. In contrast to Julia's father, she saw Juan as a happy person who did not dwell on worries. At 30, he helped out in the house and worked hard, but they still had problems to work out. They argued about how to raise their children together and how to solve problems. Teressa described some of the difficulties they had:

Sometimes because he can't handle it, he will come out and maybe say something mean to me, or curse at me. He knows that about me that I don't like to be cursed at. Sometimes he puts me down, and I think I've done a lot in life, for any man to put me down, I mean, and he knows that. I think part of the problem is because I earn maybe a bit more money than him … and I tell him, Look, you know that if you leave me right now, I could support myself, so don't curse at me, don't try to put me down. He can't deal with that.

For Teressa, maturity as a woman meant taking care of yourself and your children, with or without a man. She says:

When you have your children, you have your bills, you have your problems, but you deal with them. With or without a man…. What makes me more of a woman is that I say to myself that if you [her boyfriend] are here today, you know, [and gone] tomorrow, I'm still the same type of woman, because I do support myself. And I'm proud of that…. And if it wasn't for that, when I dropped out of school and went on public assistance, I don't think I would have felt like the way I do now. 'Cause it's basically depending on my check and depending on maybe looking for someone to be with just to help me pay my bills…. I've been struggling since I had Julia. I've been struggling. Things haven't changed, but now I can deal with them even better, and I think that makes me a woman…. My mind is more clear now. I can consider myself, that I had Julia as still a child and she helped me become who I am now. But there's no way I can consider myself the same person as a woman. Who I am now, no way. I'm a much better person now.

Teressa said she gave 100% to her relationship with Julia's father, but she said: "This time, I'm gonna keep some for myself." She wished she had waited a little longer to get involved in a new relationship—"taken some time for myself and my daughter. Just being together, and just going out and not worrying about someone telling you what time you're getting home, and I wanted that freedom so badly."

Julia's father had started using crack. After 5 months of stealing from her and not knowing when he would appear, Teressa told him:

> Stop, stop, stop ... I told him, If you come back and you don't have any money, then I'm just going to ... ship you somewhere. I tell you you're not living here anymore.... I told him, leave, leave. Just get out of my life. And I sent him to his mother [in Puerto Rico] ... and he was there for 2 years. And now he's like the perfect person, right now.

Teressa said she had been too sensitive and shy in the past and too caught up with Julia's father's concerns: "just thinking about him, and I didn't think about my friends which were important to me, my family." When she left him, she says: "I began to realize who I was and this is who I am. I was a different person when I was with him." Out from under the stress of trying to maintain this relationship, Teressa was able to recognize her strength in what she had accomplished:

> I'm 100% happier with who I am now, now that I'm 25, 'cause I'm sure I could have accomplished more, but I finished high school. And I have a great job. And I compare myself sometimes to other young mothers and other people that sometimes don't have kids and still live with their parents, and I think that I've accomplished more than like other teenage parents and other people in general that don't have children.

At the 6-year follow-up, Teressa believed she could solve life's problems as she encountered them. With a wisdom that seemed beyond her years, she says:

> We all have problems. And we have to just deal with them. We can't dwell on that, we just can't, because today I may solve a problem, tomorrow I'm sure I'm going to have another one.... When I was younger, I thought that was the main problem, that once I solved it and if I dwell on that problem, it's gonna get better ... and that's why I'm a stronger person now: Because I solved some of my problems, some of them will always be there, in my path, and I don't have to worry about them anymore.... I have to forget about the past and deal with my present and my future, which is my children.

The other mothers in this sample who worked and lived independently of their own mothers often shared Teressa's concern with career advancement, as well as her optimism about and determination to reach their goals. Julie looked forward to finishing her bachelor's degree, getting a good job, moving out of the Bronx into the suburbs, having a house or an apartment, having a nice car, being married, and having another child. Asked if she thought these things would happen, she said:

> If I put my mind to it, it will happen, because I'm the type of person as I say, when I want something I get it. I have to go for what I want and that's the way I am. I want the best for my daughter and I'm trying to show her that she could do it too.

The discovery by these mothers of their own strength and independence was often precipitated by problems with or the break up of their relationship with their child's father. As Sherry described her realization:

> We were separated for about 8 months. He left me, I graduated from college. He felt he needed to re-explore his love for me.... So, I decided I could do two things. I can sit in my house and cry for my husband to come back or I could just let it go. So what happened was I blossomed. I blossomed into this creature that I had no idea I could become. I was very active. I had a lot of fun. I met a lot of people. I started working.

Also common among these interviews was a definition of *independence* that included both self-reliance and having a plan for the future. Anne, newly pregnant with her second child and now an administrative assistant for Child and Family Services, stressed that she would stay with this job, although she could earn more somewhere else, because of the medical benefits. She had also learned that independence is not about not needing help:

> Before I wanted a lot. I still do, but I wanted a lot but it was like I didn't want help.... I felt it could be done. It could be done by myself. I don't need you to help me. I don't need whatever. Like I feel that everybody needs somebody to get somewhere, you know? It's like now I think I've learned to expect more ... that if you need help it's there for you to ask for it ... whereas before, I couldn't accept it.

Like Teressa, other mothers also planned for a future of possibly caring for their children alone. Johanna described the changes she saw in herself:

> I think now I'm more independent. Before, I think I kinda wanted someone to depend on. But, when I didn't get that, I had to become independent for myself. 'Cause I saw me depend on me. Although, my boyfriend and I live together, we split the bills now. But I'm always prepared for that, Oh, I don't have the rent this month. I'm not going to get put out because you don't have the rent, you know. I have all the rent, just in case. So I'm more independent ... and I think he knows that, because I'm quick to say it. We could break even, you could leave with what you came with and I'll still be me, you know. I'm more independent, I don't depend on nobody for nothing.... Me, independent model. That's my definition. Basically doing things on your own, like I said, not depending on anyone. Always prepared for what's to come. Prepared for what you may not expect. Basically that's independent. Paying your own bills, you know, not having to answer to anyone but the face in the mirror.

Sibylle, happily married to her child's father, Gordon, said being an independent woman was:

> ... working, and going to school and taking care of Alexia. Like I told Alexia, and like I tell Gordon ... if you're not around I have to make sure that I can provide for

her. If we grow apart, and no longer can have the friendship that we have, for whatever reason, then I have to still be … I have to be an independent woman to take care of Alexia. If I'm not an independent woman, then I would have to see myself again, going backwards, and I don't wanna go backwards. I would fall, it would seem like you're gonna just dig yourself a hole, and that would be really not good.

For these women, welfare carried with it a sense of intolerable dependency. Sherry described what had helped her accomplish her goal to finish her associate's degree in accounting:

Desire … wanting to be the best, not wanting to have a difficult life, to be a burden on anybody. I mean I was a teen parent, and I had my son very young. But I still saw girls that were my age or younger or older who did not know, who had no idea. They would just be welfare recipients for the rest of their lives. They had no idea of how to get out. So I didn't want that. I didn't want to have to go to an appointment to see a social worker and have to give her my whole life history, and be dependent on a check that comes each month.… I wanted to get an income tax return. I want to get my paycheck, I want to go somewhere and just work and have good things, I want to have a bank account, travel, and do things that I wanted to do, have a house, that 's all.

CHARISE: REACHING FOR INDEPENDENCE AND A PLACE OF HER OWN

Charise's story is representative of the experiences of the group of working mothers who lived with their own mothers at the 6-year follow-up. When her daughter, Laureen, was born, Charise was 16. She had only completed Grade 9 and was living with her mother. She had had a long relationship with Laureen's father and planned to marry him. As she said:

I've been with him for 7 years. He's the only man I've ever been with so I see myself with him for a long time. He's nice, he takes care of Laureen when I'm tired. He brings me gifts when he gets paid.

Charise stuck with him even through his jail sentence for selling drugs. Commitment for her meant:

stay by them through thick and thin, whether they don't have a job or whether doing wrong, you let that person know that you are going to be by them so they can do right, and keep on talking to them, like keep them from doing drugs.

By the 3-year follow-up, Charise had found a job as a nurse's aide and planned to keep going to school at nights to become a registered nurse. She had a good relationship with her mother, who, she said, "respects me not just as a daughter but as a friend. She worried that her mother would be lonely when Charise got married and lived in her own apartment. She felt that she had become a woman: "I think I am woman. I have a daughter. That's the child." She had become very religious and believed that, along with her aunt and mother, she had been "saved." She believed God had opened doors of opportunity for her. Like all of the other mothers who worked and lived with their own mothers, Charise had had the involvement of her own father in her life. He was separated from her mother, but he also used to give them money. At the 3-year follow-up, he worked in New York and was helping her find an apartment.

However, by the time of the 6-year interview, Charise's sense of stability had been undermined and a great deal had changed. Charise had broken up with her child's father when Laureen was about four and a half. "He had his girlfriend," but he saw Charise off and on and maintained a relationship with Laureen. However, he was in jail again by the 6-year interview: "He went to jail a year ago. He hasn't seen my daughter in a year and a half. He's going to be locked away for a long time. So that's made my life kinda hard." In fact, the loss had thrown Charise's life and identity into chaos. A great deal seemed to have come ungrounded.

Charise was back living with her mother. After living in her own apartment for a year and a half, she had moved back to her mother's apartment when her mother moved away; her mother had returned and now they were sharing once again. As she says:

> I live with my mother. I'm saving and I just can't find an apartment. My mother just had twins.... My sister is 4, the twins are 1½, and my little brother just came back from Virginia, he's 13. So it's crowded right now. I don't like that situation. I just don't have any privacy and it's just too crowded. She has her life and I have mine. I'm too old to be with my mother.

Charise was still in the nurse's aide job after 4 years. She loved her job: "I just like helping people. Just hearing them say thank you." She still planned to return to school to become a registered nurse: "I know it's going to happen," she said, "I have faith in myself." Contrasting herself with her mother, Charise said she wanted a career and more:

> My mother doesn't have a career, she doesn't have the education. She graduated from high school but she never went to college. Nobody in my family ever went to college, only my aunt and she's nothing ... so I'm going to go to college and make something out of myself. My uncle made it but he lives down south with my brother. I'm going to be different from everybody ... because I don't want the same thing they have.... They have to sacrifice for everything and I'm not going to take that. I want something better. I want a car. I want a house. I want a home. Even if it's just me and my daughter, this is what I want for her and for me. I want to put her through college. My mother couldn't put me through college. That's what I want to do different.

These dreams may have been instilled in Charise by her grandmother, who passed away when Charise was 13. Charise said her grandmother

taught us [Charise and her brothers and sisters] everything.... If my grand-mother was alive, we would all be in college. She had five grandchildren, and she had more than that, but the ones she knew was only five of us. We would have been in college and she had money, my grandmother had money.... We wouldn't have no kids. We were scared, we respected her too much to even think about boyfriends. As soon as she passed away, I was like 12 or 13, and that's when I got pregnant. You know, if she was here, I would have had an education, then fun. That was her thing. Education, then fun. Sometimes I'm upset because I didn't listen to her, I regret not listening ... [But] I'm doing okay.

Charise was very aware that becoming involved with a man or getting pregnant could derail her plans:

If you're pregnant, all your stuff has to wait and I'm not getting pregnant. I don't know ... nothing, nothing can stop me now. My daughter's 6. She's very mature. She's out of that baby stage. She's not a toddler, so that's good. I'm not proud that I had her so young but I'm glad I got her out of the way for now. I don't want to start over. See a bunch of young girls having babies, not working, not going to school. I'm not going to be like that ... because you're not doing nothing with yourself. People say they have babies for love and 'cause they don't have noth-ing ... well you're not really going to have nothing if you have babies, you know, what are you giving your child? Nothing. Love ... you can't survive on love. It really is not love. You need money. You need love. You need help.

Being a teenage mother, she said, is "horrible ... it's not good. They say it's good. It's not good. It's cute but it's not good." For Charise, being a woman meant:

First taking care of yourself and don't leave the men to take care of you. I don't want anybody to take care of me.... I'm not looking for it.... That's the one thing, take care of myself and my child ... just to stand up for yourself.

Explaining where this radical independence stems from, she went on to say:

A lot of women let men beat up on them and tell them what to do and you know, keep them in the house, and there's a lot of secrets out there, but I see a lot of young girls going through that. It's not just the old people. There's a lot of young girls that let their mate tell them what to do and hitting and abusing them, not just physically but mentally. I went through that with my baby's father before, so I know how it feels ... I learned not to let a man do what he did to me. I learned a lot. Before I was shy and dependent upon other people. Like my mother ... I knew she would babysit for me. I knew that if I spent my whole check on clothes, that she would feed us. A lot of things have changed.

Charise did not want to be involved with any man right then. Men, she said, wanted too much control. It was a problem she felt that faced every woman:

> It's just guys, period. Everybody tells me their situation, "He don't want me to go here." I think it's just the guys ... that's how they want their girls these days.... I think they have low self-esteem. You know, if I see somebody looks better than them, then they think I'm going to go out and talk to that guy. I guess they do it, you know.... They just don't want you to be around nobody, communicating with no one but them. I don't need no man right now. I want to go to school.

Church also played less of a role in her life now. Looking back to when she was "saved," Charise said:

> They say that you are born again, you are a Christian.... I never understood it though. I think I was just doing it because my aunt and my family was doing it, that's why. I never did it for me. Now they throw it in my face or whatever, "You going to church again." I'm not ready for the church.... I pray at night.

Charise's father, a public school janitor, was now very present in her life and took care of Laureen on weekends. Although Charise said he had never been there when she was young, he had begun to get closer after his son, Charise's half brother, was killed:

> I guess now he looks at the things he missed out on. He tells me all the time how much he loves me, how much he cannot bring the past back but if he could, he would do everything much better, you know, different. I accept him still. I don't hate him, I love my father.

The stories of the other mothers in this group of working mothers who still lived with their own mothers had many similar features. Each told of a period of disillusionment following the breakup or loss of the relationship with their child's father. Leaving an abusive relationship with her child's father, Josie said that what was important to her at that point was:

> ... just basically getting on with my life. I've been a long time with Gerald's father and had to deal with a lot of things with him and right now just really going on and doing what I want to do to get my own life started. I was standing still for a while. I wasn't really doing as much as I wanted to ... being a little more independent.

About the period after her son's father was shot, Heather said:

I was really lost, I didn't know how to pick up and go on. I just felt really lost, like I was wandering from one day to another. That's the way I felt. But after going to church, I got to pull myself together.... Well, he's gone and I got to continue living. I've got two children. I've go to do something.

These mothers believed their earlier choices about relationships, school, and having a child had held them back. One mother said about her child:

Sometimes I wish I didn't have him.... Most of the time I feel happy 'cause he is so funny, but sometimes I feel that way. I think I could be working two jobs, I could be doing this, I can be going anywhere I wanna go. Not having to worry about a babysitter. If I can go back and change I probably wouldn't have had him.

These working mothers were also powerfully focused on moving ahead in a career (not simply a job): A word processing secretary in a bank wanted to become an accountant, a part-time drug store clerk wanted to be a pharmacy technician, a claims authorizer for social security payments who began as a file clerk expected to be upgraded to a higher level and better income, and a young woman who had just finished business school wanted to be an executive secretary. A part-time "jack of all trades" in the television industry was thinking about producing a documentary about "teenage girls who are being abused by their boyfriends, because I was kinda in that situation like that and around me I've been noticing a lot of high school girls that live around me, their boyfriends have so much control of their lives."

Some mothers were trying to cope with the needs of their own mothers. As Heather described:

I was living in a shelter for a while ... trying to get some help for me and my children, but my mom's brother died and I came back home to live with her and I was just on the verge of getting my own place ... she begged me to come back, so I came back home.

The situation deteriorated as more people came to live in her mother's apartment:

I can't deal with not having my own space and not being able to sleep in my own bed, because it's a one bedroom apartment so me and my kids sleep with my mother. Four people in one bed.

Yet the young women in this group juggled the stresses of living in overcrowded housing and caring for their child and their own mother in the context of a strong family support system. All these girls had some contact with their own father. Most also had a strong family figure who helped them envision a better future: a mother who "has always drilled into my head, I mean don't let having a baby stop you" (Glenda); a grandfather who "stressed school to me ... that was, like, the most important thing to him, and that's all he wanted for me, is for me to bring home A's" (Josie); or an aunt who said, "God is there for you if you just tell him what you want" (Heather).

Certain that they would succeed, these women believed themselves different from most young mothers; they saw obstacles as challenges and the future as holding the promise of a better life. As Josie said:

> I would like to think that people would think about me that I just, whatever crosses my path, whatever happens in my life, whatever obstacles I had to get over.... I went on and I did something with my life because I think it's really important that we are all given a life to live and to do what we can with it until it's over ... and basically I would hope I would never lose that will to just keep going, to just keep doing things that maybe make a difference to someone else's life, but make a difference to my life too.

These mothers believed they needed to be responsible for their children and become truly independent. They had to take care of themselves "financially, working, going out there, knowing how it is to pay the bills, and to finance different things," as one mother said. Being a women, for these young mothers, meant feeling "that I don't need anything to help me do anything that I wanna do. I can do everything on my own, that's just the way I am." One mother summed up the importance of self-reliance as a protection against being alone:

> I like to be really independent. I like to do things myself. I figure if I can do it myself, I don't need anybody else's help, you know, and I think it's good because you get used to knowing that you can do things yourself. If you get used to thinking that you need somebody else to do something then you're always gonna be like that and then if you're alone, you can't. So I think it's better like this.

With the possibility of living alone looming large in front of them, these young women were bracing themselves to accept life's challenges. They were likely to succeed. Some of the mothers on welfare had similar goals. Late adolescence and early adulthood was a period of transition, and some used welfare to help them move into work. Others, as we see in the next chapter, were not so lucky. Stresses and traumas overwhelmed their aspirations and goals as some began waiting for better times to come.

6

Welfare Benefits for Inner-City Adolescent Mothers: Supporting Early Adult Development

❧

The Alan Guttmacher Institute (1994) reported that, in 1993, 3.8 million mothers ages 15 to 44 received welfare or Aid to Families with Dependent Children (AFDC). Of these, 55% were teenagers when they had their first child. However, only 5% were teenagers when they established their own welfare budgets. Typically, adolescent mothers from families on welfare are not eligible to establish independent welfare budgets before age 18. The few who do are not in the custody of their families because of homelessness, neglect, or abuse. Even after they reach 18, few single mothers can meet their basic needs on welfare alone (Edlin & Jencks, 1992; Edlin & Lein, 1996).

The economic situation of young, never-married mothers changes frequently (Handler, 1995; Harris, 1997). Less than one third of young, never-married women who receive public assistance are long-term recipients. However, many go on and off public assistance several times as they juggle part-time employment, child care, and school, as well as disruptions in their relationships and poverty-related illnesses. As Handler (1995) pointed out, although the probability of being on pub-lic assistance is high at any one time for those highly visible individuals chroni-cally on welfare, half of the individuals who receive welfare do so for less than 2 years. The Baltimore study of women who became mothers as adolescents in the late 1960s and were followed for 20 years confirms the discontinuity in typical pat-terns of welfare use (Harris, 1997). Although only 29% of the mothers were never on welfare, 42% of those who ever received welfare relied on it for 3 years or less over the 20-year period of the study.

The Children's Defense Fund (1996) estimated that for New York State, the 1995 maximum monthly AFDC benefit for a single mother and two children was $577 and the lowest monthly rent was $463. This makes it clear why other sources of income are essential for mothers on welfare. Even for mothers who are working, rent represents approximately 65% of a minimum wage income.

Similarly, for mothers in the New York study, being on welfare rarely meant they did not work or have other income or support. Most shared housing costs with mothers, sisters, or boyfriends; some worked full or part time in "off the books" jobs (like in-home child care or hairdressing) or were in job-training programs. Amy described what living on welfare meant to her:

> People talk about people living off of welfare. You don't live off of welfare. I'd like to meet these people who live off of welfare so they could teach me how to live off $109 every two weeks. 'Cause that—between my electricity bill and my gas bill and my telephone bill—that's gone. And my son is growing like a weed, so it's like as soon as I find him clothes, he outgrows them. So it's like totally impossible for me to live on that. So I work and I have a job and I hate my job. But I have to take the bullshit because basically, I have to work. I need the money.

WELFARE DEPENDENCE: BUILDING ON DISADVANTAGES

Age of childbearing may have little impact on the economic status of already poor families in communities with high unemployment and high concentrations of poverty. Teen mothers from families on welfare are disproportionately likely to go on to set up their own welfare budgets (Handler, 1995). In the New York study, mothers from families that were on welfare at the initial interview already had poorer economic prospects than the mothers who were not initially from welfare families. The former were almost a year more delayed in their school achievement (where *delay* is defined as ideal grade for age minus grade completed) than mothers who were not from families on welfare (respectively, $M = 1.6, SD = 1; M = 1.1, SD = 1$); and they had achieved fewer years of school (respectively, $M = 9.4, SD = 1.4; M = 10.2, SD = 1$) even after controlling for the mother's age at delivery [$F(2, 116) = 5.2, p = .007$]. It seems that prior disadvantage may have set them up for poor future prospects.

By any standard, the majority of the young women in the New York study were poor at the time they delivered their first child. Most mothers (63%) in this study were already in families that were receiving public assistance when they became teen mothers. At each subsequent assessment, two thirds or more of the sample reported receiving or being in families receiving welfare (66% at 12 months, 70% at 3 years, and 69% at 6 years after delivery). Yet the instability of the mothers' welfare status is striking: 19% had changed their initial status within the first year, 28% within 3 years, and 44% by the 6-year follow-up. However, the direction of this change was toward more mothers going on welfare over time: 30% of the mothers who were on welfare at delivery were off 6 years later; 68% of those who had been off welfare at delivery were on 6 years later. Seven mothers did not report receiving welfare over the entire 6-year period; seven others had only one brief spell on welfare. Five of the mothers who were off at the 6-year follow-up were on welfare at all previous assessments. Only 29% were on welfare at all data collection points.

These findings are similar to those of the women in the Baltimore sample (Harris, 1997). By the 20-year follow-up of the Baltimore study, 28% were categorized as *persistent* users (defined as those who experienced welfare spells of 3 years or more). On average, the Baltimore women received welfare support for 10.7 years over the 20 years of the study. An additional 23% experienced episodes of less than 3 years and averaged 7.9 years over the 20-year study. Twenty-nine percent of the sample was never on welfare, and 20% received welfare for a period of 2 years or less.

Clearly, welfare dependence is more typically discontinuous than continuous even for initially disadvantaged teens. Although much attention has focused on adolescent childbearing as a cause of chronic welfare use, less research has explored the diversity of patterns of welfare dependence of adolescent mothers. Harris' (1997) analysis of data from the Baltimore sample is a notable exception; however, even this detailed analysis does not reveal the experiences of adolescent mothers in the 1990s. How do some get off welfare, who stays off, and why do many not escape?

Consistent with prior research, we assessed the contributions of repeat pregnancies, cohabitation with a partner, and educational attainment as predictors of different patterns of welfare use by the adolescent mothers in the New York sample. We also went beyond these predictors to analyze the mothers' own accounts of their decisions about and patterns of welfare use. The voices of these young women have been uniquely absent from debates about their welfare use. In their interviews, we heard about the educational goals that were supported by welfare use and about the crises that forced some of these women onto welfare.

SUBGROUP DIFFERENCES IN WELFARE EXPERIENCES OF THE NEW YORK MOTHERS

The mothers in the New York study with 6-year follow-up data were divided into three groups: those with one or no welfare episodes ($n = 24$), those with two episodes ($n = 21$), and those with several (three or more) episodes ($n = 48$). Mothers in the New York sample on welfare at two or more assessments had more repeat pregnancies than those on welfare at one or no assessment points (see Table 6.1). However, they were not more likely than the other mothers to have three or more children, suggesting they had more abortions. Mothers on welfare at several assessments were less likely to live with a male partner or graduate from high school by the 6-year follow-up. They averaged only 10.9 years of school ($SD = 1.6$), which was 1 year less than mothers on welfare at two or fewer assessment points [$M = 11.9$, $SD = 1.9$; $M = 12.9$, $SD = 1.8$, respectively, after accounting for the mothers' age at delivery; $F(4,176) = 2.39$, $p = .05$].

Not surprisingly, 6 years after their first child's birth, mothers who were not receiving public assistance ($n = 29$) were better off than those who were ($n = 64$). They were more likely to be married (35% vs. 10%), more likely to have graduated

TABLE 6.1

Continuity of Welfare Episodes Related to Repeat Pregnancies, Having More Than Three Children, Living with Male, and High School Graduation by the 6-Year Follow-Up

Welfare Episodes	0–1	2	3 or more	χ^2	df
≥ 3 repeat pregnancies ($n = 37$)	33%	43%	42%	11.7*	4
≥ 3 children ($n = 17$)	20%	14%	19%	1.8	4
Living with partner ($n = 40$)	67%	43%	31%	8.18*	2
High school graduate ($n = 48$)	79%	62%	33%	14.6**	2

*$p < .05$.
**$p < .01$.

from high school (76% vs. 41% of mothers receiving welfare) or to have taken some college courses (38% vs. 19%), and more likely to have only one child (62% vs. 27%). The impact of subsequent births on welfare outcomes for adolescent mothers may not be straightforward. Timing and context of these births may mediate or moderate the impact of these additional births. In the Baltimore sample (Harris, 1997), persistent users were less likely to have graduated from high school or married and were more likely to have had additional births within 2 years and to have three or more children overall. They were also more likely to have been younger than 16 at their first birth. Using data from the National Survey of Labour Market Experience, Youth Survey, Hao and Brinton (1997) found that single mothers with more children were unlikely to enter jobs or return to school, but only if they were living with kin. Whether living with kin allows support for additional children born to adolescent mothers, has important policy implications for legislators mandating residence with kin.

WHAT DRIVES THE DECISION TO GO ON WELFARE?

It is perhaps startling, given the public concern about welfare costs, that we have few ethnographic accounts of the circumstances that lead young mothers to go on or off welfare. We also know little of what adolescent mothers do with these benefits or how they manage to live on so little. The image of the adolescent mother as an uneducated, unwed, unmotivated, isolated, long-term welfare dependent who uses the benefits to support her *independent lifestyle* predominates in public policy and opinion (Payne, 1996). How accurate is this image? What do these mothers do with their welfare checks? What do they want from welfare?

Welfare entered the lives of the New York sample of adolescent mothers at many time points, from before delivery to several years following. There were several reasons behind the continuities and discontinuities in their need for public assistance. Overlapping disadvantages were incurred from family backgrounds of poverty, chronic illness, and learning disabilities. Acute illnesses, job losses, day-care changes, disruptions in relationships with those the mothers depended on for income (including the death or illness of and conflicts with their own mothers or their children's fathers) further stressed the mothers' meager financial resources. Efforts to improve their economic status through education or job training or to care for their own children rather than risk their safety in day care differentially motivated these mothers' decision to spend some period of time on welfare.

Caring for Your Own Children

Some mothers in the New York study settled for what they believed was temporary dependence on welfare because of their commitment to rear their own children. They wanted to be home with their preschoolers. As we see in the next chapter, however, the decision to stay at home may increase the likelihood that a mother will have further children, fall behind in school, and find it increasingly difficult to work.

Using Welfare to Get Ahead

For many, welfare use led to gains in employment. Of the 64 mothers (26%) who were receiving welfare at the 6-year follow-up, 17 were in school or college programs or worked at least part-time. These may be the ones most likely to get off welfare in the future.

Of the 17 mothers who had not reported being on welfare at any earlier assessment point, 10 were receiving benefits at the 6-year point; however, the welfare dependence of these mothers may be short-lived. These mothers resorted to welfare to respond to a crisis. All but one (a recovering addict) had graduated from high school by the 6-year follow-up, and all but one (whose own mother had cancer) reported low levels of stress and depression at delivery. All went on welfare 3 or more years after the initial interviews. Going on welfare represented a discontinuity in their lives that allowed them to make an upward move (e.g., following treatment for drug abuse, out of homelessness, or to escape from domestic violence), to halt a downward spiral (e.g., following unemployment or illness), or to respond to a crisis period in their lives.

Surviving Crises

These crises had many forms. Events in the lives of those on whom the mother relied for income sometimes precipitated welfare spells. One couple with three children split up. The children's father subsequently entered a college program and could not pay child support. One young mother experienced intolerable conflict with her own mother, was hospitalized for depression, and subsequently entered a homeless shelter with her children. One's husband died. The fourth, a mother of five children, went on welfare after her family could no longer support her—her mother died of breast cancer, her 90-year-old father had a stroke, and the father of her children was in a rehabilitation program for crack addiction. Three other mothers went on welfare after they were laid off from their jobs or were unable to find work after attending job training programs. Other mothers were already, as Zill et al. (1991) forecasted, too ill to work. Diseases that disproportionately affect the poor, including AIDS, asthma, posttraumatic stress disorder (PTSD), and severe depression, usurped the potential of several of the young women in the New York sample. Mother or child illnesses (including drug abuse or severe depression in the mothers or prematurity or retardation in subsequent births) drove three mothers onto welfare.

Rita, a mother of three who was hospitalized about 10 times a year because of her asthma and dermatitis, described her transition to welfare poignantly:

To me, welfare is the last thing on the money chain. You either work, no, you either own something, you either work, or you're on welfare. So welfare's like the last, you know, you can't get any more bottom than this unless you're home [with your mother]. I pray to God I'll never be like that. So welfare's like really the bottom of the barrel for a person. And it's not like I'm trying to belittle myself. Because if it wasn't for welfare, I'd probably be a statistic of suicide. Because at one point in time I was not with my husband, and I had to go to work so that way we can live, we can survive, so I can have money.... I was also pregnant with my daughter at the time. So I needed help, you know. I had two little kids at that time ... [they] were only about 2 and 3.... I could not get a job because I was seven months pregnant. How can you get a job knowing you're going to the hospital? And so I had the possibility of bills, taking care of a home, taking care of two little children all on my own. So what I felt was that I was not gonna go to my mother's house. I wasn't going there. I was not. I had my own apartment; I had my kids. That's all I need. And to stay away, to get money for my house so I can pay the bills. So I got the welfare for that. And I've been on it for, like, 3 years, so for those 3 years ... at least I got my GED. I've gotten a little bit of job training, and now I'm trying to see if I can get a job. Now with the little girl going out to school, I can maybe get a part time job, from about 9 to 12 or 9 to 2, and then go pick up the kids.

These snapshots of mothers using welfare to stay in school, care for their own children, survive illnesses, or withstand poverty crises are inconsistent with the myth of free-living, independence-seeking adolescent mothers who inspire punitive welfare policies. However, as welfare "as we know it ends," so ends the support for success and a safety net during crises for all of these young women.

RECOGNIZING THE POSITIVE

Five New York mothers who were on welfare at three or more of the assessment points were not on welfare at the 6-year follow-up (as well as 10 mothers who had been receiving welfare on at least two earlier assessments). Are these young women really off welfare? How did they do it? Will they return?

One mother, whose marriage "changed her life" from party girl to housewife and mother, did not work because her husband "never asked her to work." She stayed with her ill mother during the day, and her son lived with her mother full time. Nevertheless, this young woman lacked a high school diploma and would have a hard time finding a job if her husband could not support her.

However, the changes in the lives of the other young women in this group lead us to suggest that a return to welfare dependence is unlikely for them. Several mothers described the changes in their lives as "just waking up" from being "lazy," "miserable," or "dependent" (e.g., Angela). Some described dramatic life transitions out of abusive relationships with male partners (see chap. 8). Others located turning points in small gestures from professionals, neighbors, and kin that seemed to recognize, with pride or support, what the mothers had accomplished.

For one of these mothers, encouragement came from a doctor who "seemed so happy sometimes when I would let her know I'm going back to school." For another it was a social worker who said "that it wasn't the end of the world—because for a minute there I was depressed … and telling me about the school for pregnant teens, 'cause that's when I went back to school." Help also came from aunts, grandmothers, and women in the neighborhood who believed in the young mothers and said so. One mother whose relatives were alcoholics and whose husband's family put her down told how she gained strength when other women in her apartment told her:

> You're a good mother. You're independent, you're not like these little girls in here. I had them calling me to babysit for them.... I used to think, well you know they're right! I can take care of my child and I'm independent and I can do this and I can do that. So I just knocked out the negative things and I … I have more positive over negative. I just left the negative alone, and kept all the positive.

In the next chapter, we detail case studies of three of the young mothers who remained on welfare. These young women talk about their pride in being able to care for their children *without help* and in taking responsibility for their own children and not abandoning them (like their children's fathers or other irresponsible teenage mothers did). We also visit their resourcefulness in creating ways to live on this meager income through casual work; sharing a residence with their mothers, male partners, or others; or scrupulous budgeting. Those who were able to combine welfare with educational training seemed to have found the way to a more positive future. In contrast, the ambitions of mothers who remained at home to care for their children had often become vague and distant.

7

Living on Welfare:
Mialisa, Helen, and Vivian

Although the risk statistics presented in the last chapter for adolescent mothers paint a familiar picture of the differences in education, work, and numbers of children that subsequently distinguish welfare from nonwelfare mothers, these figures can mislead us into believing that all adolescent mothers on welfare are similar in their lack of capacity for and motivation to better themselves economically. The interview data, however, suggest a different picture. Adolescent mothers are not a uniform group. Three major subgroups could be differentiated based on their motivation toward use of public assistance. One group of about one third of the New York sample of mothers who were on welfare were successfully using welfare to accomplish the tasks of late adolescence. They were completing educational and job training programs 6 years after the birth of their first child. These resilient women showed remarkable personal strengths and optimism that pulled them forward despite multiple experiences of trauma and high levels of ongoing stress. They matured in their understanding of relationships and of what was needed to survive as adult women.

The second and largest group of mothers were subsisting on welfare by the 6-year follow-up. They were unable to overcome extraordinary poverty-related problems and stresses that, for them, included learning problems, illnesses, family deaths, and domestic violence. They had all but resorted to merely waiting for their fortunes to change. A third, smaller group of the mothers on welfare became adults overnight with the birth of their child; thus, their adolescence ended abruptly. Their attention turned to their roles as mothers, and their adolescent educational and work goals had to be set aside. Often in close relationships with their own mothers, they strongly believed in the importance of caring for their own children and mistrusted strangers with their childrens' care. They believed they had to be content and manage on their meager incomes from welfare to fulfill the responsibility they had accepted in becoming a mother; other child-care options were not available.

Mialisa represents the group of mothers who were on welfare but also worked or were in educational/job training programs. Helen was on welfare, but she lived with her sister and had a second child, an infant daughter. Her life, similar to the mothers' lives in the second group, was on hold: She was waiting for the future, waiting for her daughter to get older, waiting for a GED program in her housing project, waiting for her new relationship to sort itself out. Vivian was among the small group of mothers who, at the 6-year follow-up, managed on their meager incomes from public assistance and were focused on their responsibility for caring for their own children and reasons for not abandoning them to a stranger's care.

MIALISA: WINNING IN THE
STRUGGLE AGAINST THE ODDS

Seventeen young mothers were working or in job-training programs while receiving welfare. They were unique in their very active struggle to use welfare to get off welfare. For these mothers, welfare was not enough. Each of them was focused on making their own and their children's lives better. They shared much of the determination of the working mothers who were not on welfare (see chaps. 4 and 5), but differed in having to deal with extraordinary stress. Few had the support of the grandmothers, and none lived with the grandmother by the 6- year follow-up. Yet they had been able to engage the help of the welfare or educational system and moved forward often in the face of what most of us would consider overwhelming odds.

Limiting the number of children they had was important for most of these mothers' success. Half had only one child at the 6-year follow-up, although four mothers had three children, and one cared for five (two of her own and three of her drug-addicted sister). Most had graduated or obtained a GED by the 6 year point. Eight worked for low wages, ranging from $5 to $9 an hour (with a mean of $5.80). Nine were in job training programs or college.

Mialisa represents those young women on welfare who were also doing job-training programs and working full or part-time in low-income jobs. Her father left when she was 8 or 9 and she rarely saw him although he lived nearby. Her mother, whom she described as "very strict," would lock her in the apartment and did not want her to hang out with her friends. Mialisa described her as the "type that gives you advice about something, but it's like scolding you at the same time." Although she said she hated and rebelled against her mother when she was young, she also said she understood why her mother acted like this now that she had a child of her own to protect.

Mialisa had her son at 16. She left school in the ninth grade, but was attending a job corps program in Northern New York state to get a GED when she discovered she was 2 months pregnant. She returned to New York City to get an abortion at a clinic "where they do it for free," but she says she kept waiting until a friend could go with her:

I needed someone to come with me, 'cause I'd never done it before. I was really confused and I was scared, so by the time I did it, my mother found out about it. She approached me with one of her sisters and they confronted me about it and I told them the truth and I told them that I didn't want to keep it. So they came out real snotty about the situation and they said; "Well, if you're old enough to make it then you're old enough to have it."

Mialisa's mother went to her boyfriend's family to see if he was going to support the baby and he promised he would. However, as Mialisa says, "things didn't work out the way we wanted it, we did stay together though." He did not have a job and did not contribute to the child's support. Her mother then cut off financial support when she continued to associate with her child's father. The baby's father was 9 years older than Mialisa and already had two daughters with two other women, one of whom supported him "so he can stay there with her." Mialisa described him as "lazy":

he don't want to do anything for himself. He'd rather live off a woman, and get his money and whatever.... It's like, he doesn't have that much confidence in himself. I guess he needs someone to push him.

But she too was supporting him. When her child was about 3 years old, Mialisa moved out of her mother's house and into a new apartment in the Bronx where she knew no one. She was afraid to go out:

They sell drugs on the corner, they shoot, they throw gunshots across the street, 'cause there's a lot of Dominicans over there where I live so a lot of those Dominican men, they think they Mr. Macho and if you mess up with a drug deal then ... the only thing they think about is killing the other person who messed them up, so it's really dangerous.

As a result, Mialisa, a Puerto Rican, spent most of her day inside with her son watching TV. She complained of boredom and talked about returning to school or to her old job as a dental assistant, but did not have anyone to care for her son: "I'm waiting for somebody [a woman who takes care of children in their homes] to be available 'cause there's a lot of kids in the Bronx." She had worked for 5 months as a dental assistant with a dentist who just "wanted a bilingual person." The dentist said she was a fast learner and encouraged her to train as a dental hygienist, but problems with her child's father caused her to miss too many days of work and she was fired.

At the 6-year interview, much of the passivity evident in the previous interview was replaced by a newfound confidence and optimism. Mialisa's son, Joshua, was graduating from kindergarten and she was finishing her training as a dental assistant. Encouraged by her former employer's praise, Mialisa had found a place for herself.

Mialisa's mother was more helpful about caring for Joshua and was being paid by welfare while Mialisa was in job training. She was about to take her grandson with her for a vacation in Puerto Rico. Mialisa still described her as not the "helpful type of mother." She wondered how she would manage because her mother was in Manhattan and her next intern position was near her house in the Bronx.

She was no longer with her child's father and said things were working out better. As she examined her changed views of the relationship, she was able to see her self-transformation:

> I'm not that naive little girl that I used to be back then. I'm doing a lot of things better now than I did before.... like being motivated, period. You know, before I wasn't motivated. I just wanted to stay home, do nothing, wait for my boyfriend. It was sickening [laughs] and I got tired of it and I feel better now ... [knowing] that you can do what you want, you can hang out with whoever you want.

The depth of her earlier feelings of being trapped was evident as she talked about the obligation she had felt to financially support her child's father:

> Even though I was working when I was with him ... it felt like I was working for him, you know, supporting him financially. Because he wasn't working, so I was obligated to work, so, you know, I could help him out too, supporting him. I got tired of it, so I feel free, I don't have to be obligated to someone. Feels great ... I get to do the things that I haven't done at my earlier ages ... like going out.... Before when my kid's father was around, you know ... It's like I had to support three people, and now thank God, I don't have to do that no more. Now it's just me and my son.

When asked what led to these changes, she described her growing understanding of the complexities of relationships and said she was figuring out who to listen to:

> Some people will say things on spite, you know, just to get you mad or to see how far you go and there's people who wind up telling you the truth where you just don't want to listen, you know. So I've learned the difference, comparing them two. And I see things a lot more than I used to. Since I'm dating, you get to know them.

Although adolescence is generally a time for trying out relationships, which are typically short-lived, Mialisa's early sexual experience and rapid encounter with expectations that she make a commitment to her child's father and motherhood foreshortened her experiences of nonsexual intimacy or mutuality in relationships. Her boyfriend's dependence on her, and her loneliness and boredom as she waited for him, eventually led her to see the difference between relationships that worked and did not work for her. As Mialisa put it:

I was so naive, I couldn't recognize that. I couldn't recognize a loser from a good guy. So I got messed up, you know, down the line with a loser. But because of that loser, I learned not to deal with people like him anymore. [Laughs] So you get to learn these little experiences, you just learn from them and you go on.

Mialisa was able to establish important nonfamily and nonsexual relationships with people in her neighborhood that made her feel competent and respected. She was comfortable in her neighborhood in the Bronx where she now said everyone knew her. Unlike many of the young mothers who did not trust people outside their families, Mialisa depended on friends for support and for having fun.

She described an older man of 43 who lived with his daughter in an apartment next to hers, where he could hear the fights and arguments she had with her child's father. Although he was interested in a romantic relationship, Mialisa felt otherwise: "I knew it from the beginning, but I set him straight. I told him, 'There's like no way, I'm not physically attracted to you. I see you as a friend, a good one.' Cause he's been there." Mialisa described his friendship with great affection:

He knew most everything about me without me even knowing him. He already knew, but he saw me as a good decent young woman with a child and that I was doing my best with my son and we became friends, and we were dating, not dating. He was taking me out, 'cuz he knows I hardly went dancing, and he knew my man didn't do nothing for me. He took me out dancing a lot, took me out to a movie, even with my son. He loves my son.

She also described a real intimacy with a girlfriend of about 2 years whom she saw or talked to daily and went out dancing with. The relationship touched every important part of her life and helped Mialisa know herself better:

We trust each other. We're up front with each other. Yesterday, she was telling me something [about myself] that I didn't like, but at least I'm glad she's a good friend, that she can tell me anything. And she really looks out for me a lot. She loves my son. I love her kids. She's great.... We can trust each other with each other's boyfriends, you know, I don't have to worry about her liking my boyfriend or taking him away from. 'Cause she's up front. She'll be the type that, she'll tell me: "I like your boyfriend and I'm going to take him away from you." [Laughs] She'll tell me exactly, she won't hide around a bush. We already both tested each other on that.

However, Mialisa still struggled, with the question of what it meant to be a woman and with reconciling the tensions between her past and current views:

It's just a job. I was born as a woman so ... we're brought here to produce. It says it in the Bible.... We're supposed to have a husband and be married and you do that housely thing and produce. That's what we're here for, but I have a totally different opinion. I like to work. I like to do things on my own. There's time that you do stay home and cook and clean ... but I got to do something, I can't stay home living that kind of a life.

When asked why she does not want to stay at home, she emphasizes not wanting to be taken advantage of by a man:

> If you let a man think that that's the type of woman you are, they will take advantage ... of their clothes being cleaned every weekend, their clothes being ironed, their everything. Their food being done when they come from work. They get used to that and they get spoiled, and then they start messing up on you. They see that that's what they have at home, and then Hey, I could fool around with blahs-ee-blah. She ain't gonna find out. She's always at home! Who's gonna tell her anything.

Mialisa's transition to young adulthood was indeed a journey out of adolescence, but one she was able to make because she was able to revisit the crucial tasks of adolescence: establishing nonsexual, nonfamily intimate relationships, receiving job training, and dating.

Mothers Like Mialisa: Going Further, Getting Stronger

Mialisa's experiences were shared by the other mothers on welfare who were working or in job training programs or college. Able to cope with the responsibility of caring for children and with support from "the system" and their families and friends, these young mothers, at the 6-year follow-up interview, shared Mialisa's confidence in the future.

Shelly was in the second year of a 4-year nursing degree program when her mother died of cancer, leaving her with custody of her drug-addicted sister's three children (ages 6, 7, and 10) in addition to her own two (ages 4 and 5). She had promised her mother she would keep her sister's children together. She had help from her new boyfriend, whom she referred to as her *fiancé*. He cared for the children when they were not in school. However, Shelly was having trouble staying enrolled in school because her grades had dropped in the previous semester when her mother was dying. She spoke of how the welfare system almost derailed her progress, but again she resisted using the legal system for support:

> I was in court with the city because they wanted me to go into a two-year program instead of a four-year program. But when they made the law I was already in school and they knew it was a four-year program when I enrolled in the school. Basically these are the people that pay for my daughter to go to school. So they told me if I didn't go into a two-year college they were going to stop paying for her to go to school. So I took them to court. I felt that I was enrolled in the school before they made the law.... The judge ruled on my side.

Surprisingly, the accumulated stress from going through the court case, filling out forms, enrolling in classes, grieving for her mother (and father, who had died 18 months earlier), and getting five children ready for the new school year had not exhausted her resources. She was aware of her strength, which she described this way:

> I take on a lot of things for one person. I can handle a lot to be so young. My mother did the same thing, I say I get the strength from my mother. But the strength that I know my mother had, I think I go further, a little further than she does. I think every generation grows up stronger.

Marilyn, a part-time secretary, also struggled to go farther. She wanted to get a degree in accounting so she could have a career, not just a job. She described her teenage years as *chaos*. Caught between an addicted mother and an inability to negotiate school demands, she had fallen behind in her senior year:

> I moved out of my mother's house when I was 17 ... she got into drugs and I had to go through a big thing to testify to get my sister out. Right before that what made me move out is she would leave and leave me in her house with my sister and her boyfriend's baby. I couldn't go to school in the morning, so they expelled me. They wouldn't let me back in until she [my mother] went in and she wouldn't go back in because I wasn't in the house. And I had 6 months to go before completing my senior year, so I had the baby. I stayed home with her for a while and then I went and got my GED ... Six months and I would have had a high school diploma, instead of a GED. She wouldn't go and sign me back up. So me and my sister moved in with my grandmother.... My grandmother was my rock that kept my sanity there.

Tanecia, who was in business school to become a legal secretary, said she had "gone through a stage" after her mother's death: "My mother passed away ... and Martin [her children's father] dumped me with three kids." Unable to cope with school and her children, she took them to the Department of Child Welfare Office:

> "I going to put you away until I get what I'm going for and I can't do it with you because it's very hard for me." I just closed my eyes and took them there and I changed my mind. As we sat down I looked at my daughter and I was like I can't do it to them. It's my kids and I've got to struggle.... I come home from school and I have to cook, clean, get my kids ready for the next day. I have to do it. It's my responsibility. But at that time I was just closed, I was focused just on school and with my mother passing away I screwed up very bad.

Tanecia was fortunately able to get help from a Department of Children and Families (DCF) affiliated program. She described how valuable the opportunity was for her:

They wanted me to keep my kids so they really helped me. Last year I was very disappointed, very down. And they brought me up and I learned … I never had feelings for kids. I would talk nasty to my kids and I totally changed. I don't hit them, I punish them. I got rules in my house and the kids sometimes aggravate me but I have my rules. And they really helped me.

Anna, the youngest mother in the sample, dropped out of school in Grade 9 and had her only child at 14. She had been raped at age 7 by a stepfather who also beat her mother. She was homeless when her mother "fell into drugs and also got incarcerated." She went to a shelter for adolescents, but then, she said, "We had to run for our lives … because they felt that I was too young to take care of Jay, and they wanted to separate us." She became dependent on friends and eventually on a physically abusive boyfriend for a place for her child and herself to stay:

It was either be homeless in an abandoned car, like I saw myself once before or stay here where Jay was going to be warm, and Jay ate, even though I had to put up with what I had to put up with.

Yet she described herself as a "survivor, you know, the one that can take on anything, the drag racer, the horseback rider, you know what I'm saying, the racer." At 18, she got her own apartment; at 20, she entered a college program that allowed her to get credits toward a nursing degree and GED certificate. Although her mother was recovering from her addiction and was out of jail and could help with her child, Anna also struggled against depression and feared that some tragedy would derail her, but she pushed herself forward on behalf of her child. Asked where her strength came from, Anna answered:

Being tired, being tired of seeing your mom on drugs, being tired of running the streets, you get tired. You want to accomplish something. You want to make a foundation. You want to because you think about your baby, that's the first thing that made me see was Jay. Jay has brought me off of the cloud of suicide. I've never regretted Jay, never will regret him because Jay opened up a lot of light to me. You know because I used to also be suicidal, you know, because of certain things that happened in my childhood with men, my mother's … which is my stepfather, my uncle you know.… You don't want to see Jay helpless like you find yourself at that moment. You don't want to see your baby helpless. You want to be like 'If he goes to do this I want to be there to help him. I can't leave him alone because nobody's helping me. Who's going to help him? So why not stick with him and help him and he; be my buddy and I'll be his. And Jay has always been a buddy of mine. I probably wouldn't be here if I didn't have Jay … I wouldn't have been here.

HELEN: WAITING FOR TOMORROW

What was different about the other young mothers who were living independently on welfare? Why couldn't they take advantage of the system and make something of themselves? This is the group we perhaps hear most about, but in this study they represented less than half of the mothers (43%, $n = 40$). Most of these young women did have more subsequent children than mothers who, like Mialisa, worked or went to school. This group also had a remarkably high level of serious health problems (asthma, PTSD, depression), learning difficulties (leaving them unable to read or do math), domestic violence, and illnesses among their children (asthma, prematurity, disabilities, and psychiatric problems) or own mothers (drug abuse, cancer, heart disease). It is difficult to choose a representative of this group. Each of these mothers seemed an exception. However, they reported in common, overwhelming poverty and health-related stress accompanied by feelings of self-doubt, discouragement, and inertia.

Looking back at the interviews over the course of the study, we see this helplessness growing in the face of overwhelming obstacles. Many of these young women started out well (finishing high school, getting their own apartments, and working), but by the 6-year follow-up were defeated by repeated failures in their attempts to deal with their problems. Their discouragement showed as they narrowed their goals, focused on caring for their children, and waited for the future. In the face of almost constant stress, they began first to drift and then fall behind. They seemed to lose the motivation to do well that having a child to care for initially brought them. Discouragement with their repeated lack of success eventually overwhelmed their will to act on their own and their child's behalf.

Helen was just finishing Grade 8 when her son, Andrew, was born in July. By September, however, she returned to school hoping to go in to nursing so she could "work with babies in a hospital." Three years later, Helen was living in a homeless shelter. Andrew's father had died in jail. She was about to enter Grade 12, but she did not graduate. Her mother, a long-time alcoholic, minded her child for the first 2 years so Helen could go to school, but the conditions for the grandmother's continued support were unpredictable and onerous.

Looking at Helen's early motherhood experiences, we first see a remarkable ability to tackle multiple stress to keep moving forward. However, doubts about her ability to manage grew with the deterioration of her relationship with her mother and the death of her baby's father. At the 3-year follow-up, Helen described how hard it had been from the beginning:

> It was hard because I was young. I was 15 years old and I was still in Junior High School ... and I was on my mother's budget and she wasn't giving me enough. She was giving me, like, $50 and what can I do with $50 with a baby ... can't do nothing. So then I had thought of working after school at [a grocery store] and she used to buy Andrew Pampers because she ain't give me money, so she just used to buy his Pampers but when I started working she stopped giving me money completely and said that the money that I get, I can buy for me and my

baby. So it's kind of hard. Then like I almost got fired a few times because I had to stay home with Andrew because it was days that we got into arguments and she said "I'm not babysitting" and nobody else was there.

Helen said her mother did not like her child's father:

She didn't want me around him. She didn't want him to give me no money for the baby. She would keep me in the house all the time and sometimes she would go around and tell her friends things about me, you know … and have her friends watching me. So if they see me with him, they would tell my mother and she would, you know, hit me and all of this when I was pregnant.

Her mother's temper was at its worst when she was drinking. Helen found assistance from a social worker who helped her get into a temporary residence where, in turn, she got help with finding her own apartment.

Moving to a shelter improved Helen's relationship with her mother because she could now get up and walk out when they had arguments. She also said her mother had stopped hitting her sisters. Helen said her mother had "slowed down a lot" since she moved out because:

she knows if there is a problem in beating up, if there's a problem with them I already told her I'll come and take my little sisters to my house and I will tell her she cannot come in. She knows that I'll do that.

By then, Helen had taken Andrew to day care, although she worried frequently that his "wild" behavior (jumping off chairs and landing on his butt, trying out car doors, taking cookies from stores) would cause him to get hurt or in trouble. She said her sister told her: "He won't live, he's not minding you." She worried that, like his father, he would die young. She vigilantly tried to protect him, monitoring what he watched on TV and correcting his misbehavior.

Despite her clear ability to find help in coping with her responsibilities as a teenage mother, Helen did not have the feeling she could manage alone. She felt like she was still a teenager (and she was). She considered her mother grown, but she saw herself as "just a teenager and a mother." She did not have to take responsibility for all the bills and for getting things fixed when they broke down like her mother did. In fact, she was ambivalent about leaving the shelter for her own apartment:

I'm ready to get my own apartment now. I'm looking. They're giving me places, but then again I really don't want to leave. I just want to stay where I'm at 'cuz they is a lot of help. There is a lot of help there and, I don't know, I just feel kind of comfortable there.

Three years later, Helen was living in her second apartment with her son, her new baby daughter, and her 16-year-old sister. She spent most of her time listening to music with her sister. Her life was stalled while she waited for things to get better, and she lacked the motivation she had shown earlier to take on challenges. She now wanted to get a GED because, as she said: "I need an education to take care of my kids and I want a job and get off public assistance." She still wanted to be a pediatric nurse, but she said: "My building is putting together a GED program, so it's gotta be easy," and she was waiting for the program to start.

> She hoped to get married to a nice man, because she says: I'm a family type of person, I like for my children to be around somebody that's nice and respects me and respects them, especially because Andrew's father is deceased so he needs a father.

She did not mention her relationship with the father of her infant daughter until asked directly about having a current boyfriend, and then she described the relationship as poor from the beginning:

> We was friends but he was with somebody else and he has a lot of problems with his ex- girlfriend but we are together, I think it's still on shaky ground. I'm still ready to be like forget about it in some cases.... He got other girls, problems with girls and I don't have no time for that.

Indeed, his former girlfriend was expecting his child, but Helen said: "Now he kinda makes it like it's me and him together 'cause he's going through too many problems with the other girl, and me and his mother are close." Helen said if she had known about the other girl, she would not have "kept my baby, it wouldn't have been no chance."

She settled into taking care of her children. She felt responsible for them:

> My mother always told me "You have children. You take care of them. You had chances, you know, not to have it but you chose to have them so you have to take care of them." That's one thing that stays in my mind. I had them and I have to take care of them.

However, Helen often worried about her ability to care for them:

> Mostly ... I don't have low self-esteem but sometimes I think about, like am I doing the right thing with my kids and I call my mother a lot and I ask her ... especially if they get sick and I wonder about that and getting my house together ... things like that. I worry about saving up for furniture because my mother is real good at it.... It's like, will I get my kid's life together?

Andrew had a discipline problem that Helen found hard to control:

I have to repeat myself over and over "stop, stop, stop." You see Andrew do something and I'm like "stop A" and he's like "I'm not doing nothing." Andrew is in school ... he's not a problem ... but he don't like to work.... If he don't like it he's not going to do it.

In the previous interview, Helen had hoped that, by the time Andrew was 20, he would finish school, go to college, and get a good job. Now her hopes for him were less ambitious. When asked for three wishes for him when he was 20, she hoped he would "finish school, have a job [maybe building things], and still be living to have a job and finish school."

She said she wanted to move "real bad" because there were shootings and drug dealing in her neighborhood and because she only had two small bedrooms for herself, her son, and her daughter. Again, Helen, no longer worked on her own behalf or sought help to initiate change. Speaking of the community housing group that regulated the housing project where she lived, she wishes they would recognize her need for more space:

They don't want to move you, they don't want to do nothing. As your kids grow up these are small bedrooms, you know, you would think they would probably move you out of them apartments and move you to another apartment instead of leaving you in that little apartment, you and your kids all squashed up. They don't do none of that. They don't want to move you. You got to talk about getting a lawyer or ... I think they are a bunch of nosey people [laughs]. I just want to go to their GED program and after that ... I don't go to their meetings ... I don't associate with them. I don't associate with nobody there.

Six years after her first child's birth, Helen had lost the earlier drive to care for herself and her child. Overwhelmed by the loss of her first boyfriend and the absence of her mother's support, it was not clear how she would regain momentum or redirect the downward slide now set in motion by her lack of education, second child, and poor relationships. Living day by day, she had little chance of realizing her dream to be a nurse.

Mothers Like Helen: Overwhelmed by Stress and Adrift

Helen's encounters with extraordinary stress, conflicts with her mother, and focus on the present characterized the lives of several of the young women in this group who were living in their own apartments and on welfare. Their ability to seek or even envision a better future appeared blocked by a kind of helplessness in handling their current problems. Like Helen, many of these mothers were dealing with extraordinary stress, adjusting as their children's father left them, went to jail, or died; as their children or parents died; or as chronic unemployment, frequent moves, family problems, and financial problems overwhelmed them.

After the birth of her son, Nancy worked to support him briefly, but then had two subsequent births—a daughter with a genetic problem and a premature son. Both of these children died. Pregnant again at the 6-year follow-up, Nancy prayed for a healthy child. Her mother had begun to work late in her life and Nancy thought she would do the same thing: "In the future, hopefully I'll be somebody, or in school, or working." When asked what her ideal job would be, she continued: "I don't know, I like working with people. I don't know. I don't put my mind to it anymore, 'cause before I used to always be in school or doing something. But now I've dedicated myself to my kids...."

Sakinah had a less traumatic family situation. Her mother and boyfriend continued to support her financially and emotionally, and she had only one child. In the first few years after her child was born, she finished high school and got a job in an insurance company. She was hoping to learn car insurance and go to college to be a broker. At the 6-year follow-up interview, however, she had begun to drift and her plans were vague. She had not worked for 9 months after being let go after an absence due to illness. She said she wanted a secretarial job: "Working on computers and things like that. Work with people. I'm just versatile, whatever it is, you can teach me and I can learn." However, she said:

> It's hard. I go to temp agencies. I take tests. I'm just waiting now, I just can't find a job. I don't know, it's just hard. But it's been nine months since I haven't been working and it's just like, I moved so that took up some time, but now I guess you could say four months, there has just been so much on my mind, I'm moved. I'm settled, now I could take a job.

Sakinah also considered enrolling in a community college to "take a couple of classes ... maybe going to school will help, you know, get into the work study program, something like that.... I may be able to find a job that way," but she had not sent her transcripts to the school. With little more than staying versatile and hoping for a chance to work, Sakinah's plans were vague and undirected. Like Helen, faced with apparently insurmountable unemployment, she had begun to slow down her drive and wait for the future.

Jennifer's child's father was in jail by the time his child was 2½ years old and he subsequently died, leaving her surprised at having total responsibility for her child. She worried constantly about how to pay her bills on public assistance and blamed herself for not working, but she could not think what kind of job she would like and could not seem to get started. Asked what the ideal job would be for her, she said:

> I don't really have anything ... on the top of my head.... I always fantasized that I wouldn't have to work. I would have everything [laughs]. Everything would be, you know, done for me. I would have, but I don't know. I always wanted to work in a hospital ... I don't know.

When asked what she could see herself doing there, she continued:

Being in charge … I don't know what department or what it is, but being in charge. But just basically working there. Doing something, so I won't be choosy, just get me a job. Until I can decide, this is what I wanna do.… I was thinking about going into a, uh, nursing assistant program to do that. But I haven't … I was gonna go to one, but I don't know, I missed the interview, whatever it is. But that probably would be it, what I would wanna do.

It is hard to know what would help Jennifer define her goals or gain the motivation to start out working.

Ebony, a mother of two, earned a little extra money doing hairdressing. She said she wanted to get an associate's and a bachelor's degree, but did not know what she would study. She said: "I like dealing with people, but this woman's hair, no, not like that.… I wouldn't mind being like a correction officer, or something. Or working in a hospital. You know or something like that."

For these mothers, vaguely defined goals replaced past hopes and provided little direction to guide their actions. Indecision seemed to immobilize them. Like Helen, Isabel described the anxiety and despairs about the future that undermined her ability to make plans. She had no help with her two children, "no one to sit down and talk to me or try to help me." She was haunted by an incomprehensible fear that something bad would happen to her:

What I worry most about … That I ain't going to be able to make it … Something might go wrong, but I won't be able to take care of my kids or something like that … Somethings going to be bad or I'm not going to be … Somethings just gonna happen and I don't know what it is … I keep thinking something's gonna go wrong or I'm not going to be about to take care of my kid or something like that. I keep thinking that. I always think that. I always be stressed, all the time.

Life held no certain future for Isabel, and planning made little sense:

No one really knows what they want out of life. You can go to work, you can go to school, you can get a mansion, you could be rich, and still not be happy! It's like, what is it that you gotta find that's going to make you content? You don't know! You know, none of us asked to be on this earth, but we're here … And what is it, violence? Drugs? You understand, and it's like what are you living for? And you can have all of these things all of these positive things, and then get shot or hit by a car. And then where does all of you go, you know? So, it's just crazy. That's why you can't plan. I mean, people … Have their way of doing things. The way that's best for them. So I don't plan anything … I know what I want, and I just go for it. And I just look at life as it comes. I try to enjoy every minute I can, because you never know what's going to happen. Anything can happen.

These young mothers are unlikely to identify their problems as depression (Leadbeater & Linares, 1992). Both the mothers and those around them interpret depressive symptoms as an inability to get going or just laziness. These women blame themselves for this laziness and do not seek help. However, untreated symptoms of depression (e.g., the inability to make decisions, irritability, paranoia, anxiety about the future, self-criticism, withdrawal, and alienation of supports) make coping with stresses even more unlikely. Moreover, higher levels of depressive symptoms are associated with increases in stressful life events (Leadbeater & Linares, 1992), poorer educational outcomes (Leadbeater, 1996), and a greater likelihood of problem behaviors in the children of these mothers (Bishop, Leadbeater, & Way, 1998; Leadbeater & Bishop, 1994).

VIVIAN: TAKING CARE OF A MOTHER'S RESPONSIBILITIES, ONE DAY AT A TIME

Twelve young women were receiving welfare while still living with their mothers 6 years after delivery. A commitment to rearing their children, despite the financial sacrifices required, kept them from working or getting job training. In contrast with the other mothers on welfare, who have been described, these women were more content with just mothering, and their supports were more plentiful. Their initial response to having a child was to *automatically* become an adult. They focused on the responsibility of caring for their children, and their futures as working women became increasingly unpredictable.

These mothers' education had been put on hold at the delivery of their first child. Only 2 of the 12 had gone farther than Grade 10 at delivery and only 2 had received GEDs 6 years later. The future was unpredictable. Focused on the present, they lived day to day. They felt that public assistance was not enough, but it made it possible for them to care for their children without depending on others.

Four of these mothers shared housekeeping, and sometimes babysitting, with the grandmothers; eight of the grandmothers could not help with day care because they were working, ill, or alcoholic. Some of the adolescent mothers had moved out of their mother's apartment for a time, but later returned to care for an ill mother or younger siblings. Although the grandmothers were rarely able to provide day care or material help, they were frequently described by the young mothers as their closest friends to whom they could talk about anything. Relationships with other family members, especially sisters, were frequently close as well.

The word *responsibility* peppered the remarks of this group of women who focused on caring for their children. They felt that babysitters, other than family members, could not be trusted; leaving a child with a stranger was not an option, at least not until the child could talk. They gained their identity and a sense of dignity from the fact that they did not abandon their children to the care of others. They took on the responsibility for rearing the children themselves.

Vivian represents this group of mothers. Seventeen when her first child was born, she had only finished Grade 9. Six years later, the mother of three children, she had not returned to school. She describes how the birth of her first child both slowed her down and sped up her entry into young adulthood:

> You got to realize that you have your responsibility, 'cause before you didn't have a child you could just get up and go. Now that you got that child, you gotta sit there, try to find a babysitter, try to get all that stuff together. It's just ... it slows you down a lot.... Especially if you have it at a young age. Your youth just goes right past you. You just automatically turn into an adult, no matter what age you have that child. You're taking care of it ... your youth goes on past.

Vivian was reluctant to give up her youth entirely, however. When asked what being a woman meant to her, she said:

> When I was small, a woman to me was a woman that was responsible, mature person herself, in a decent respectful way. And to me,... somehow I consider myself a nice decent woman, but then I see women like dresses and shoes, and I don't like dresses. I consider myself a young, young, woman ... I still consider myself a teenager 'cause of the way I dress, and sometimes the way I act. But a woman to me is a woman that considers herself in a respectful way. With dresses and working, and looking decent and not showing herself too much. That's the way I see a woman. I think I got a few more years to consider myself a woman.

Like many of the mothers in this group, Vivian saw her future through her children's eyes and said she would like to have her GED:

> 'Cause a high school diploma is very important to me. 'Cause when my kids grow up, I don't want them asking me, mommy, did you finish high school? And I be like, no. And they be wondering why. And I really don't have no excuse why. And if they see that I didn't finish, they'll probably go, Well, if she didn't finish, why should I?

She had no plans to return to school. She said she wanted a job to get off welfare, but again had no plans:

> ... it's doing something with your life instead of being home all day, doing nothing and depending on welfare, whatever people call it. That's no good, 'cause that's just making them lazier and I don't wanna do that. And I really wanna go out an get a job and find a job.

Vivian wished her mother, who was strict about a lot of things like eating all your food at the table and being in on time, had been more strict about her attending school.

> As far as school-wise, she wasn't strict. Because it was certain days we would stay home, and she wouldn't force us to get up out of bed. And see, we figured

she didn't care, so why should we?... And I wish she probably would have forced us to try to get a job. But she never forced us to get no summer jobs, working papers or nothing like that.

When asked what her ideal job would be, she said she would like to be a secretary—that it was what she had wanted to be since she learned to type in junior high school: "I love typing, but now what's really out there is computers. That's why I wanna learn them." She had tried to go to a GED program and wanted to enter a new program where she could also learn about computers, but she could not get child care she could afford and trust. She said: "I gotta make sure I have a good babysitter ... that wouldn't mind watching them just in case I got extra hours or whatever. My mother charges too much." Her mother wanted to go back to her own job as a nurse's aide or she would charge $60 a week (two thirds of Vivian's $185 biweekly welfare check) to look after Vivian's three children.

Vivian said that, once her children could talk, she would have no problems with a babysitter. Until then, however, "I'm not going to trust nobody with my kids." Even in the face of this unresolvable day-care problem, like the other mothers whose lives were stalled on welfare, Vivian located her difficulty in her own lack of motivation:

What I would like to do is put my mind really to it and keep it on my mind. What I do is think about it one day, and forget about it the next.... And I won't think about it until maybe a week later on. If it was to stick on my mind, and I was really thinking about it I would find some way, somehow, to do it. I just gotta keep my mind on my goal. The kids' father keeps saying I'm not ready to really go to school and take my GED and start working.... He says, I'm still young and have a life ahead of me. I said, I don't know what's ahead of me. I don't know what's in my future.

A kind of generalized uncertainty kept her from making plans and bound her to a day-to-day existence. When asked what she would like to see happen in the future, she had a hard time answering and finally said:

I don't know. I don't know, I'm saying, you could want a whole lot of things to happen. But then when they happen, there's always something else that you want. So really, I'm not the type of person that plans things. You know? I just know what I want, and I just go for it. So I really can't tell you 'cause I don't know. Just happiness and, I don't know, luck, I guess. I don't know. I don't know. So much stuff that people want, you know. You just really don't know, because when you have, when you get certain things you're still not happy. It's not that you're not happy, but just like you're still missing something in your life.

Not having enough money was a constant worry for all of the mothers in this group. Vivian was proud that she could take care of her own kids without depending on other people, but she believed only in "getting things you really need." She refused to get cable TV, although her kids wanted it, because she needed to get them summer clothes and she needed car fare. She weighed having cable TV against getting a phone:

> I gotta try get my phone back on, that's important. I need a phone. But there's only so much money, and so for this money, I said ... I could be putting that toward my telephone bill.... This public assistance, they don't give you much to take care of all of that. They don't give you enough to take care of your kids.

From Vivian's perspective, welfare allowed her to depend on herself to care for her children. In this way it was, somewhat paradoxically, the source of her independence and respectability as a woman. She was proud of her ability to manage her own money and take care of her own children.

Being responsible for her own children was paramount in Vivian's positive view of herself:

> For me to be so young and have three kids, I figure I'm doing pretty good. And, it's so shocking, 'cause I don't need help from anybody. I don't need my sisters. And that's what really amazed me, 'cause I be sitting there wondering, I got three kids and I'm taking care of them all by myself. And it's so shocking because I thought I would never be able to do it. I thought I would go insane when I had the first child. And I guess I just sat there and realized, I got pregnant, I got the responsibility now.

Vivian mentioned several times that she was the only one who would take care of her children: "I know I got things to do, because they are mine. Ain't nobody gonna help me,... I just got to take care of them." Her greatest worry was "dying and leaving my kids alone." "Especially," she went on, "since I don't got no job, and nothing to give them when I die."

It came as a surprise that Vivian's children all had the same father with whom she was still involved. She did not mention him until asked directly to talk about her oldest child's father. She said that, although they had had some ups and downs, she was still involved with him and described him as understanding and caring. She did not seem to expect him to provide financially for her or *her* children; he came over to play with their oldest girl sometimes, but "then he'll go home and go to sleep, 'cause he be so tired." He did not bother much with his other two children because the youngest, Vivian explained, was "too small," and his middle daughter, who was born prematurely and had a speech defect, "can't really talk. So he can't really do that much with her." Even so, she found it remarkable that they are still together:

> And for him to still be with me with three kids, that's so amazing. And we've been together for ten years, going on eleven. And for us to be together for that long, I feel as though we haven't changed. And that's amazing because most people don't last that long.... He still cares. That's what's so amazing.

Vivian said he worked, was starting college, and did some volunteer work so she did not see him as much as she wanted. She would have liked them to live together, but mentioned no plans for that to happen. Vivian also wanted her own apartment and kept filing applications for subsidized housing, but she said:

> They keep telling me that they don't got enough room for us, so there's no where else for me to move. [My mother's] got a three bedroom so they think that she's got enough room. So they tell me I'm on a waiting list, so I gotta wait.

Apartments advertised in the newspaper were completely out of reach, Vivian said:

> "Most of them charge five [$500 a month], and public assistance is not gonna pay that much. I gotta find one that's gonna fit my income ... and my mother won't want me to go anyway."

Expecting little from the future and having no plans make it unlikely that Vivian will get off welfare. She has become an adult with responsibilities for her children. However, as much as this ideal competes with current ideal roles for single women, it is unlikely Vivian will change her attitudes or goals.

Mothers Like Vivian

The other mothers in this group similarly emphasized their rapid transitions to being an adult and having sole responsibility for their children. Day-care problems prevented working. Shelly said being a woman was:

> to be older. I feel when you're a woman you have responsibilities. You have to be alert more, you have to be reliable ... when you pay your own bills, nobody pay them for you.... Take on responsibility. That's being a grown-up, a woman.

All struggled to make it day to day with the limited income welfare provided. Two supplemented their income by caring for other people's children. Only one mother in this group, Tory, lived with a boyfriend, who she said accepted her children but was "scared of commitment" and unreliable. These mothers were unable and unwilling to return to school or get work, hampered by the lack of dependable day care. Like other mothers in this group, Tory feared something might go wrong if someone else cared for her children:

> Well basically all I think about is my kids. I live day-by-day, Are my kids alright? What I'm afraid of is somebody [later revealed as her child's father, who was abusive] taking my kids from me.... I got scholarships and stuff for basketball ... 'cause, I was supposed to go on a basketball scholarship and get an associate's degree, but I never went. Never got a GED, no nothing.... Nobody to watch my children.... Who can I trust watching my child? If I leave this person

with my child, would they try to molest my child, beat my child, or would I come
home and my child would still be my child when I get there?

Jamaica also described her slowed-down life and rapid transition to adulthood:

When you have a child, it like, slows it down, because there's certain things that
you miss. And you become more of an adult quicker than what you should have
been. So if I can do it all over, I would wait.... It just seems like, things just went
so quick. You know like it could have been a little slower, that's all.

She was 2 weeks short of 18 and had finished Grade 11 when her first child was
born. She never returned to school. Now the mother of three, she focused her life
on caring for her children and looking for an apartment. She, her daughter, and
twin sons shared one bedroom in her mother's five-bedroom apartment where 11
other people also lived. About going back to school, Jamaica said:

I want to go to school for X-ray technician.... It's, like, delayed, 'cause my problem
is, every time I want to get involved into something, I always have to sit back and
wait, because the only one that I trust with my kids is my mother. So I wouldn't, you
know, it's like hard trying to trust people with your kids.... Most of the time when I
get jobs and stuff I have to leave the jobs. Because I don't have a regular babysitter,
so once I get my own apartment, things will work out differently, 'cause I have no
choice but to have a babysitter. But then my kids will be a little older.

Although some mothers shared Vivian and Jamaica's hope that things would
get better when their kids went to school, others were more entrenched in a present
of overwhelming responsibility. Tia, mother of two, said she was "a simple person
... I'm basically home. That's all I do." She imagined a future with a good job,
maybe meeting a nice man and getting married, but she could not say what kind of
job she would like to do. She only finished Grade nine and said: "Nowadays, I hear
that it's harder to get a job if you haven't finished schooling," but she said dealing
with public assistance was hard because there was not enough money. Her own father was an alcoholic and did not work, and her children's fathers were never involved and were "in and out of jail." For now, she cared for her own mother (who
occasionally drank and never left the house) and her two children. Most days her
sister and her sister's children also stayed with her. Tia also babysat three other
kids before and after school to supplement her income.

The young women in this group were perhaps closest to the stereotype of adolescent mothers (e.g., dropped out of school with little education and not returned,
and rapidly having more children). Their lives focused on their responsibilities as
mother for these children. Although some might return to school or job training
when their children went to school, their own lack of education and aborted plans
will make this later transition unlikely.

Welfare clearly serves different needs in adolescent mothers' lives. Universal welfare reform policies that are insensitive to these differences can unwittingly undermine the potentially successful mothers who persist, despite obstacles, while failing to overcome the obstacles that keep other mothers from even trying to leave welfare. Although the first group of mothers described in this chapter were able to take advantage of welfare education and job training programs, and thus will likely move off public assistance, their numbers were small. Entering and staying in educational and work programs requires persistence and a personal drive that were defeated by the overwhelming stresses for the adolescents in the second and largest group of welfare users. Without addressing the problems of illness, stress, and domestic violence that these women were experiencing, they were unlikely to become self-supporting. Indeed, as their levels of depression and discouragement increase, it is likely that the stresses that defeat them will also increase, creating a downward spiral that will be increasingly difficult to halt.

Valuing of traditional roles for mothers allowed the third group of young women to make do with meager incomes to protect their children. Child-care providers and programs that could guarantee child safety were not available to counter these strongly held values, and the likelihood that these women would realize their adolescent career goals was rapidly diminishing.

These differences also demonstrate the potential for advantages of using welfare to encourage young mothers to grow up more slowly and focus on the tasks of late adolescence. Success at this stage of development can create trajectories that end welfare dependence. Failure to overcome obstacles and too early rejection of adolescent goals can also create trajectories for negative outcomes that are not easily overcome.

8

Resilient Relationships: Men as Fathers and Partners

Many have argued that the rise of adolescent parenting as a social problem stems less directly from the age of the mothers than from their status as single parents (Furstenberg et al., 1987; Lawson & Rhodes, 1993; Nathanson, 1991). As noted earlier, the number of births to teenagers has actually declined since the 1950s, whereas the number of out-of-wedlock births has soared (Children's Defense Fund, 1993). Nevertheless, policies aimed at reducing the number of children born out of wedlock, or supporting these children once they are born, have rarely incorporated roles for men. On the contrary, policies directed at unwed adolescent mothers have been unequivocal in assigning them custody of and responsibility for their children.

Welfare assistance has traditionally been denied to households that include an able-bodied man, creating financial disincentives for parenting couples to stay together (Burbridge, 1995). Where attention has been given to unwed fathers, it has focused on mandating the mothers' cooperation in establishing paternity to enforce child-support legislation (Levin-Epstein, 1996). However, this legislation was designed to sanction *dead-beat-dads* for failure to provide support rather than enable the biological fathers of children of adolescent mothers to demonstrate their ability to provide for their children. The biological fathers of the children of adolescent mothers often differ greatly in their age, employability, and life circumstances from fathers in divorcing families. Unemployment, drug involvement, and imprisonment, which all disproportionately affect young, inner-city poor men (William T. Grant Foundation, 1988), also directly impairs these men's capacity to provide financial support to their children. There is clearly a need to rethink the issues of paternity identification and child-support enforcement as it relates specifically to the strategies for family formation among young unwed couples to enhance their abilities to support their children in the long term. This chapter focuses on the couples in the New York study who maintained involvement with each other.

THE INFLUENCE OF FATHERS ON ADOLESCENT MOTHERS AND THEIR CHILDREN

There is not a great deal of prospective research on the types and effects of the involvement of the biological fathers of the children of adolescent mothers. Although research indicates that the economic contributions of noncustodial fathers, in general, remains low, especially for minority families, qualitative studies of young, low-income fathers found that many were strongly committed to their children and often provided noneconomic support (like child care) when they could not add to the household income (Furstenberg, 1995; Sullivan, 1989). These fathers may provide a range of formal or informal supports in addition to or instead of direct economic support, including acknowledging paternity, maintaining contact or emotional bonds with their children, providing child care, and giving clothes, diapers, and other material support (Adams, Pittman, & O'Brien, 1993; Sullivan, 1989). Some authors have argued that the involvement of these fathers is hampered more by negative stereotypes, as well as by their economic, educational, and residential circumstances, than by their lack of concern for or commitment to their children (Adams et al., 1993; Lamb & Elster, 1986; Sander & Rosen, 1987; Sullivan, 1989; Watson, Rowe, & Jones, 1989). Many involved fathers initially live with their own or the adolescent mother's family and typically depend on them for financial support (Marsiglio, 1987). These living arrangements can support young families, but they can also exaggerate competing demands for loyalty to kin versus partner. Moreover, by early adulthood, many of these fathers are in new relationships, have additional children, and face the challenges of negotiating the competing interests of more than one family.

For adolescent mothers, support from a male partner is positively related to residential stability, overall life satisfaction, psychological well-being, and social participation (Cooley & Unger, 1991; Leadbeater & Linares, 1992; Spieker & Bensley, 1994; Unger & Cooley, 1992; Unger & Wandersman, 1988). On a less positive note, early marriages or cohabitation are associated with less maternal education for African-American and White mothers (Unger & Cooley, 1992).

Less research has investigated the effects of father involvement for the children of adolescent mothers. Cooley and Unger (1991) found that involvement of a male partner was associated with greater overall cognitive stimulation, which in turn was related to fewer problem behaviors and better academic achievement in the children of adolescent mothers at 6 to 7 years of age. Following a small group of adolescent children born to adolescent mothers in the late 1950s, Furstenberg and Harris (1993) reported that youth who had long-term relations with a resident, biological father or stepfather were more likely to have entered college or found stable employment after high school, were less likely to have become teenage parents or have been in jail, and were less likely to report depressive symptoms. However, these close, residential relationships were rare. These findings do not hold for adolescents with close attachments to a nonresident father—a situation that, in fact, predicted an increased likelihood of teenage childbearing, particularly for male children.

A great many gaps remain in our knowledge about the role of fathers of children of adolescent mothers. Most research has not considered the role of biological fathers separately from that of stepfathers or other male partners, despite the possibility that biological fathers may have reasons related both to emotional attachments and ethology to be more invested in how their offspring do (Lancaster & Lancaster, 1987). Measures of father involvement also generally tap presence or absence, rather than qualitative differences in or the closeness of father–child relationships (Way & Stauber, 1996). In addition, we know little about the parenting skills, stresses, competencies, or problems of fathers who are or are not involved with their children (Lamb, 1988). A father's reasons for not being involved with his child, the mother's reasons for not being involved with the father, and the quality of the relationship and level of conflict for couples that remain involved all may have important implications for the durability of these relationships and their influence on their children (Leadbeater, Way, & Raden, 1996). Almost no research has focused on the reasons for stability or instability in the relationships of poor, unwed couples.

THE EFFECTS OF CHANGING
PATTERNS OF FAMILY FORMATION

Patterns of family formation have changed over the past decade for all sectors of American society. Women and men are marrying later. Today, more never marry than in the past. These individuals live alone or with a partner without marrying. There is no simple explanation for these trends. In the past, differences between the rates of marriage for Euro- and African Americans were attributed to cultural differences that, in the case of African Americans, emphasized kinship obligations and maternal–child bonds over affinal attachments. The socioeconomic conditions for African Americans as a result of slavery and racism also disrupted family stability and imposed a need for flexibility in family roles (Tucker & Mitchell-Kernan, 1995).

Research also shows that recent demographic and economic changes disproportionately affect family formation for inner-city minorities. The percentage of African-American men ages 20 to 24 who were married fell from a peak of 44% in 1960 to 13% in 1990. Statistics for Hispanic men in 1960 are not available, but by 1990, only 27% of Hispanic men in this age group were married. In addition, marriage rates for inner-city women are associated with the *male-to-female sex ratio,* defined as the number of marriage-appropriate men per 100 women, reflecting differences in birth, immigration, and mortality rates in young men and women (Kiecolt & Fossett, 1995; Sampson, 1995; Schoen, 1995; Testa & Krogh, 1995). Given that the rate of marriage is low for both employed and unemployed men who have fathered children out of wedlock, reviewers have suggested that demographic and economic changes must also be considered in transaction with women's increased economic independence (through welfare or employment), changing gender roles, attitudes toward marriage, parental obligations, out-of-wedlock births, and welfare dependence (Danziger, 1995; Furstenberg, 1995).

Hatchett, Veroff, and Douvan's (1995) research on the predictors of instability in the first 3 years of marriage for African-American and White working couples in their early 20s in Detroit is relevant in understanding the patterns of family formation among young minority couples. For African Americans, greater marital instability was predicted by the husband's anxiety about his ability to provide for a family and his drinking or substance use, as well as by gender role inflexibility (i.e., husbands holding more traditional views and wives advocating more flexible participation in household tasks). Premarital children (which possibly motivated the marriage) contributed to the early stability of marriages, whereas births in the first few years after marriage had a destabilizing effect (possibly as a result of increasing financial and role strains). Also contributing to marital instability for African-American couples were difficulties blending premarital kin bonds, interference on the part of the husbands' family, and noninvolvement of the wives' family. Finally, African-American husbands' disapproval of their wives' friends was predictive of stability, rather than instability, in the marriage. Explaining the latter counterintuitive finding, Hatchett et al. (1995) suggested that, "maintaining a distinctive friend network apart from her husband's allows a wife to continue a marriage regardless of her level of unhappiness" (p. 196).

The picture that emerges from these sociological and demographic perspectives on family formation in inner-city couples is that young marriages, lacking a secure economic base for their existence, depend on the Herculean ability of the couple to resolve gender role conflicts and balance the marital relationship with demands of kin and friends while maintaining a sufficiently strong affectionate bond to stay together. This must be achieved in the context in which marriageable men, because of their relative scarcity, have greater freedom to seek new partners, and where changing roles for women are challenging traditional gender role divisions of authority and labor.

Reflecting these difficulties, few adolescent mothers and their children's fathers form stable and long-lasting families. The declining involvement of recent cohorts of fathers of children of adolescent mothers has been documented (Chase-Landsdale & Vinovskis, 1987; Osofsky, Hann, & Peebles, 1993). This decline becomes more pronounced as the children leave infancy (Furstenberg & Harris, 1993; Leadbeater, Way, & Raden, 1996; Unger & Wandersman, 1988). Again, African-American children of adolescent mothers are disproportionately affected.

Using data from the 1986 National Longitudinal Survey of Youth (NLSY), Marsiglio (1987) reported that only 15% of African-American fathers of children born to adolescent mothers lived with their first child shortly after birth, compared with 48% of Hispanic and 58% of White fathers. For White fathers, residence with their child was positively related to the fathers' older age, Catholic religion, and rural residence, However, none of these factors predicted involvement for African-American or Hispanic fathers (Marsiglio, 1987). Other research has found that Hispanic adolescent mothers are more likely to be married or living with a partner than African-American or White adolescent mothers (Salguero, 1984;

Wasserman, Rauh, Brunelli, Garcia-Castro, & Necos, 1990). However, more African-American than White adolescent mothers live with their own families, remain single, or marry later (Unger & Cooley, 1992).

Anecdotal evidence from qualitative, longitudinal case studies of 20 young couples (Furstenberg, 1995) underscores young fathers' difficulties in sustaining commitments in the face of inadequate resources, weak emotional attachments between the partners, or competition from relationships not only with kin, but also with friends and new romantic partners. A stable relationship before the pregnancy, support from both extended families, financial capability, and limited additional childbearing allowed a few young men to honor their commitment to "doing right" for their children (Furstenberg, 1995).

INVOLVEMENT OF THE CHILDREN'S FATHERS IN THE NEW YORK STUDY

Data from the New York study yield reasons for instability as well as stability in relationships between adolescent mothers and their children's fathers. Given the difficulties and expense of contacting the young fathers directly, all data were collected in the interviews with the adolescent mothers.

On average, these fathers were 20 years old at the delivery of the first child—3 years older than the mothers' mean age. The range in the fathers' ages, however, was great: from 15 to 33 years. At delivery, most of these men had completed Grade 11; 36% had graduated from high school. Only 17% were in school and 64% worked at least part-time.

Seventy-eight percent were in relationships with the mothers when the child was born, and 68% of the mothers said the biological father was contributing (money or supplies) to the child's care at that time. Three years after the birth, only 26% of the mothers said they had a close relationship with the child's father, although 35% said the child and father had a close relationship. *Close* was defined as frequent and emotionally positive contact because few lived with or financially supported their children at that point.

By the 6-year point, these numbers had declined further, with only 12% of the mothers and 34% of the children in close relationships with the biological fathers. Fourteen (11%) of the fathers lived with their child; two were the primary parent. At this point, nine (10%) of these young men had died (up from 4% three years earlier), 25% were in jail (up from 19%), and the numbers selling or using drugs increased to 24% (up from 14%). Relationship problems were frequently reported by the mothers: 26% of the men were in new relationships, 29% were described as irresponsible, and 26% were described as physically abusive or excessively controlling. Clearly, expectations that these young couples will marry or even that many of these fathers could "do right" by their children are misplaced. The diminishing potential of the young fathers in the New York study to ease their children's economic straits or contribute to their well-being in other ways is evident.

Moreover, only a few mothers entered into long-term supportive relationships with men other than their first child's father. Fifty-six percent of the mothers had a second relationship; 19% reported three or more relationships. Yet only 21% of those in a second relationship and 47% of those in a third described the new relationship as emotionally close at the 6-year follow- up. Only nine women were married. The mothers expressed concerns about their new relationships similar to those just listed. To these they added worries about being hurt again in the new relationship, concerns about their new partner's relationship with their child or children, and, particularly, doubts about the stability of the new relationships.

Effects on the Children of Their Father's Involvement

Previous research with the New York study focused on predictors of the fathers' continued involvement with adolescent mothers and the consequences of their involvement for their children (Leadbeater, Way, & Raden, 1996). Findings when the children were approximately 3 years old show that the children of involved fathers had higher externalizing scores on the Child Behavior Checklist (CBCL) than those with noninvolved fathers [respectively, $M = 26.8$ vs. $19.9, SD = 12.5$ vs. $9.9; T(79) = -2.63, p < .01$]. The relative contributions of father involvement, after accounting for the effects of ethnic differences and levels of maternal depressive symptoms, explained a small but significant amount (5%) of the variance in the children's externalizing behaviors [$F(4, 71) = 5.47, p < .001$].

Analyses of interviews with the mothers suggest that the association between father involvement and the children's externalizing behaviors might be related to the levels of hostility and conflict in the couples' relationships, inconsistent parenting styles (the mother was typically the limit setter, whereas the father set few or no limits with the child), and, infrequently, the father's own problems (e.g., drug use, depression). However, by the 6-year interview, child problem behavior was no longer related to father involvement. Whether assessed as frequency of contact or quality of relationship with the mother or child, father involvement at this point had no effect on the level of child problem behavior reported by mothers or teachers.

As Furstenberg (1995) noted, custody is not granted to the fathers of the children of adolescent mothers; custody is granted to the mothers and access must be earned by the fathers. In the New York sample, the price was not just paying household bills or child support. When the young women spoke of their relationships with the children's fathers, it was clear there were other conditions for access to the children. Almost without exception, the women referred to their child as *my* child and the biological father as *my* child's father. There was a disturbing lack of reference to *our* child. Parallelling societal expectations that young women take primary responsibility for their children, most mothers believed that they are the only parent who could be counted on to care for their children. In contrast, parenting was optional for the young father: he could leave if the mother was no longer attractive to him, if he met someone else, if he fathered another child, or if closeness in the relationship with his child's mother floundered. Being a good father was tallied from evidence of the young man's contributions to the child's care. The mothers valued behaviors that relieved them of their full-time role as caregivers, including the father's willingness to babysit so the mother could go out with friends, to independently care for or take the child out, and to help with the child's school work.

RELATIONSHIPS THAT ENDURED: MATURING TOGETHER, OUTLASTING SEPARATIONS

In the New York study, only 14 couples stayed together over the 6-year period of data collection. The stories of these couples reveal the changes, compromises, maturation, and commitment that allowed these relationships to endure. Only three of these relationships represented stable, continuous commitments. The other couples had reunited after painful separations, outlasting the conflicts they faced and demonstrating resilience in their willingness to recommit to each other and the responsibilities of parenting their child together. These relationships were tested while the young men were attending college, hanging out late at night with their friends, seeing other women, serving jail sentences, submitting to drug rehabilitation, or exercising domineering or abusive attitudes. Often both members of these young couples began their early 20s wondering what they had missed by having a child so young, wishing they had waited, wishing they had had more time to be alone, and longing to have the freedoms and enjoyment of what they called their "missed" adolescence.

The young women's lives also underwent critical turning points in these tumultuous early years of their relationships. One woman entered an emotionally devastating and abusive extramarital relationship. Other women found themselves and their autonomy as they survived their fears of living alone and recognized their efficacy as single parents who could take charge and succeed. The couples that survived separations came back together often on a more equitable footing, struggling to balance the authority and power in the relationships.

For these young couples, being a good husband was a separate matter from being a good father, and marriage was a separate decision from that of being a parent. The mothers summarized what was important in their own relationships with their child's father: mutual trust, being able to talk about almost anything, and doing things alone with each other. What caused ongoing distress between the parents were boredom with the relationship, perceived interference from the father's parents, conflicts over child discipline, and the mother's jealousy of the child's relationship with the father.

Resilient Relationships: What Protects Them?

Resiliency researchers (e.g., Garmezy, Masten, & Tellegen, 1984; Jessor, 1993; Rutter & Rutter, 1993) have consistently identified individual intelligence, religious affiliation, and a positive relationship with an adult mentor as protective factors for children growing up in high-risk environments. However, the protective factors for these resilient relationships were not merely the sum of these individual assets.

The narratives of two women, Sibylle and Sherry, describing their long-term relationships with their children's fathers, illustrate processes that protected the relationships that endured. Recurrent themes in these interviews suggest that the stability of these relationships reflected:

- a considered decision to marry rather than merely drifting or escaping into a relationship based on parenting demands
- extended family members who modeled what to avoid in a marriage
- extended family members who offered material support and advice
- the growth of self-respect and self-determination in the young women
- the flexible reassignment of gender roles

Given the small number of couples in the New York sample that formed stable relationships, these data are necessarily anecdotal. They may not represent a larger population of inner-city, young couples, and they do not represent the men's viewpoints. However, these data do offer insights into problems and protective factors at the level of the relationship rather than the individual. To our knowledge, no research has examined these protective factors. Hence, although not generalizable beyond this study at this point, these data may help stimulate and frame future research.

Sibylle and Gordon: Making the Decision to Marry in a Community of Single Women

Six years after the delivery of their daughter, Alexia, Sibylle and her partner, Gordon, were married and happily nestled among supportive, female, extended family members. Sibylle worked as an advocate for the homeless, Gordon as a manager at a store. Their enviable marriage epitomized the traditional ideal of a working couple who were committed to each other and to the education and well-being of Alexia, who was still their only child.

Sibylle was one of the few women who used the pronoun *we* when talking about her life with Gordon and Alexia. At the 3-year interview, they were not yet married, but she described their relationship this way:

> He doesn't want to leave me and I don't want to leave him because he's always been there for me. He's more than just my boyfriend, he's also my best friend. We have the most wonderful conversations and we relate to each other a lot. It's not a forced thing where because you are her father you have to marry me and you're stuck with me. It's because we want to be together, be a family. We've never been separated or had arguments, thank God, and he's never had anybody else either and I've never because we think we'd be disrespecting each other....

Even at the 6-year follow-up, the relationship, now a marriage, was a happy one. They had become "like a trio." Despite occasional worries about bills, Sibylle said things were running smoothly, as she is quoted in chapter 5 as saying: "It's just the basic routine where it's working and bringing in enough money to pay the bills and take care of our necessities and that's basically it."

This resilient couple beat the odds in many ways. When Alexia was born, Sibylle was 15 and Gordon was 23. Both came from single-parent, mother-headed households. Sibylle was raised by her grandmother after her fifth or sixth grade, when her mother became a drug addict. Sibylle said her mother went downhill when Sibylle's brother's father left her. Sibylle appears to have stumbled in the face of her mother's drug addiction. She became involved with Gordon at 13—about the time her mother was no longer able to care for her. She became sexually active and pregnant by 15.

When Alexia was born, Gordon had graduated from high school. He was 8 years older than Sibylle. Gordon's mother was "addicted to numbers," but she cared for him until he moved in with Sibylle and her grandmother after Alexia was born. His father was not part of his life. He was involved with deviant friends.

Extending Families Modeling: What to Avoid and Offering Support.
Sibylle's downhill slide stopped with the birth of Alexia. On Alexia's behalf, and with the support and encouragement of her grandmother, Sibylle took control of her future, resisting all pressures to marry out of tradition or dependency. Her mother's mistakes in becoming an addict influenced Sibylle's views about the necessity of making *either* Alexia *or* Gordon the priority in her life. Her mother became an addict after a failed relationship, but Sibylle challenges this:

> How can you destroy yourself because of a man? You know, you have to be strong for us [her children]. How can you let a man ... If one heads down the wrong path you can't follow that path.... You've got to want better, because you have to have your priorities, I guess, straighter. Emotionally, she wasn't strong enough to deal with what she had to deal with.

Like Sibylle, several of the young mothers voiced their desire not to end up like their mothers in a marriage that did not work. However, only a few were able to construct a vision of marriage that could transcend their mother's fate. Beebe, a 21-year-old homemaker with three children by the same man, articulated her stubborn fears of marriage. Her highly religious partner was several years older than she and he wanted to be married, but after 7 years together, she still refused:

> I was always the type of person that didn't wanna marry. 'Cause I saw my mother. She had marriage and, like, I don't know. It didn't work out for her. She brought home some Jamaican, like he ran off. So I didn't want to be in the same predicament.... I always felt that marriage is to condemn yourself even though I live in a marriage environment. I didn't want to condemn myself to the papers ... people say oh, I have three kids, but I'm not ready for it yet. Even though I have kids and responsibilities of a mature middle-aged woman, I feel that I'm still not ready for marriage. I don't know when I'll be ready for it. Not now.

Despite problems in their own marriages, the grandmothers, who were the mothers of either the adolescent mothers or the biological fathers, often played a role in supporting the couple's relationship, particularly through providing material support like day care. However, extended family support for marriage, per se, was rare. Only 3 of the 14 women said their families encouraged their marriage. Most said their families either actively disapproved of marriage or did not mention their support.

Sibylle loved and respected her grandmother and knew what her grandmother expected from her. Her grandmother had paid for her to go to Catholic school and was angry about the pregnancy:

> She yelled, I cried. I knew what she wanted. I don't blame anyone but myself.... It just happened and I don't regret [Alexia].... I know I should have waited. It would have been better for my education, but it happened and I never regret it and I love her so much.

Sibylle's interviews at both 3 and 6 years showed what she had learned from the contrast between her mother's lifestyle and her grandmother's care. She would never treat her child like her mother treated her. Her grandmother had modeled how to parent a child with discipline and love. She wanted to do the same.

Although positive relationships with extended family members often aided young families, they also frequently presented competing demands for the couple's attention. This was especially true for the young men whose divided loyalties to their mothers and wives were frequently mentioned as a source of problems in these relationships. Competition from kinship obligations was clearly present for Sibylle and Gordon, but Sibylle had empathy for Gordon's concerns about his mother: "The same level that I have for my grandmother, his level is his mom ... so we've got about even with the family."

A Considered Decision to Marry.   Sibylle could not take Gordon's commitment to Alexia or herself for granted. Although she hoped he would take on the responsibility, she initially refused to marry him despite pressure from her Puerto Rican family and several proposals from Gordon. She iterated her view in several places in both interviews: "When you're forced into a relationship and you're not ready and you didn't argue it out and you didn't understand the person then it makes it very difficult to be together."

There was little doubt even in relatively stable relationships, like Sibylle and Gordon's, that decisions about childrearing and decisions about marriage were highly distinct. Childrearing was accepted as a mother's responsibility, but it was a father's choice. The importance of mother–child bonds over her attachments to the child's father was evident in Sibylle's decision making. Initially, she did not want to be trapped into a bad relationship. She repeatedly insisted that Gordon's decisions to become a father and a husband must each be separate and voluntary. At the 3-year interview, she said:

I always told him, heh, just because I am having a baby doesn't mean you have to be a dad. If you are not ready for it, don't take on the responsibility. He told me, no I want to be, I want to be her father, and I told him that doesn't mean you have to be my husband, that's a different story, and he understood that and he respected that.

At the 6-year follow-up, Sibylle was still telling Gordon:

as her mother you owe me respect, and certain things that go in our relationship. But as for being partners, that's just me, you know, that has absolutely nothing to do with Alexia, and that's what I wanted to make absolutely clear.

Sibylle did not agree to marry for 3 years, and then only after a 6-month course that included "just basic stuff about just marriage, and with doctors and the church, and we looked at all types of marriages." She finally married when she was sure of his commitment. By this time, their marriage was also important for their daughter's sake. Alexia was beginning to ask questions about their relationship, and Sibylle wanted to make sure Alexia knew what was "right." Reflecting her traditional family beliefs, Sibylle explained, "She knows I had her before I got married and that might not be the way I want her to do it."

According to Sibylle, Gordon also changed a lot because of Alexia: "He took responsibility and faced up to it." Before Alexia was born, Gordon was "hanging out with the fellows who were not looking out for his best interest and were doing things wrong." He turned away from these friends when he took responsibility for Alexia. With wisdom beyond her 21 years, she also noted that their relationship had mellowed:

[Before] he was more lovey-dovey and cute and so forth, and now it's just because there's so many other things going on with Alexia and just with work and stuff. It's, it's ... you don't go through that as much, you know, being cute and going places and stuff ... before we did a lot of that and now it's more basic routines and waiting for vacations.

Gordon's role in maintaining his relationship with Sibylle was clear. He was able to give up friends who were getting into trouble, and he insisted on taking responsibility for his child. He worked and contributed financially to her well-being. However, these actions did not earn him the title of husband in Sibylle's eyes. What allowed the marriage to take place was his commitment to and respect for Sibylle. He could have felt rejected by her insistence that she would not marry him, but she said he thought of her as "just being stubborn." In her eyes, he was a good friend—a partner with whom she could communicate. He did his part with their child, but also insisted that they go out without Alexia. He talked to Alexia when she was bad and worried over her when she was sick. He came home after work.

The importance of Sibylle's lengthy consideration of Gordon as a marriage partner is consistent with research findings on the effects of timing and planning marriage decisions on outcomes for women who spent most of their childhood years in group foster homes (Quinton & Rutter, 1988). Outcomes for institutionalized women were, in general, worse than those for a comparison group of women who were raised with their parents. However, the difference was accounted for largely by the greater tendency among the institutionalized women to marry deviant men with whom they had a conflicted, nonsupportive relationship. Decisions to marry that were the result of "impulsive ventures or drift" were more likely to result in marriages to deviant partners and reflected a pattern of poor coping strategies. Commenting on this study, Rutter and Rutter (1993) asserted:

> The young people who married in haste ... usually showed a general tendency not to plan their lives, associated with feelings of helplessness about their life situation and a belief that there was little that they could do to affect what happened to them. But, also, they lacked family support and experienced severe family discord, conflict and distress. The girls leaped into pregnancy and/or marriage in a forlorn attempt to make their situation better. (p. 270)

The roots of her personal resilience are not hard to find in the interviews with Sibylle, and these are consistent with findings reported in chapter 3. She appeared an articulate, strong-willed, and principled young woman. Her religious upbringing from a reliable parent figure who conveyed a clear statement of her values, and the opportunities afforded by her Catholic private school education, set Sibylle apart from many of the other mothers. The clearly negative example of her drug-addicted, unhappy mother also stood out for her as a life story to be avoided at all costs. Her mother's firsthand example of what it means to go down the wrong path inspired Sibylle to take charge of her own life. She was determined not to treat her child as she had been treated. Her carefully considered decision about her marriage to Gordon reflected what she had learned from her mother's unhappiness in relationships with men. Her grandmother provided a model of care rooted in a commitment to education and children that formed the core of Sibylle's family values. Gordon's maturity, commitment to Alexia, respect for Sibylle, and employment also held the couple together.

Beyond these aspects of individual resiliency, a clear configuration of protective factors provided the foundation for Sibylle and Gordon's marriage (two supportive extended families, a well child, and two jobs). These factors only rarely came together for other young women in the New York sample. More often, the young women's strength and determination were overwhelmed by men who were deviant, domineering, unfaithful, or unwilling to share household or parenting responsibilities; by nonsupportive or absent extended families; by inadequate education or employment skills; or by health problems (see chap. 9). All of the remaining couples that were together at the 6-year follow-up had separated and come back together. This more typical pattern of resilient relationships is exemplified in the relationship of Sherry and Rick.

Sherry and Rick: Separation and Self-Discovery

Most of the other couples that were together at the 6-year follow-up had endured separations ranging from a few months to several years. These separations were related to the man's or woman's affairs, domestic violence, jail sentences, and even, in the case of two of the young men, entry into college. With their own mother's unhappiness in relationships often paving the way, the young mothers could never take for granted the future with their male partners. However, their interviews demonstrate that surviving the separations did indeed strengthen their relationships. The self-determination that emerged for the young women in the face of these separations allowed a growth in self-respect.

Frequently unwanted and unanticipated, the separations from the child's father initiated an identity crisis that forced the mothers to reevaluate their life plans. Anticipating the responsibility of caring for their child alone, often for the first time, these young women gained strength taking on this task. They believed they alone could do it. No one else could love their child as they did. No one else could give their child what they could. It was up to them alone to make their child's life better than their own. They proved to themselves that they could live alone. When they reentered partnerships with their children's fathers, it was on a more equal footing.

The Growth of Self-Respect and Self-Determination.   Sherry and Rick's relationship exemplifies the struggles encountered and the maturity gained through a painful separation and reunion. Lacking family support (but not interference), they reached stability in their relationship only after both partners underwent a crisis of identity and a redistribution of their traditional gender roles. Sherry described herself as having "blossomed" during her separation from her child's father.

Like Sibylle's mother, Sherry's was addicted to drugs. Sherry had been a good student and hoped to go to college. However, by the time her son, Michael, was born, her mother had moved to Puerto Rico and Sherry was intent on escaping her family's problems. She was highly committed to her relationship with her son's father, Rick. They were one of the few couples that lived together immediately after their child was born. Rick worked, but his family was in Sherry's words, "hard to please, offensive, lazy, and not helpful with Michael." Sherry stayed home and looked after Michael and Rick worked. At the 3-year interview, she was thinking about a wedding and wanted to have another child, but everything changed when Rick left her. Sherry says: "He had to re-explore his love for me. [He said;] I don't think I love you like I used to because we got together so young, and I need some time alone." They were separated for 8 months.

By the 6-year follow-up, she had an associate's degree, was working in a steady job, and was again thinking about having a second child. She saw her relationship with Rick as greatly transformed. He had been unlucky with jobs, but, according to Sherry, they could talk, they loved the same things, they agreed on movies, and they had the same hobbies. She also described Rick as "crazy about my son" and said he accompanied Michael to Little League. In several places in the interview, Sherry described the change in their relationship as a change in herself:

> [Before] if he needed to go do anything, I couldn't do anything. I had to stay home.... I was good ... things happened in my life where I was really good, I was like trying to be the perfect housewife, the perfect sister-in-law, and I got treated badly. And I realized that sometime you can be too nice.

Accustomed to success as a student, Sherry had to deal with her inability to be a "perfect wife." Contrary to the Puerto Rican traditions Sherry believed in, Rick's family did not insist that he provide for her and their child. Instead, they encouraged him to leave. Sherry was outraged with their response when Rick once lost his job and his wallet in the same week. His family had suggested he go to Puerto Rico to relax. She said:

> His mother had this great deal for him, everything was like, oh, he's depressed. Let him go to Puerto Rico. And I was like, well look, he has a wife who's doing all this stuff and you are going to leave her alone.... I told him, when you get back, you're gonna have no driver's license, no registration, no social security card, 'cause remember you lost it and you didn't go to Puerto Rico to get it back. You get back, you're gonna have no job and you're gonna be like $500 in debt because you went to Puerto Rico.

With her beliefs in the dependability of family and marital relationships plunged into doubt, Sherry fell back on her own resources and, ironically, attracted Rick back:

> I decided I could do two things. I can sit in my house and cry for my husband to come back or I could just let it go. So what happened was I blossomed. I blossomed into a creature that I had no idea I could become. I was very active. I had a lot of fun. I met a lot of people. I started working.... I just blossomed. I did whatever, whatever the hell I wanted to do. I did it whenever I wanted to do it. And that killed him. He couldn't take it. He noticed that he missed me, he noticed that he loved me, and I didn't want to get back together. I said nope! I'm sorry, we can't get back together. I don't love you anymore.... I got the job that I'm working in now and I was making good money and I decided that maybe I should give him another chance. Just because that was only the first time we had ever split up since the time we had met ... and thank God everything is going fine, but I had the best time of my life when I was alone.

Sherry reentered the relationship making the distinction, as Sibylle had, between her relationship with Rick and her son's relationship with him. She now knew she could take care of Michael herself. She said they were together now because they "loved each other ... we're not together because of Michael.... If we were not happy, we would not be together just 'cause we have a son." She also said she reentered the relationship stronger, no longer dependent on Rick:

I'm stronger. I used to focus my life around my husband and his family.... I always felt like I needed them for some reason.... There was a point in my life when my husband was the center of attention as far as I thought. I wouldn't be complete or be able to survive if he wasn't in my life. And that is was like, hello, that's not true.... So, that's even better. I know the reason I am with him is because I want to be with him now. Not because I'm dependent on him. So I've come to learn that even if I'm alone I can do anything, just as well as if I'm with him.

By the 6-year follow-up, Sherry's mother had also returned, sober and able to help her with child care. This support bolstered Sherry's new independence in her relationship with Rick. Their eventual marriage was Rick's idea, but Sherry hoped it would solidify their relationship:

What decided me to get married was the fact that he said when we first split up, it was too easy.... He could walk out even though we had a son. There was nothing ... I mean there was a [kind of] marriage, that's my husband, we were together for 11 years. But a lot of people don't realize how big a step marriage is. I mean really getting married. I thought it wasn't going to be different ... but when that priest said "husband and wife" I thought I was going to faint.

This awe was, in part, a return to Sherry's ideal of the traditional Hispanic family. Few of the adolescent mothers went to the altar without ambivalence. For Trisha, for example, the experience of marrying was not so positive. Trisha met her child's father when she was 14, she was pregnant at 16, and they married when she was 18. Trisha's mother was also on drugs. As Trisha described it:

I really had nobody and ... I met up with the wrong group of girls. My husband took me away from this bad crowd saying, You don't need to be with them. You are a much better person. Those type of girls can lead you into drugs and having babies. So I kind of cut myself off from them.

Trisha said her husband talked her into marriage, although she was not ready. Again in her words:

My wedding wasn't planned. I didn't have a wedding, I went to City Hall.... I walked out the first time because there was a void, something telling me, listen you are not ready, and I always think about that little voice because ... they say if you have second thoughts then you shouldn't get married.... I wanted to date different guys. I loved my husband but I was curious.... I felt that I was going to be tied down.

Although living with her child's father at the 6-year follow-up interview, Trisha still longed to be single and had been attracted to other relationships. She and her child's father had recently separated for "a couple of months." She complained that her husband was not showing her that he loved her and was not helping with the housework, although she worked. She wanted him to be more romantic, bring her gifts, and help her out more. She was trying to work things out with him because she said her son missed him too much.

The Struggle Toward Flexible Gender Roles and Shared Responsibility

The increase in self-determination these women gained from making it alone created new problems in their relationships. Traditional gender divisions of household tasks and child care were no longer tenable in these households. Authority, once assumed by husbands, had to be shared by women no longer willing to submit to the men's authority. To stay in the relationships, men had to be able to adapt to their demands for equality. Sibylle described the importance of the changes in her relationship with Gordon:

> We've reached a different level in our lives, where we understand we're adults now and we don't need to ... like his father was really into ... I had to ask permission to go out. Had to ask permission to go shopping with my friends. I'm like, I don't have to ask for anything, just have to inform you. "Honey do we have anything planned for Saturday? No oh, 'cause I'm gonna go out." That's it. I don't have to ask you if I can go out shopping. So I got away from the typical Hispanic situation that happens a lot. And I ... was able to pull my husband with me. Get him to another level.

Rick also changed. As Sherry saw it, he separated himself somewhat from his dependence on his family, who had pulled him too much away from his responsibilities to her and Michael. He was able to take her side against them. Initially, his family's belief in traditional Hispanic gender roles did not extend to pushing Rick to take responsibility for his child and wife, but he had begun to change. As she said: "[His family] sees the male role model as not having to do dishes, not having to change a diaper. And he's not like that anymore." His loyalty to her and Michael had increased. However, at the 6-year follow-up, Rick was still unemployed, unable to cook, and reluctant to clean the apartment. It is unclear whether Sherry's hope that he would be "totally different" if they had another baby would be realized. As her roles and responsibilities as a working mother continued to expand, it was also not clear what part Rick would continue to play as a marital partner. Beyond being there for his son and celebrating his son's Little League successes,

Rick's aspirations for the future or for their marriage remained obscure in Sherry's recounting of their relationship.

Struggles over the husband's "right" to command obedience were described by many of these women. Problems with jealousy and trust turned into fights about "going out alone," "speaking to other men," or "going out with friends." The young men's ability to take on some household chores and care for their children alone were changes valued by these young mothers. The relief provided to these young women by gender role flexibility allowed for their greater autonomy in work, school, and with kin or friends. In contrast, surprisingly few mothers voiced concerns about their husbands' unemployment or education level. Seemingly, unemployment could be the result of bad luck and uncontrollable circumstances, whereas macho attitudes could be changed.

Despite these resilient couples' efforts, the probability that poor unwed parents can increase their children's financial security through marriage is clearly limited. Increases in poverty of children under 6 and adolescents under 18, even when their parents are working (National Center for Children in Poverty, 1990), demand renewed attention to the problems of the fathers of the children of adolescent mothers. The effects of the inner-city, drug culture on the maintenance of poverty need to be studied: Disadvantages that stem from it (such as imprisonment, drug involvement, and missed educational opportunities) decrease the possibilities for constructive involvement of these fathers. Relationships and children with new partners, excessively macho or abusive behaviors, and drug- or violence-related crimes severely limit the likelihood that the biological fathers of the children of adolescent mothers will become long-term sources of support to their children, even if paternity is established. We visit some of these problems in the next chapter.

Many mothers were reluctant to become involved in new relationships when their relationships with their children's fathers ended. As Sharon says, "I just came out of one relationship that ended bad, so I can't see myself in another one." The long-term effects of involvement in new relationships for both the mothers and their children have not been studied.

Most primary perhaps is the need to question our typical conceptualization of the unwed adolescent mother as a single parent. Our research demonstrates that this inadequately represents the complexity of their early struggles toward family formation. Many of the adolescent mothers believed the biological fathers should be involved with their children and attempted to foster the fathers' ties with the children with little guidance on how to deal with the serious conflicts in these relationships that threatened to derail them. Moreover, these young couples are negotiating their transition to parenthood in the context of stresses that take their toll on all families: poverty, unemployment, and kin conflicts. Policies that support resilience in couples, rather than further compromise these relationships, are badly needed.

Relationships That Hurt: Escaping Domestic Violence

With Tricia Harmon

Jadine is an African-American mother who had her first daughter when she was 16 years old. Her child's father was 10 years older. He made her feel grown up. Pregnant again at 19, she describes the episode that made her leave this violent relationship, fearing for her life:

> so I was pregnant with twins. He actually beat me so bad that his whole white shirt was covered with my blood. So I pulled a knife out on him, don't you know he took that knife and put it to my throat and said, "Bitch, don't you ever pull a knife out on me." So I actually seen the look on his face that he would kill me and that's how the man could get rid of them twins and get away from 'em. That's one reason why I took off. And you know, when you're a battered woman, you're a battered woman. But I was a battered teenager, I was young trying to be grown and look what I got myself into.

Like many abused women, Jadine was alone with her children. One of her sisters died of AIDS, one "died mysteriously" and was found dead in her apartment. She does not want to be around her other family because "they don't set no [good] example." At first, Jadine submitted both to her child's father's beatings and his claims of love, but the door in and out of this relationship did not continue to revolve. Watching her young daughter watch him beat her up and fearing she would be killed eventually made her realize, "this man don't love me because if he loved me he wouldn't beat me like that." She says:

He used to beat me up, you know, for no reason, he used to put his hands on me and for years I used to go through that and then I tell myself I'm gonna leave him alone. I ain't going through that. Then he called me on the phone crying, I'd fall for it and go right back to him and then next two days he'd be beating on me again. Then you know I just sat down, I was like, I'm going to die or I'm going to get up and you know, just have to walk away and be strong. Because the way he was beating me up you know one blow to the head and he could'a killed me.... My daughter used to sit down and watch this and ... I used to just watch her. It used to bother her to see me going through it so I just said I ain't going to let my kid go through [this]. I'm just gonna get up and I'm gonna get away from him and that's what I did.

At 22, Jadine looks back on this relationship, ironically, saying: "I missed my teenage years because I wanted to be grown and be with an older man but it wasn't worth it because all I got was pain."

Research examining violence between adolescent mothers and their male partners is scarce. These women may be particularly at risk for domestic violence both as pregnant women and as adolescents entering serious dating relationships. Pregnant women have twice the risk of abuse by male partners as nonpregnant women (Martin, Holsapfels, & Baker, 1992; McFarlane, 1991; U.S. Senate Committee on the Judiciary, 1990), and abuse frequently escalates in severity during pregnancy and the child's infancy (Campbell, 1986, 1989; Campbell, Poland, Waller, & Ager, 1992; Fagan, Stewart, & Hansen, 1983; Helton, McFarlane, & Anderson, 1987; McFarlane, 1991; Stacey & Shupe, 1983). Forty percent of physical abuse by male partners begins during women's first pregnancies (Martin et al., 1992).

In addition, dating violence typically increases as commitment level increases (i.e., it occurs more frequently in relationships where the involvement is reported as *serious*; Arias, Samios, & O'Leary, 1987; Cate, Henton, Koval, Christopher, & Lloyd, 1982; Henton, Cate, Koval, Lloyd, & Christopher, 1983; Laner & Thompson, 1982). Gamache (1991) wrote that violence often begins when the couple "perceives that they have entered into an exclusive, marriage-like relationship" (p. 73). In studies of college and high school students, dating violence was reported by 12% to 65% of students (Sugarman & Hotaling, 1989). Although the relationships between adolescent mothers and their male partners have frequently been described as transitory and short-lived (Chase-Lansdale & Vinovskis, 1987; Musick, 1993), the existence of a child may foster a greater degree of seriousness in the relationship.

Many have argued that higher levels of physical or sexual abuse in the childhood experiences of pregnant and parenting adolescents also leaves them vulnerable to abuse or sexual exploitation in relationships with men, compared with their nonpregnant or parenting peers (Boyer & Fine, 1992; Bullock & McFarlane, 1988; Musick, 1993; Rainey, Stevens-Simon, & Kaplan, 1995; Russell, 1986; Spieker, Bensley, McMahon, Fung, & Ossiander, 1996). This may particularly affect poor teens. According to the National Center for Children in Poverty (1990), poor children do experience sexual abuse at alarmingly higher rates than nonpoor (4.8 in 1,000 poor vs. to 1.1 in 1,000 nonpoor).

In one of the few studies of prevalence among pregnant teens, Boyer and Fine (1992) reported that as many as two thirds of a sample of 535 ethnically diverse women from Washington state who became pregnant as adolescents had been sexually abused (averaging self-reports of unwanted touching [51%] or being forced to look at sexual objects [35%] and attempted rape [42%] or rape [44%]). Musick (1993) also reported that 61% of a sample of 445 teens in Ounce of Prevention programs for pregnant and parenting teens in Illinois reported sexual abuse. However, these high figures may depend on encompassing definitions of *sexual abuse*. Rhodes, Fischer, Ebert, and Meyers (1993) found 22% of an urban Illinois sample of pregnant and parenting African-American adolescents reported at least one incident of unwanted kissing, fondling, or sexual intercourse.

A wealth of research has documented the physical and psychological trauma that women suffer as a result of violence in heterosexual relationships (e.g., Aguilar & Nightingale, 1994; Douglas, 1987; Dutton & Painter, 1993; Follingstad, Rutledge, Berg, Hause, & Polek, 1990; D. Martin, 1981; Mitchell & Hodsen, 1983; Musick, 1993; Walker, 1979; K. Wilson, Vercella, Brems, Benning, & Renfro, 1992). The debilitating effects of histories of victimization on the psychological distress, self-esteem, economic strains, social supports, and risks for repeated pregnancy in young women who become mothers as adolescents have also been studied (Boyer & Fine, 1992; Musick, 1993; Rhodes, Fischer, et al., 1993).

Researchers have suggested that adolescent mothers may be more vulnerable to abusive relationships than other adolescent females because they have fewer sources of support, as well as greater socioeconomic stress and psychological dependence in relationships with men (Musick, 1993; Sugar, 1993). The stigma of having an out-of-wedlock child may also increase pressure to remain in a relationship with a man even if he is abusive.

Although the majority of women leave abusive relationships, to our knowledge, no study has determined the reasons for, or nature of, transitions out of abusive relationships for adolescent mothers. The obstacles to leaving have also not been identified for this group.

Using quantitative and qualitative data from the New York study, we examined some adolescent mothers' experiences of being in and getting out of abusive relationships with their male partners. Research on domestic violence often compares ever-abused versus nonabused groups as if abuse status is a static event. However, like the majority of outcomes for adolescent mothers that we have reviewed (i.e., school dropout, welfare use), the experiences of abusive relationships differ along many dimensions, including severity and duration, as well as whether the problem is past or current. Our analyses compared four groups of adolescent mothers to allow for comparisons of women who had left abusive relationships with those who were currently in an abusive relationship, as well as to those who reported negative or conflicted, but not abusive relationships and those who reported only positive relationships with male partners.

Abuse was defined as physical abuse resulting in physical injuries (black eyes, bruises, torn ligaments, etc.) or sexual abuse (rape or forced participation in sexual acts). It also involved extremely controlling, jealous, or threatening behaviors (e.g., "When I was with him I couldn't work; I couldn't go to school; I couldn't go to the store; I couldn't visit my mother; I had to be careful of what clothes I wore."). Two methods were used to differentiate the abuse groups at the 6-year follow-up. Open-ended descriptions of the mothers' relationships with each of the male partners they had been with since their first child was born were coded from written transcripts of the qualitative interviews to distinguish: (a) mothers who were currently in a relationship with a male partner in which they were currently experiencing or had previously experienced physical abuse or excessive control, (b) mothers who were formerly abused by a male partner but who were no longer involved with that partner, (c) mothers who experienced previously or were experiencing negative/conflicted relationships (without abuse) with a male partner or partners, and (d) mothers who reported only positive (romantically involved/warm, close, emotionally supportive) or neutral (not especially negative but not warm) past and current relationships with male partners. All interviews were rated by two independent coders with 98% agreement.

In addition, mothers were asked directly about sexual and physical abuse as part of a health questionnaire at the 6-year follow-up. The questions included: "Has anyone ever forced you into contact with private parts of their body or yours?" If they answered yes, they were asked to identify who did it, when it happened, and how long it continued. "Were you ever hit or beaten up by anybody in your family or outside of your family?" If the answer was yes, these mothers were again asked who did it, when it happened, and how often. Agreement in determining abuse group status between interview and questionnaire data for relationships with male partners was high (100% for mothers coded in the nonabuse groups and 85% for mothers coded in the abused groups). Discrepancies were in the direction of coding abusive relationships from the open-ended interviews that were not acknowledged in the questionnaire. All were resolved by discussion.

Of the 93 former adolescent mothers, 41% ($n = 38$) had experienced abuse by a male partner at some time in their lives. Eleven women (12%) were currently involved in a relationship in which they were experiencing ($n = 8$) or had experienced ($n = 3$) physical or sexual assaults or excessive control. The mothers who were in relationships with previously abusive partners were in some ways more like those who had ended abusive relationships, but their categorization with those currently in abusive relationships is a more conservative strategy for data analysis contrasting these groups. Twenty-seven mothers (29%) had ended an abusive relationship. Twenty-nine (31%) described relationships with former or current male partners that were primarily conflicted/negative, and 26 (28%) described their former and current relationships as either positive or neutral.

As Table 9.1 shows, the groups were similar in racial composition, percent living with their own mothers at delivery, percent of high school graduates, and educational achievement by 6-years postpartum. It may seem particularly surprising

TABLE 9.1

Percent of Mothers in Each Relationship Group by Race
or Ethnicity, Residence, Welfare Status, and Educational Outcomes
at Delivery and the 6-Year Follow-up

	Positive	Negative/Conflicted	Past Abuse	Current Abuse
Number in Group	**26 (28%)**	**29 (31%)**	**27 (29%)**	**11 (12%)**
African American (*n* = 59)	73%	45%	41%	27%
Hispanic (*n* = 34)	27%	55%	59%	73%
Status at Delivery				
On welfare (*n* = 59)	46%	72%	63%	82%
Living with mother (*n* = 71)	85%	79%	63%	82%
Status at 6-Years				
On welfare (*n* = 64)	50%	76%	74%	82%
Lives with mother (*n* = 20)	23%	28%	19%	9%
Employed (*n* = 34)	46%	21%	48%	27%
Graduated high school (*n* = 48)	54%	45%	59%	46%
Lives with male partner (*n* = 40)	54%	38%	41%	36%
Mean grade completed (*SD*)	11.2 (2.1)	11.4 (2.1)	11.7 (1.6)	11.8 (1.9)

that the abused women were able to maintain stride with the others in terms of educational achievement. However, most were not financially dependent on their partners, and few lived with them on a day-to-day basis. At both delivery and 6 years postpartum, fewer mothers who reported only positive relationships were on welfare than mothers in the other groups. At 6-years postpartum, mothers who left abusive relationships and mothers in positive relationships were similar in employment rates. Their employment rates were double the rates for mothers in the other two groups.

Abuse group differences in mothers' early and concurrent experiences of stressful life events and depressive symptoms were also evident, as shown in Table 9.2. Although differences between groups were only trends at delivery,

TABLE 9.2

Means (and Standard Deviations) for Depressive Symptoms, Life Stress, and Emotional Support From Family at Delivery and 6-Years Postpartum for Relationship Groups

	Positive	Negative/Conflicted	Past Abuse	Current Abuse	Univariate F
Number in Group	26	29	27	11	
At Delivery					
Depressive symptoms	11.45 (6.07)	12.61 (5.57)	13.21 (7.20)	13.35 (9.15)	ns
Stressful life events	8.83 (4.98)	12.15 (5.44)	12.89 (5.83)	11.67 (6.79)	2.64[t]
Emotional support from family	13.73 (4.46)	12.45 (5.23)	10.73 (4.90)	9.56 (6.34)	2.49[t]
6-Years Postpartum					
Depressive symptoms	5.42[a] (6.34)	9.53[ab] (6.74)	11.30[b] (8.51)	21.91[c] (10.82)	11.94***
Stressful life events	7.15[a] (4.41)	12.14[b] (5.28)	15.44[c] (7.62)	16.55[c] (6.06)	10.90***
Emotional support from grandmother	115.62 (33.83)	116.81 (28.31)	107.41 (31.11)	100.05 (35.23)	ns

Note. Different superscripts ([a,b,c]) indicate that differences between groups are significant.

[t]$p < .10$.

***$p < .001$.

121

by the 6-year follow-up, several significant and meaningful differences emerged. Mothers reporting concurrently abusive relationships reported levels of depressive symptoms that were significantly higher than all other groups at the 6-year follow-up. This group also reported the least emotional support from their own mothers at both assessments, although differences between groups did not reach statistical significance. Both currently abused mothers and mothers who ended abusive relationships reported higher levels of stressful life events than mothers who had not previously experienced abusive relationships. It is likely that stressful life events like moves, financial strains, child-care problems, and conflicts with relatives increased as these women separated from their abusive partners. However, women who left abusive relationships appeared to be coping better with these stresses given that their levels of depressive symptoms were dramatically lower than those in the current abuse group, and given that their levels of employment were as high as mothers in the positive relationships group.

Consistent with past studies (Boyer & Fine, 1992; Rhodes, Fischer, et al., 1993), cross-tabulation of the relationship groups with the mothers' reports of abuse by someone other than a male partner on the health questionnaire showed that mothers in the currently abused group were at higher risk: forty five percent of the currently abused mothers reported past physical or sexual abuse (by a parent, stepparent, uncle, or babysitter). This compares with 15% of the positive relationship group, 31% of the negative relationship group, and 22% of the past abuse group. Also consistent with past research, more mothers in the abuse groups had repeat pregnancies (but not more children) within 3 years after their first birth (71% of those who left abusive relationships and 89% of those in abusive relationships) than mothers in the group who reported only positive relationships (40%). However, frequency of repeat pregnancies in mothers in the current and past abuse groups did not differ from those reporting negative but not abusive relationships (78%), suggesting that repeat pregnancies may not be related to abuse per se. Can psychological dependency explain group differences?

In her anecdotal study of sexually victimized adolescent mothers, Musick (1993) reported that a primary characteristic shared by these women was a "psychological neediness, the legacy of severe and often protracted emotional deprivation, beginning early and continuing throughout the adolescent years" (p. 101). She argued that this neediness leaves adolescent mothers vulnerable to lives that revolve around "pleasing and appealing to males" and sexual exploitation. We investigated within-group differences in the New York sample of adolescent mothers' experiences of interpersonal dependency, self-criticism, and efficacy across the abusive relationships groups. The Depressive Experiences Questionnaire for Adolescents (Blatt, Schaffer, Bers, & Quinlan, 1992) was used to tap differences in the personality styles of these young women.

It has been argued that multiple experiences, including childhood experiences with parents, can contribute to the differences in these depressive personality styles (Blatt & Homann, 1992). According to Blatt et al. (1992), individuals with excessive interpersonal concerns are preoccupied with the affection of others, feelings of loneliness and helplessness, fears of abandonment, desires for intense closeness, and "difficulty in managing anger for fear of losing someone" (p. 83). However, individuals endorsing high levels of self-criticism have excessive feelings of guilt, emptiness, hopelessness, worth-lessness, and inadequacy. They feel unable to assume responsibility, are ambiv-alent about relationships, and tend to assume blame. Efficacy, at the opposite pole from self-criticism, describes "goal-oriented striving and feelings of per-sonal accomplishment." Interpersonal and self-critical depressive personality styles may be highly differentiated in an individual; more typically, however, there is some overlap.

In the New York study, the assessment of these personality styles was col-lected at the 6-year follow-up only. The data allow us to investigate the associa-tions of feelings of excessive dependency, self-criticism, and lack of efficacy to leaving or remaining in abusive relationships. As these psychological problems could be either a cause or effect of involvement in abusive relationships, tempo-ral relations could not be examined. The results of qualitative analysis of the in-terview data are used to illustrate the association between these personality styles and the young mothers' efforts to cope with, change, and/or leave abusive relationships.

As shown in Table 9.3, the groups of abused and nonabused mothers did not dif-fer in reported experiences of interpersonal concerns or in efficacy, but significant differences were found in their levels of self-criticism. Mothers in currently abu-sive relationships experienced dramatically higher levels of self-criticism than the other mothers. Mothers who had left abusive relationships and those in more nega-tive relationships also reported more self-criticism than mothers describing posi-tive relationships with their male partners.

Interpersonal dependency and self-critical personality styles are only slightly correlated in this sample ($R = .14$). Twenty-two (24%) of the mothers in this study had scores above the mean for both. Nevertheless, findings of higher levels of self-criticism in the abused mothers provides a window into the psychological ex-periences of these women. The irritability and ambivalence toward relationships of self-critical individuals may contribute to the abusive relationships they co-con-struct with their partner or it may be a consequence of the abuse. Downey and Feldman (1996) have begun to explore the associations of a similar construct that they call *rejection sensitivity* for intimate relationships and adolescents' engage-ment in violent relationships.

The data in Table 9.3 show higher mean levels of self-criticism in the cur-rently abused group (.76) compared with the past abuse group (−.21). It may be that leaving an abusive relationship requires overcoming, in part, feelings of in-adequacy and self-blame in the face of critical, overcontrolling partners. We elaborate on this view by discussing the interview materials. All but one (91%) of the mothers in the current abuse group scored above the overall group mean for self-criticism, whereas 56% of both mothers in the past abuse and negative rela-tionships groups scored above the mean for self-criticism. In contrast, only 23% of mothers reporting positive relationships had scores for self-criticism that were above the mean. The dynamics of how self-criticism is related to coping with

TABLE 9.3

Dependency, Efficacy, and Self-Criticism Among the Four Abuse Groups at 6-Years Postpartum

	Positive	Negative/Conflicted	Past Abuse	Current Abuse	Univariate F
Number in Group	**26**	**29**	**27**	**11**	
6-Years Postpartum					
Interpersonal Concerns	-1.19 (0.66)	-1.07 (0.82)	-1.16 (0.58)	-0.86 (0.86)	ns
Efficacy	0.12 (1.07)	0.48 (0.92)	0.58 (0.78)	0.42 (1.19)	ns
Self-criticism	-1.19[a] (1.28)	-0.40[b] (1.16)	-0.21[b] (1.26)	0.76[c] (0.83)	7.43***

Note. Different superscripts ([a,b,c]) indicate that differences between group are significant.

***p < .001.

abusive relationships are evident in the interviews with these mothers at the 6-year follow-up.

LOSING SELF-CONTROL:
THE DYNAMICS OF SELF-CRITICISM

Several mothers who left abusive relationships recalled their experiences of becoming immobilized in abusive relationships as a loss of self. They also frequently blamed themselves for letting the abuse happen. Recovery from their abusive relationship also disrupted their ability to commit to new relationships. For example, Jadine, quoted at the beginning of this chapter, describes her abusive boyfriend's out of control anger, but blames herself: "I was trying' to be grown and look what I got myself into." Like Jadine, Angela also says her child's father "would argue with me, he would downgrade me, he would beat me up, kick me." She talks directly about retreating to becoming "stupid" to protect herself. She describes the process of being emptied of her thoughts and identity to avoid her partners' criticism, saying *she* was stupid:

> He just had me so I was dumb. I was stupid. And it was like if we was walking in the street and somebody looked at me, 'Oh, why you looking at him.' So I wouldn't even look at people. I always used to turn my head or put my head down. Or if I saw a group of guys on the corner, I would be so nervous. 'Cuz I wouldn't want them to say nothing to me, because I didn't want to get in trouble, you know?

Leah also describes herself as her own worst critic, saying:

> Most of the time, a person will tell me something and I would actually believe what they were saying. And I would put myself down and say no, you're no good, you're not this you're, I mean I really put myself worse than what the person has. And I tell myself I really have to stop doing that if I wanna get anywhere in life, 'cuz I can't believe what people say.

Anger fueled the mothers' own part in the fights. Like Jadine, some mothers fought back or even started the fights. Despite their own aggressiveness, they also began to feel powerless when they were overwhelmed by their partners' strength, and they began to adapt to their partners' control over their lives. Deven describes first being beat up by her child's father when she was 6 months pregnant. She got involved in a new relationship, but this boyfriend also "started doing drugs and became violent and abusive." At first she was the more violent partner, but when he became drug involved he changed and began to fight back. She explains:

> I was flinging things all around the house, Like when he would get mad, I would throw things, 'cuz that's like our family. We throw things, it's like, you get us mad and we'll pick up whatever's near us, and we'll just fling it across the room towards you. We might not hit you but you'll get the point. So I was

flinging things and he'd go 'you're crazy' … and he'd walk out the door, like this girl's gonna kill me one day. And he never would think about touching me or anything…. But then once he started getting into drugs and stuff, it's like he changed.

Recovering a sense of self-sufficiency, as we describe next, marked the route out of these abusive relationships for these self-critical women. Few were economically dependent on the men who abused them. They were able to support themselves on welfare or by working. Some of the women reported finding their sense of self in the realization that they had continued going to school or work and that they had sole responsibility for their children despite their partners' abuse. Like women who overcome other adverse circumstances to move ahead, this growing self-sufficiency helped women in abusive relationships to move out.

INTERPERSONAL DEPENDENCY IN ABUSIVE RELATIONSHIPS

Also reflecting the data in Table 9.3, desires to cling to abusive relationships because of fears of loneliness or abandonment and desires for intense closeness were rarely heard among the adolescent mothers in the abuse groups. Only one of these mothers, Marie, who was among the resilient group in chapter 3, described enduring an abusive relationship with her partner. She did so in terms suggesting that loneliness and fears of abandonment were the unbearable alternatives she was avoiding by staying in the relationship. She says:

I thought of committing suicide because I wanted out so bad, because I felt like I couldn't go to my mother … she's [was] still kind of very upset, because I couldn't go to college…. I felt like I was just isolated, I was alone my first New Years after I had my son, I remember I stood in bed watching the countdown by myself. You know, while my son's father was in a party. And then when he comes back from the party he put the gun to my head, you know, he's drunk….

She spent her first year of college alone, then her son and his father came to live with her for the summer. He resumed the abuse: "He beat me every single day, he even raped me." Yet even when she ends the relationship to gain safety, Marie still talks about her painful loss of love. She says, "After I went through that whole time and it's like after, I have a courage in cold kind of safety and say 'I want you to get out of my house' … It hurt me a lot because I did care about him. He was my first love."

In contrast to the highly self-critical mothers who left abusive relationships, often angry and feeling they could only rely on themselves, Marie remained needing and willing to trust in a relationship with a man. It seems it was her partner's ability to love and not hers that she came to question. She completed her college degree and entered into a stable relationship with a new partner who she says is "totally the opposite than my son's father.... He's been really good to me and he's like my best friend." But she vows, "I would never go through that again. I would never give a chance to anybody to walk all over me like my son's father did."

MOTHERS WHO LEFT ABUSIVE RELATIONSHIPS

The qualitative data from the interviews with the young women who left abusive relationships by the 6-year follow-up reveal a great deal about the dynamic processes of coping with, leaving, and recovering from abusive relationships. Mothers who ended abusive relationships describe the loss and recovery of control over their own lives with a remarkable degree of self-awareness. The three mothers in the group who remained with abusive partners reported on the processes of resilience that allowed their relationships to survive. One of these resilient relationships is described in the previous chapter by Sherry. Her growing strength in being able to care for herself and her child clearly enabled her to reenter this relationship on a more equal footing with her partner.

The other eight mothers who were in abusive relationships each reported levels of depressive symptoms indicative of clinical levels of depression. The interviews revealed that each had also experienced either debilitating traumas or had severely limited personal and social resources that made leaving their relationships with their male partner overwhelmingly difficult. We discuss these personal vulnerabilities and the contexts that trapped these eight women in abusive relationships at the end of this chapter. We turn first to the women who left abusive relationships. First, we describe the rise in their own feelings of self-criticism and loss of self as they attempted to cope with their abusive partners. Second, we describe the resources and personal changes that they experienced as they transitioned out of these abusive relationships.

Why Do They Leave?

No single picture can be painted of the characteristics of the abuse in terms of its intensity or duration or of the reasons that some women left these relationships. Some described relationships that started out well, but deteriorated when their partners became addicted to drugs. Others described increases in the abuse as the relationships became closer and their partner's jealousy became more restrictive. Some described single episodes of physical or sexual assaults that immediately motivated a breakup, whereas others endured long periods of abuse and reconciliation before leaving. One mother was pregnant as the result of a rape that occurred at a party, and she stopped seeing the abuser immediately after.

Some mothers talked about breaking off the relationships by just telling their partners to stop seeing them or by moving, themselves, to another residence (e.g., with relatives who offered protection). For some, leaving was a slow and difficult process of choosing between bad options including loneliness, suicide, and homelessness. Liz, whose mother and sister were abused, says she told her partner before they got married, "I will not go for it. You put your hands on me, I will pack my stuff and I'm out the door. He never believed me." After an argument that ended in a physical fight with her child's father, she made good on her threat:

> I went and called my mother and told her what happened. She was worried about my eye. She told me to go to the hospital. Everything was fine with my eye. Then I went and put a police report in [when] he went to work the next day. I called [my sister] and she told me to come move with her. I packed up me and the kids' clothes and was gone the next day. He went to my mother's house, thinking I went back home. So he didn't know where I was at. He asked some people and actually tracked me down from going to see my mother. So he knew where I was at then. Basically that was it.

Other mothers feared they might be killed by their partners if they left. They found relief only after their violent partners were imprisoned for assaults on others or for using or selling drugs. As one mother says, "When I did try to get rid of him, he just wouldn't go." She would tell him to leave and he "would leave but then he would come right back." He was arrested for an unrelated crime. At the 6-year follow-up, she wanted to move because she feared his release from prison would put her and her children back in danger. He had vowed he would take her children when he was released from jail. As she puts it:

> [My son's father] always said he was gonna come back.... He talks about how he's gonna come back and he's gonna do this and he's gonna do that. I'm trying to move, I want to move, ... he's just possessive.

The Dynamics of Recovery: Gaining Self-Sufficiency, and Managing Anger and Distrust

Emotionally, the road out of these relationships was in part a struggle with anger and an inability to trust people. Commitments to new relationships, like Marie's, were rare. Only 1 of the 27 women in the group who left abusive relationships was married at the 6-year follow-up, compared with a third of those in positive or currently abusive relationships and 14% of those reporting negative relationships. Many of these women who left abusive relationships were economically self-supporting through welfare or work and they felt efficacious in providing for their children (but not in protecting them from witnessing the abuse). Recovering from abusive relationships required gaining self-control; this was characterized by an extreme dedication to self-sufficiency—a feeling both that others could not be trusted and that they did not need other people to care for them or their children. Managing the anger that they felt, especially in relationships with their children and new partners, also proved difficult. As they describe it, self-control (both in the sense of trying to regulate their emotions and of never depending on anyone) replaced their experiences of being controlled by their male partner.

Angela, who described her retreat to stupidity to protect herself, describes her transition out of the abusive relationship with her child's father as gaining independence—by refusing to depend on anybody:

> I want to achieve things. Your know what I am saying. I want so much. And I'm not gonna depend on nobody. You know, because when I was with my son's father, I didn't have no identity. Every little thing. I mean, it could be going to the store, I depended on him. He had to come with me to the store. I had no identity. I didn't have myself. So after I broke up with him and it was so hard breaking up with him. He was abusive and everything. So after that I just really became independent.

She now refuses to be made stupid, but has to deal with the anger of being constantly alert: "I like kind of tend to think back on my relationship with [my child's] father.... I always tell myself that I'm not stupid anymore, you know. Keep my eyes open, and just little things piss me off."

Angela's hypervigilant independence clearly has interpersonal costs. With her stronger sense of efficacy in "wanting to achieve things," she cannot rely on others for the help she will likely need to achieve her goals in the context of the poverty that surrounds her. She says, "I don't trust no man." Now involved in a new relationship with someone she really cares about, Angela is preoccupied with fears that he will cheat on her. Reflecting her old immobility, she cannot risk either confirming or disconfirming her fears:

> I would like to spend my life with [my new boyfriend], actually. But I don't trust him. It's hard for me to trust him. I mean, I won't go and see ... where he was at. I'm not the type of person to be drilling you and asking questions. If you're going to do it. You're going to do it.

Leah similarly describes her recovery from the abusive relationship with her two children's father as a need to become self-sufficient. After he beat her up, she describes the course of "building up my confidence little by little," referring to the need to move forward alone and managing her anger so she would not harm her children. She says:

> I just had to change. I couldn't, I mean for a while I was really down. I didn't go to counseling, 'cuz I've never been to counseling for it. But ... I didn't see no use for it. I mean, I already felt bad and stuff like that. But when I saw myself, that when I got angry, I used to scream at my kids, to take my anger out. They were the only people there. I noticed, I can't be doing that. That's harming them besides myself, because that's not right. And I told myself you gotta change.... The kids are going to do exactly what you're doing. They're going to do it later on when they're mad, they're going to scream, they're going to yell.... All your frustration that you're taking out, they're going to do it even worse. So I told my-

self I had to stop. From there on, I, you know, built up my confidence little by little, but I did it.

Leah adds that her new husband "just helped me a bit more." But says her temper continues to get in the way of her ability to commit to this relationship. She says:

> People tell me, I'm a very hard person to love. Because I think, like my husband, he, I know he loves me. And I can feel the love but I push him away. Kind of because I guess I feel a lot of people have said the word love … but they didn't really mean it. And now for the first time there's a person who actually really means it, instead of pushing it closer to me I push him away … I guess I'm afraid of getting hurt.

Vivian also generalizes a feeling of mistrust to new relationships. She is aware of how this mistrust affects her relationships with others, but she cannot stop it from happening even in the interview. Asked how she thinks about herself differently now, Vivian says, she is more judgmental and cannot accept help:

> I would see things different when I was younger in the past. It was easier. I wouldn't judge anybody and now I judge everyone. Like I was sitting here and you are like funny and I was like thinking "I don't like her." Like I told you, I went through that with [my son's father]. I don't trust all the men. I don't know how but I don't trust someone else. Sometimes it's my fault because like when they try to give me something and they ask me to do something for them, I say "Oh, that's why you gave it to me? Take it back. I don't want it." Sometimes I don't mean it like that, but being what I went through with my son's father, that's the way I see them. I think that's why I act like that.

In her evolution out of an abusive relationship with her drug-addicted partner, Deven describes how her will to fight back emerged in recognizing the contradictions between her own efficacy and her partner's control of her. She says "everything I had was mine, but I couldn't have it unless he was there." Deven describes the changes in herself as she tries to deal with her relationship with her child's abusive father. First, she tried to change it by crying and fighting, then she just adapted and tried to maintain her own goals and responsibilities despite the relationship. Finally, she left the relationship in a decisive act of resistance that conveys both her courage and the extremity of the abuse she had endured. She says:

> In the beginning I was crying, and fighting, and I was throwing things and all types of stuff. But towards the end, I just like, I, I'm the type of person, I adapt to things if I have to. For a little while, and I take as much as I can, but then it's over, and that's it. And I just say that's it, and I've had it and it's gone. You know, so in the beginning I fought it, and then I just said, well, if you wanna throw your life down the drain, that's your business, and I'm not gonna let mine go with you.

And I continued, I went to school. He was doing all these things, I went to school, I worked, I took care of Patrick, I took care of our house, and bought all the groceries and did everything I had to do. And the day just came that I came home one night ... I went out with his sister-in-law, I came home, and he decided to hit.... So, I got up the next morning and I called my mom, and I told her. I said, "I'm leaving, call Oregon and tell them that I'm coming." And I got up, I packed up our clothes, I took the cat, and I walked out the door. And that was it. And I never went back.... But when I left he was threatening and everything. He said, he was gonna kill me. He was like, "I'm gonna kill you." I was like, "Okay, so come and find me. I'm in Oregon." [Laughs] I was like, "I'm in Oregon, come and find me, come kill me. Come on."

Her determination to recapture control over her own life culminated in her dramatic move to Oregon. Back in New York at the 6-year follow-up, she reflects back on the changes in her attitude toward submitting to the abuse:

I'm doing what Deven feels like doing. [The interviewer asks: What do you think led to that change?] I think it was my boyfriend, me leaving this way.... Our relationship was very bad. He started doing drugs, and doing all types of negative things, and finally the day came that I just couldn't take it anymore, and I realized that everything I had was mine, but I couldn't have it unless he was there, because he wouldn't let me. And, that control that he had over like, my entire life, I realize that I don't want anybody to be that much in power of me. So now I'm like, taking more control of myself and not letting anybody have that kind of influence over my life.

When asked what being a woman means to her at the 6-year follow-up, Deven defines her new independence as being emotionally and financially self-sufficient even emotionally:

Um ... just being like, taking on your own responsibilities, and not letting everybody else control you.... I think that I've always felt that when you start taking care of yourself, that's when you're really a woman.... I mean financially and emotionally, everything. Just, just making sure that you have control of your life, and not anybody else.

LaRue also describes her transition out of a relationship, which was the "first time anybody ever laid a hand on me," as the growth of self-sufficiency in looking out for herself and her children. At first she did not care what happened to her, then she was forced by the demands that being a mother made on her to redirect her efforts and start again. She explains:

On top of that, you know, he hit me. And that was terrible. I went through that and that's the first time that happened to me. I was so shocked that I let it happen because I didn't know what to do. I figured well, let me let him do whatever because if I try to leave he may try to kill me or something. So I didn't do anything. And after that it's like I didn't care about myself. I didn't really feel that good and I think that's why I started hanging out and going out with different people. But then I realized and said; "Why am I doing this to myself?" You know. I am only hurting myself and dragging everybody else along with me, I don't need to be hanging out with these people. You know, I just work up I guess and I just realized; "You're wasting your time doing this. You're a mom. Be serious. Do something. Stop hanging out with so many different people.

Thinking about what she had written in her diary, she recalls herself weighing the cost of her relationship with her abusive partner:

Sometimes I look at myself because I also have a diary at home and I write things, and its like, I always go back and look at stuff and I just realized, you know, I was just getting more depressed, getting myself hurt even more emotionally. I didn't need that. So I guess I just changed and being with the other person, not the abusive person, the other person that didn't want to be a father figure, I'm like "Why do I need all this? I don't need all this." Let me just forget about this situation and just take it from number one.

The unfortunate paradox here is that as these young abused women increasingly commanded self-sufficiency in the control of their own lives, they also felt the need to separate themselves emotionally and physically from potential supports. Angry and unable to trust intimate partners, or even strangers, they may have difficulty gaining the resources they need to maintain their independence. Their acceptance of counseling or assistance from others is damaged by fears of being reengulfed by obligations to repay what they receive. Because of the ways they have paid for their relationships with their abusive partners, the potential costs of accepting support or intimacy appear to be too high. Nevertheless, the recovery of self-control from recognizing that they had the resources to support themselves and their children did renew their chances of making a successful transition to early adulthood.

In contrast to the mothers who were able to end abusive relationships, the mothers who were still experiencing abuse at the 6-year follow-up interview were challenged by illness, disabilities, and extreme or traumatic stresses in addition to the abusive relationships. In this context, they were unable to gain the self-sufficiency that would allow them to leave.

MOTHERS WHO REMAINED IN ABUSIVE RELATIONSHIPS: DEPRESSION, TRAUMA, AND CHOICES

Uniformly, the small group of eight women who remained in relationships that were currently abusive were also living with stressful life events, traumas, and mental health problems that immobilized them. Their choices were reduced to ambivalent cycling between bad alternatives. The stresses of dealing with financial dependency, multiple partners, frequent moves, or homelessness were weighted against the possibility of trying to please or change their partners. Their ability even to use welfare to achieve financial independence was frequently disrupted by multiple moves. They were also frequently unable to care for their children. Two of these mothers had children removed by child welfare services and two others had sent their children to live with other relatives. Also extending beyond their health problems, a variety of compounding stressors (repeat pregnancies, multiple children, lack of education, lack of family willing to care for them) reinforced their beliefs that their best chance was to try to live with or improve their current relationships with their male partners.

Monique's experiences typify this group. Multiple traumatic stressful life events derailed Monique's early positive start toward her early adult goals to go to college. When Monique got pregnant at 16, she was happy. She says: "I didn't think about getting no abortion. I'm glad I'm pregnant. Now I got somebody to love me, and to accept me for me.... I don't have to worry about nobody putting me down or telling me what I can't do."

Her mother was strict and was angry about the pregnancy. Monique also believed her mother favored her sisters. Showing her resiliency, she was proud to prove to her mother that she could finish high school. She also took some college courses and made plans to enter nursing school. However, by the 6-year follow-up interview, her life had changed dramatically. Responding to the interviewer's initial request to "Tell me about what's been going on," Monique says:

> Well, [in] the last 3 years, my mother was burned out and we stayed in the shelter for 3 months, and I was hospitalized for two months [with severe burns]. And after that I had an apartment in [another state] and my apartment was broken into when I was in the hospital, so I lost everything that was there. And then [my child's father] wound up shooting my boyfriend in the head and I went through that whole thing. [Her boyfriend had been raping her and beating her up in front of her child.] After that I went back ... and I tried to get my life back together. I didn't really get back on my feet until ... when I started nursing school ... I worked in the hospital for 7 months and then I became pregnant with my second child and after I had my baby, it was like, ... I just started having anxiety attacks and a lot of aches and pains and I started going to the doctor like every other day. Calling 911 like every day. It became part of my life.... They said I was severely depressed. I was also hospitalized, they put me in a mental institution, I was there for like 2 weeks 'cuz I had a nervous breakdown from all the stuff happening.'

Monique cries at several points in the interview. She says her new boyfriend and father of her new son "abuses her emotionally." He threatens her with violence if she tries to leave. At the time of the 6-year follow-up interview, she had just left her son with her boyfriend's relatives and was in New York with her own mother. She recognizes the need to protect herself in this relationship:

I need to get away from my boyfriend.... He's not good for me. He's using me and he'll tell me to my face ... you're not going nowhere ... 'cuz I could do anything to you and you'll stay still' and he is right. But I don't want him to know that he's right ... but I'm assuring that he's right by staying there [so] I had to get up and go.

Blaming herself for the PTSD that she cannot control, she says her boyfriend is getting tired of her being sick. In her words:

He hasn't been very good at all.... He put me through a lot of stress when I was pregnant with my son [cheating on her]. And even now, and I'm mad at myself, because I should let him go, but it's like I don't know why, I just keep allowing people to just hurt me.... When I went through that thing with calling 911 every day, he told me one time,... "I'm getting sick of you being sick." And it just hurt my feelings but you know I kinda realized that I'm putting everybody's life on hold, everybody's got to stop when [I'm] sick. And then he was like, there's nothing really wrong with you, they keep telling you there's nothing really wrong with you, but I can feel the pains, you know?

Highly self-critical, Monique says, I am always "criticizing myself or putting myself down." Unlike the mothers who left abusive relationships, Monique has no resources left to counterbalance her self-criticism. She has left her new son with her boyfriend's family and she feels her emotional problems are damaging her daughter, who also experienced the apartment fire and was a witness to her mother's abuse and her boyfriend's death. She is immobilized by her continuing anxiety attacks. She says:

I just feel like something's wrong with me. I have cancer somewhere, nobody can find it.... When I came here at Thanksgiving, I was so convinced something was wrong with me, I was having chest pains and I couldn't breathe and all that, but that was like ... all that was anxiety. And even now I have chest pains, I have a lot of problems with my left side, you know, a lot of pain.

Despite almost daily trips to the doctor or emergency department, Monique has been treated only once in the hospital for her symptoms. The 2-week stay helped her, but she relapsed when the stressors built up in her life again. She says:

They helped me. I had group therapy and you know self-assertive classes or something. I don't know what it was called, but, you know, it helped me a lot when I was there. 'Cuz I couldn't bear to talk about the fire and talking about the shooting. I couldn't deal with it ... [being in the hospital] gave me a chance to open up and when I got out I felt better about myself. They said I should have continued therapy, you know. I was supposed to continue seeing the psychiatrist after I got out of the hospital but I didn't stick with it. I figured, oh. I'm OK now. I can deal with everything now and everything just started coming back. Like now, the shooting, right around this time every year, I start having flashbacks or something.

Frequent moves from her boyfriend's house to her mother's and back disrupt the brief periods she has spent in outpatient therapy. She refuses medication, thinking she should be strong enough to get better on her own. However, she is now feeling too defeated. She says:

> everybody expected me to pick up and go. I mean "Come on Monique," you know how you used to be just pick up, brush that right off, and go. And I can't do it this time. I have tried and tried, but I can't do it.

Similar mental health problems, compounded by stressful life events, also held the other seven mothers in place. Several were struggling with recurrent episodes of severe depression and suicidal thoughts. Like many of the sexually victimized women in Musick's (1993) study, many of these women also had histories of abuse. Yet at the 6-year follow-up, only one of these women was in treatment. Trisha was a resident in a drug treatment program, which she entered as an alternative to having to give her third child up to her mother's custody. She wanted to get back on track—to finish her GED and enter a home attendant program. She wanted her children back. Trisha was sexually abused at age 10 and raped at age 20. She was addicted to cocaine, which her child's father (also an addict) sold. She was waiting for him to get out of jail for a drug-related crime and she planned to continue in the relationship. She believed his abuse of her was motivated by the drugs they were on, and she expected he would be clean when he was released from jail. They had been together for 10 years and she says:

> When we first go together we didn't get high. We were okay.... Because of us using and him selling, we did a lot of things to hurt each other.... I feel that the drugs played a major role with his inconsideration and my mistrust.... It was really because of drugs that he was so inconsiderate and very untrustworthy.

The program she was in gave her hope that "life can be better without using drugs" as well as a support system from the women who were there with her. She said the program was also showing her "how to deal with my anger and my hostility so I don't get high." She says:

> I don't get mad I get angry. My first step is not upset, it's anger. And then I just blow, see I am past upset. I just can't get upset today, I got to get angry and I don't like that about me. I really don't, I don't get violent, you know abusive, angry but I can say some really harsh stuff.

But trusting others and herself is hard. Trisha says, "I don't trust nobody but my Higher Power."

Myra also had a history of being the victim of multiple abusers, including her own mother, stepfather, and a former boss. After she moved out of state to be with a new boyfriend, she says, "then he started hitting me and then he started letting his mother curse me out and stuff." At the 6-year follow-up interview, which was conducted by phone, she was pregnant again. She was financially dependent on and living with her abusive boyfriend's family. She said she could not move back to New York because she had no one to stay with. She says, "I would have to go to a shelter." She also believed she had "an emotional attachment" to her current boyfriend. She said, "He's the only one I have right now. He's the only one I have period." With a long history of lost relationships, she wanted to marry this man. He was religious and could provide for her financially. She hoped to win his approval by going back to school after her pregnancy and getting her GED so she could work. She said she wanted to marry to stop the cycle of unstable relationship that is plagued her. Self-sufficiency was not an option for Myra. As she says, she wanted to marry:

> because I don't want to break up with my boyfriend and go find somebody else and break up with them and find somebody else and I want be with one person. We've been together for 3 years, I know him so well, I figure if we got married and we both had good paying jobs, we wouldn't have the problems we have. We could be happy. 'Cause I know he cares about me and I care about him.

She knew he cared about her because he was a "nice, decent person" and he did not leave her for his "daughter's mother when she asked him to marry her." She compared herself with this other woman, trying to understand why he stayed with her:

> I don't know why he didn't [marry her], but she offered to marry him; and she's got a good paying job and at least she's got something going for herself. But she's got four other kids besides his daughter, so maybe that's why he didn't go with her, and they are all from different fathers. So I don't know whether that was the reason that he didn't go or that he didn't want to leave me. Or he knew that he wouldn't be able to take advantage of her like he does me or be ruler over her. 'Cause he can rule over me. I think that's probably why. If it's not those, I guess he loves me, because he wouldn't wanna hurt my feelings because I came all the way down here to be with him. That's what he says, so maybe that's it. He didn't want to hurt my feelings.

Another mother, Tia, also moved from one excessively controlling relationship with her child's father into another, with her current partner. Her children's father went to jail for his involvement in a murder. She describes her new overcontrolling partner as "a good person with her kids," but she had to do what he wanted:

> Now I feel free because I'm not with the kids' father. When I was with him I was like locked in. I couldn't go anywhere. And now it's different. I'm not suffering. I suffer but I'm not suffering the way I used to suffer with the kids' father. So it's

a difference ... 'cuz I have a boyfriend and he doesn't let me breathe either but [I] try to change. Make him change.

Brenda also stayed with her abusive husband and tried to "work with him." He hit her when she was 6 months pregnant and is still "cursing her out all the time" and threatening to leave her. He also wanted her to go to school and work, in contrast to her other children's father, who made her stay at home. She married her new partner 3 months after they met. She had four children and was 8 months pregnant at the 6-year follow-up interview. She says she did not have to work because she received disability insurance. However, her own intellectual resources for getting out of this relationship are also limited by this disability. She only finished Grade 10. She had meningitis as an infant and was left disabled. She explains:

Certain things I don't understand. I can't explain it.... My allergy's [IQ's] below other peoples ... certain things you might tell me I might not understand ... so that kind of slowed me back a little bit too on the things that I want to do.

Like the young women who ended abusive relationships, those who stayed in these relationships experienced severe psychological distress, depletion, and self-blame. Those who left found personal efficacy: they became self-sufficient by caring for their children and accomplishing things at work or school. In contrast, these avenues out were largely overwhelmed for the mothers in the current abuse group by the unremittingly stressful contexts of their lives. Two had benefited from brief periods of hospitalization for psychological problems, but most were not receiving treatment. Their often severe mental health problems were poorly understood by both these women and their families. Their anger, fears of homelessness, and difficulty trusting others, as well as the negative stigma of not making it on your own, prevented them from seeking help. (Referrals for service were made at the 6-year follow-up interviews for these mothers.)

Overall, the story of abusive relationships among the women in the New York study was one of getting out of these relationships. Personal efficacy in caring for their children and concrete resources, including stable welfare or work and family who they could temporarily live with, allowed most of the abused young women to regain their self-control. Their independence was marked by a determined self-sufficiency. Although they remained angry and unable to trust relationships, those who ended abusive relationships regained their determination to make their own and their children's lives better. These mothers were able to utilize their own resources and public supports to their transitions to early adulthood. Welfare gave some the financial independence that allowed them to leave and helped them resume their education. In contrast, the eight mothers who were in abusive relationships had few personal resources, or family resources, or public services to counteract the severe stresses in their lives. These mothers and their children are unlikely to move forward without outreach and comprehensive intervention programs to address their severe mental health problems and concrete service needs.

Adolescent Mothers as Co-Parents: The Effects of Maternal Care, Grandmothers' Involvement, and Day-Care Experiences on Child Competence and Problem Behaviors

With Wendy Hoglund

The stereotype of adolescent mothers as "children having children" stems directly from the belief that they are too young to parent. Yet the majority of adolescent mothers are over 18 years of age (Alan Guttmacher Institute, 1994), so their perceived immaturity does not reflect the mature physical, cognitive, or emotional capacities that are normative by late adolescence. In many domains, 18-year-old women are considered adults. They are old enough to make adult choices about driving, smoking, drinking, sexual activity, and employment. They can enlist in the armed services, live independently, or receive welfare. Many begin college. They are also adults in the eyes of the law. They can consent to health care and are subject to adult court proceedings. They can purchase a gun. Yet at 18, women are not considered old enough to parent.

Beliefs about the parenting immaturity of adolescent mothers most likely arise from the economic immaturity of these young women relative to older parents—quite simply they are less educated and command lower wages (Mathews &

Ventura, 1997). In addition, age differences between parents and parented have increased dramatically since the last 1960s. First births occur, normatively, at increasingly older ages. Whereas 8.6% of 18-year-old women and 11% of 20-year-old women had births in 1960, only 5.6% of 18-year-old women and 6.5% of 20-year-old women had births in 1980 (Heuser, 1980). With these cohort differences, births to teens appear increasingly off-time. However, because perceptions of adolescent mothers' parenting immaturity are confounded with their economic immaturity, the negative effects of maternal age and poverty on child outcomes are difficult to disentangle (Brooks-Gunn & Furstenberg, 1986; Ketterlinus, Henderson, & Lamb, 1991; Klerman, 1993; Muslow & Murry, 1996; Schellenbach, Whitman, & Borkowski, 1992).

Moreover, despite the stereotype of adolescent mothers as single parents, their children are rarely parented by these young mothers alone (Kontos, Howes, Shinn, & Galinsky, 1997; U.S. Bureau of the Census, 1990). Typically, extended family members, particularly grandmothers, and other day-care providers are also involved. With a few notable exceptions (Apfel & Seitz, 1991; Burton, Dilworth-Anderson, & Merriweather-de Vries, 1995; Chase-Lansdale, Brooks-Gunn, & Zamsky, 1994; Spieker & Bensley, 1994), the influences of extended family and out-of- home care on child outcomes have not been addressed in studies of adolescent mothers' parenting skills. Nevertheless, with legislation demanding that adolescent mothers on public assistance live with an adult and work (Personal Responsibility and Work Opportunity Reconciliation Act [PR&WOA] of 1996), the effects of extended family and child-care services on the development of these children take on increased importance (Collins & Aber, 1997; Zaslow, Moore, Morrison, & Coiro, 1998).

In this chapter, we consider the effects of differences in adolescent mothers' welfare and work status, depressive symptoms, stressful life events, number of children, number of housing moves, and parenting sensitivity on their children's problem behaviors at the 6-year follow-up. We also examine the effects of the grandmothers' involvement and the children's child-care experiences (type and duration) during the first 5 years of life on the development of these children's competence and problem behaviors as rated by kindergarten or first-grade teachers. First, we review what effect poverty has on parenting and children's development.

POVERTY, PARENTING, AND CHILD SOCIAL COMPETENCE

Children under 6 years of age of minority-group, adolescent, mother-headed families fall into several high-risk categories for persistent poverty (National Center for Children in Poverty, 1998). Inner-city adolescent mothers who are exposed to persistent poverty in their families of origin face both the disadvantages of their own backgrounds and ongoing poverty in parenting their children (Klerman, 1993). McLoyd (1990) cogently argued that "poverty and economic loss diminish the capacity for supportive, consistent, and involved parenting and render parents more vulnerable to the effects of negative life events" (p. 312). Factors that diminish the capacity for sensitive parenting are also experienced at higher levels in poor communities, including maternal depressive symptoms, limited support, chronic stresses, childhood history of abuse or ongoing abuse, and domestic violence (Klerman, 1993; Muslow & Murry, 1996). The links among poverty, child problem behaviors, and poor school achievement have been extensively studied.

Children in poor or low socioeconomic status (SES) families are at higher risk for behavioral problems (Campbell, Pierce, Moore, & Marakovitz, 1996; Egeland, Pianta, & Ogawa, 1996; Leadbeater & Bishop, 1994; McLoyd, 1998; Shaw, Owens, Vondra, & Keenan, 1996). Predictors of child problem behaviors for poor children include physical health risks (prenatal exposure to teratogens, prematurity, asthma, etc.), home environment risks (lack of cognitive stimulation), family problems (maternal depression, coercive interactions, domestic violence), and environmental problems (neighborhood violence and high concentrations of poverty; McLoyd, 1998).

Not surprisingly, the risks for cognitive, behavioral, or health problems in the children of poor adolescent mothers are similar to those of low socioeconomic children in general. For example, preschool children of adolescent mothers are at higher risk for cognitive deficits and behavior problems than children of mothers who delay childbearing (Camp, 1996; Chase-Lansdale, Brooks-Gunn & Paikoff, 1992; Dubow & Luster, 1990; Ketterlinus et al., 1991; Miller, Miceli, Whitman, & Borkowski, 1996; Moore & Snyder, 1991). Research also supports the long-term stability of early behavior problems, showing moderate associations between early problems and deviance in childhood and adolescence (e.g., Campbell, Ewing, Breaux, & Szumowski, 1986; Egeland, Kalkoske, Gottesman, & Erickson, 1990; Egeland et al., 1996; Lerner, Inui, Trupin, & Douglas, 1985; Rose, Rose, & Feldman, 1989; Verhlst & van der Ende, 1992; Zahn-Waxler, Iannotti, Cummings, & Denham, 1990).

The trajectory toward lower levels of school achievement is also set in motion early in poor children's lives (McLoyd, 1998). Persistent poverty has detrimental effects on child IQ, school achievement, and socioemotional functioning, and also increases children's exposure to health risks (e.g., fetal alcohol syndrome, environmental lead) that lead to learning abilities. As preschoolers, poor children are at risk for less home-based cognitive stimulation (Zill et al., 1997), and they may receive less assistance in behavioral and emotional regulation (Alpern & Lyons-Ruth, 1993).

Problematic parent-child interactions can compound risks for cognitive, emotional, and behavior problems (Alpern & Lyons-Ruth, 1993; Field, 1992; Hubbs-Tait et al., 1996; Lyons-Ruth, 1992; Miller et al., 1996; Wolkind, Zajicek-Coleman, & Ghodsian, 1980). As poor children enter school, inadequate readiness skills elicit or co-occur with lower teacher expectations for their success (Alexander, Entwisle, & Thompson, 1987). Small deficits in preschoolers' cognitive and behavioral school readiness can make substantial differences when these children enter school programs that lack adequate resources to assist them in developing these readiness skills (Pianta, Steinberg, & Rollins, 1995; Pianta & Walsh, 1998). High concentrations of peers with similar deficits in schools in poor neighborhoods can also augment early social skills deficits. As the children of adolescent mothers become teenagers, they are more likely to fail a grade, drop out of school, and have or father a child themselves (Furstenberg et al., 1987; Horwitz et al., 1991).

Research suggests that strict, highly directive, but warm, parenting and higher educational expectations among parents can protect against school failure, whereas harsh, inconsistent parenting and exposure to acute and chronic stresses increase the likelihood of negative outcomes (Jarrett, 1995; McLoyd, 1998). The parenting skills of adolescent mothers may be particularly compromised by depression, stress, and lack of support (Hubbs-Tait et al., 1996; Klerman, 1993; Schellenbach et al., 1992), augmenting their children's risks for problem behaviors and inadequate school readiness.

THE NEW YORK STUDY: ASSESSMENT OF CHILD BEHAVIOR COMPETENCE AND PROBLEM BEHAVIORS

Teachers' assessments of the children's *competence* at about 6 years of age were collected using the Vineland Adaptive Behaviors Scales, Classroom Edition (Sparrow, Balla, & Cicchetti, 1984). The Adaptive Behaviors Scales yield an overall competence composite, and the subscales include communication (what the individual understands, says, reads, and writes), daily living skills (personal care, household tasks, use of phone, etc.), and socialization (interpersonal relationships, use of play and leisure time, and responsibility and sensitivity in coping skills). Compared with standardized scores normed for a large group of children representative of several ethnic groups (scaled with mean scores of 100 and a standard deviation of 15.), the New York children's scores for the Vineland Subscales fell within the adequate range (communication $M = 95.5$, $SD = 14.0$; daily living skills $M = 99.67$, $SD = 16.8$; socialization $M = 94.3$, $SD = 13.0$; adaptive composite $M = 95.8$, $SD = 14.8$).

Assessments of the children's problem behaviors were collected from the mothers when the children were about 3 and 6 years of age and from the children's kindergarten or first- grade teachers at about 6 years of age. Maternal reports of child behavior problems were obtained at the 3-year follow-up using the CBCL/2-3 (Achenbach, 1992) and at the 6-year follow-up using the CBCL/4-18 (Achenbach, 1991; see Appendix A). These measures yield scores for internalizing and externalizing behaviors as well as total problems. Teachers' reports of child behavior problems were obtained using the TRF of the CBCL (Achenbach, 1991), an essentially parallel measure to the CBCL/4-18. Additional items tap school-specific behaviors related to anxiety (e.g., overconforms, afraid of mistakes), social problems (e.g., cries, feels unloved), aggressive behaviors (e.g., defiant, disturbs others), and attention problems (e.g., difficulty with following directions, fails to finish work).

Levels of mother-reported child problem behaviors at 3 and 6 years of age were moderately stable ($r = .48$; Bishop et al., 1998; Leadbeater & Bishop, 1994). Only four children (5.6%; two males and two females) scored above the CBCL cutoff for clinically significant problems (Achenbach, 1992) at both time points. Mother-reported total problem behavior scores at the 6-year follow-up (range

5–80, mean = 31.7, SD = 18.0) were significantly higher than teacher reports [range 0–99, mean = 22.7, SD = 20.0; $t(78)$ = 3.29, p < .01]. Mothers reported higher levels of aggressive behaviors, somatic problems, and thought problems than teachers. In contrast, teachers reported higher levels of attention problems than mothers. Girls were more likely to score above the cutoff for clinically significant problems on the teacher-completed CBCL (n = 11) than boys [n = 3; χ^2 (1) = 5.81, p = .02]. Five children (one male and four females) scored above the cutoffs on both the mother- and teacher-completed CBCLs at the 6-year follow-up. The correlation between mothers' and teachers' reports of total problem behaviors was low (r = .21, p = .06). This is consistent with previous findings (Achenbach, 1991) and may reflect differences in the children's behaviors across school and home settings.

Correlates of Child Competence and Problem Behaviors

Demographic, maternal, and child behavioral correlates of child competence and problem behaviors outcomes are displayed in Table 10.1. Correlates of competence differed among the Adaptive Behaviors Overall Competence Composite and Competence Subscales. However, several significant associations were found. Child problem behaviors reported by both mothers and teachers were associated with lower competence scores. Children with mothers on welfare at delivery were less competent both in overall scores and in communication skills at school entry than children in families not on welfare. Higher levels of maternal depressive symptoms, stressful life events, housing moves, and number of children in the family were also associated with lower child competence. Significant correlates of more child problem behaviors included higher levels of maternal depressive symptoms, lower quality grandmother support and acceptance, more stressful life events, more housing moves, and number of children in the family. We discuss and expand on these findings as we examine differences in the sources of preschool caregiving for the children in the New York study. We focus on differences in the parenting skills of the adolescent mothers, the grandmothers' involvement, and the children's out-of-home child-care experiences.

THE EFFECTS OF ADOLESCENT MOTHERS' PARENTING STYLES ON CHILD OUTCOMES

Although confounding the effects of young age and economic immaturity, studies comparing parenting styles of adolescent and adult mothers have identified a long list of deficits in the parenting of adolescent mothers compared with those who delay childbearing until age 20 (Klerman, 1993; Osofsky et al., 1993; Raeff, 1994). On average, adolescent mothers are more punitive, vocalize less, show less empathy, and are less responsive. They have premature expectations for developmental milestones, show more negative and less positive affect in mother–child interactions, and report intervening less frequently in potentially hazardous situations. They are also more likely to have a child who is abused (Leventhal, Horwitz, Rude,

TABLE 10.1

Correlations of Maternal Demographic, Depressive, Support, and Stress Variables at 1 and 6 Years Postpartum With Child Behavior Competence at 6 years and Problem Behaviors at 3 and 6 Years of Age

Variable	1	2	3	4	5	6	7	8	9	10	11
Behavior Competence											
1. Overall[a]											
2. Communication[b]	.81***										
3. Daily Living[c]	.93***	.62***									
4. Socialization[d]	.87***	.55***	.77***								
Problem Behaviors											
5. Mother-report: 3-years[c]	-.34**	-.28*	-.30*	-.35**							
6. Mother-report: 6-years[e]	-.38***	-.32**	-.37***	-.38***	.48***						
7. Teacher-report: 6-years[f]	-.35***	-.28**	-.27**	-.43***	-.01	.21^t					
Demographics											
8. Mother's age	-.01	.00	-.02	.07	.03	-.01	-.05				
9. Ethnicity	-.01	.06	-.02	-.00	.14	.04	.11	-.02			
10. Last grade	.11	.19^t	.03	.07	-.07	.04	.01	.69***	.17*		
11. On welfare	-.19*	-.25**	-.3	-.16^t	-.02	.00	.11	.02	-.17^t	-.23**	

continued on next page

TABLE 10.1 (continued)

Variable	12	13	14	15	16	17	18	19	20	21	22	23
Behavior Competence												
1. Overall[a]												
2. Communication[b]												
3. Daily Living[c]												
4. Socialization[d]												
Problem Behaviors												
5. Mother-report: 3-years[c]												
6. Mother-report: 6-years[e]												
7. Teacher-report: 6-years[f]												
Demographics												
8. Mother's age												
9. Ethnicity												
10. Last grade												
11. On welfare												

Variable	1	2	3	4	5	6	7	8	9	10	11
Maternal Symptoms											
12. Depressive symptoms: First year	$-.16^t$	$-.16^t$	$-.13$	$-.15^t$	$.33^{**}$	$.47^{***}$	$.06$	$.06$	$-.04$	$.04$	$.05$
13. Depressive Symptoms: 6-years	$-.24^*$	$-.12$	$-.31^{**}$	$-.23^*$	$.22^*$	$.45^{***}$	$.24^*$	$.14^t$	$.07$	$.13^t$	$.13$
Grandmother Support											
14. Quality: First year	$.12$	$.13$	$.11$	$.07$	$-.23^*$	$-.33^{***}$	$.07$	$-.09$	$.01$	$-.09$	$.05$
15. Quality: 6-years	$.09$	$.14$	$.05$	$.04$	$-.23^*$	$-.29^{**}$	$-.11$	$.08$	$.08$	$.11$	$-.09$
16. Acceptance: First year	$-.04$	$.02$	$-.06$	$-.04$	$-.20^*$	$-.31^{***}$	$.00$	$-.03$	$.08$	$-.03$	$.05$
17. Acceptance: 6-years	$.04$	$.03$	$.01$	$.12$	$-.26^*$	$-.29^{**}$	$-.01$	$-.09$	$-.03$	$-.08$	$-.00$
18. Lives with Grandmother: First year	$-.06$	$-.15^t$	$-.07$	$.04$	$-.20^*$	$.13$	$-.18^*$	$-.17^*$	$-.15^t$	$-.21^{**}$	$.09$

Continued on next page

TABLE 10.1 (continued)

Variable	12	13	14	15	16	17	18	19	20	21	22	23
Maternal Symptoms												
12. Depressive symptoms: First year												
13. Depressive symptoms: 6-years	.29**											
Grandmother Support												
14. Quality: First year	-.47***	-.08										
15. Quality: 6-years	-.46***	-.32***	-.48***									
16. Acceptance: First year	-.54***	-.07	.69***	.20*								
17. Acceptance: 6-years	-.43***	-.29***	.48***	.78***	.63***							
18. Lives with grandmother: First year	.06	-.13	.09	.14^t	.05	.07						

146

Variable	1	2	3	4	5	6	7	8	9	10	11
19. Lives with grandmother: 6-years	.01	-.03	.05	-.05	-.24*	-.06	-.06	-.07	.02	-.08	-.09
Maternal Stress											
20. Stressful life events: First year	-.21*	-.27**	-.17t	-.14	.25*	.41***	.10	.00	-.04	-.07	.05
21. Stressful life Events: 6-years	-.21*	-.25*	-.17t	-.23*	.17t	.45***	.32**	-.24**	.05	-.18*	.17*
22. Repeat pregnancy: first year	-.22*	-.19*	-.17t	-.19*	.36***	.18*	.11	.13t	.11	-.23**	.07
23. Number of children: 6-years	-.18t	-.25*	-.11	-.14	.19t	.27**	.08	-.02	.04	-.11	-.14t
24. Housing Moves: 6-years	-.16t	-.03	-.14	-.26*	.25*	.21*	-.03	-.13	-.07	-.09	-.07

continued on next page

TABLE 10.1 (continued)

Variable	12	13	14	15	16	17	18	19	20	21	22	23
19. Lives with grandmother: 6-years	$-.14^t$	$-.16^t$	$.23^{**}$	$.20^*$	$.15^t$	.11	$.19^*$					
Maternal Stress												
20. Stressful life events: First year	$.56^{***}$	.11	$-.63^{***}$	$-.35^{***}$	$-.57^{***}$	$-.46^{***}$	$-.02$	$-.17^*$				
21. Stressful life events: 6-years	$.26^{**}$	$.50^{***}$	$-.04$	$-.20^*$	$-.15^t$	$-.17^*$	.03	$-.11$	$.34^{***}$			
22. Repeat pregnancy: First year	$.16^t$	$.18^*$	.04	$-.08$	.01	$-.03$	$-.03$	$-.06$	.12	$.19^*$		
23. Number of children: 6-years	$.17^t$	$.14^t$	$-.09$	$-.16$	$-.19^*$	$-.13$	$.19^*$	$-.06$	$.20^*$	$.26^{**}$	$.27^{**}$	
24. Housing moves: 6-years	$.22^*$	$.13^t$	$-.34^{***}$	$-.34^{***}$	$-.29^{**}$	$-.42^{***}$	$-.25^{**}$	$-.28^{**}$	$.26^{**}$	.12	.07	$.15^t$

Note. $^a n = 76.$ $^b n = 75.$ $^c n = 73.$ $^d n = 74.$ $^e n = 92.$ $^f n = 79.$
$^t p < .10.$ $^* p < .05.$ $^{**} p < .01.$ $^{***} p < .001.$

& Stier, 1993; Zuravin & DiBlasio, 1992). Although the results of other studies reveal fewer significant differences (Baranowski, Schilmoeller, & Higgins, 1990; Chase-Lansdale et al., 1994; Philliber & Graham, 1981), the higher risks for poorer parenting skills among adolescent mothers compared with adult mothers cannot be dismissed. Substantial within-group differences in parenting skills, however, are also evident.

Factors that buffer or enhance associations between risks for inadequate parenting skills among adolescent mothers and impairments in children's socioemotional development have begun to be investigated (Battle, 1995; Brooks-Gunn & Furstenberg, 1986; Culp, Appelbaum, Osofsky & Levy, 1988; Leadbeater, Bishop, & Raver, 1996; Miller et al., 1996; Osofsky & Eberhart-Wright, 1992; Reis, 1988). This research shows that developmental outcomes for children (generally assessed as infants or toddlers) relate to within-group differences in the adolescent mothers' depressive symptoms, warmth or sensitivity, strictness, and valuing of education (Bishop et al., 1998; Leadbeater & Bishop, 1994; Leadbeater, Bishop, & Raver, 1996; Way & Leadbeater, 1999). Poorer child outcomes also relate to more controlling grandmother involvement (Apfel & Seitz, 1991; Chase-Lansdale et al., 1994), and greater support from the baby's father (Leadbeater & Bishop, 1994; Shapiro & Mangelsdorf, 1994). However, adolescent mothers may become more competent in interactions when their children can take a greater role in initiating and maintaining these interactions (Raver & Leadbeater, 1995). In studies of interactions with older children, women who became mothers as teens were not less responsive than older mothers (Darabi, Graham, Namerow, Philliber, & Varga, 1984; Philliber & Graham, 1981). Increases in these mothers' own resources and experiences as parents may also contribute to their more successful parenting skills when their children are older.

Stability and Predictors of Maternal Sensitivity and Child Outcomes

In the New York study, the effects of differences in maternal sensitivity for child behavioral outcomes were examined using videotaped and interview data collected at several time points. Videotaped play interactions between the adolescent mothers and their children at 12 and 20 months were independently coded for sensitivity (warmth) and insensitivity (control and conflict) using the Care-Index (Crittenden, 1981). Coders were blind to all other data and trained to reliability by Dr. Crittenden. Interview ratings of parenting sensitivity (at the 6-year follow-up) were coded from open-ended questions eliciting information about the mother's perceptions of her parenting behaviors and her child (see Appendix B, Questions 11–13 and 32–37). Sensitivity was coded on a 4-point scale indicating the presence or absence of each of the following parenting behaviors: (a) awareness of the child's physical needs, (b) physical and verbal expression of affection, (c) empathy towards the child's feelings, (d) pride in what the child does, and (e) positive dialogue between the mother and child. Insensitivity was also coded by summing a 4-point scale: (0) *no indications of neglect, nonresponsiveness, or excessive control;* (1) *insensitivity in acknowledging the child's needs;* (2) *angry, intrusive, or excessively controlling mother–child interactions;* and (3) *neglecting or distant mother–child interactions.* Consistent with the videotape ratings, the final sensitivity score was calculated as a total of the sensitivity ratings minus the insensitivity ratings. Insensitivity scores are also considered separately.

As shown in Table 10.1, ratings of videotaped interactions of maternal sensitivity were modestly stable across assessments at 12 and 20 months ($r = .30$). Insensitivity ratings were less stable at 12 and 20 months ($r = .22$). Mothers who were more sensitive at 12 and 20 months had lower insensitivity ratings at the 6-year follow-up ($r = -.23, p < .05; r = -.17, p < .10$, respectively). Although these correlations are small, they are of particular interest given that they are assessed across differences in both time (approximately 30 months) and method of data collection (videotapes vs. parent interviews).

Consistent with past research (e.g., Dishion, French, & Patterson, 1995), bidirectional influences of maternal sensitivity and child problem behaviors are also suggested by the correlations in Table 10.2. Not surprisingly, video ratings of child problem behaviors and concurrent video ratings of maternal sensitivity and insensitivity are significantly correlated. Video ratings of child problem behaviors at 12 months were also significantly correlated with both mother and teacher ratings of child problem behaviors at the 6-year follow-up ($r = .43$ and $.21$, respectively). Ratings of maternal insensitivity at 12 and 20 months were also associated with mother reports of child behavioral problems at the 6-year follow-up ($r = .22$ and $r = .17$, respectively). Insensitivity in the video taped interactions at 20 months was also associated with mother reports of child problem behaviors at 36 months ($r = .26$) and 72 months ($r = .17, p < .10$).

Neither parenting sensitivity nor insensitivity were significantly associated with teacher-reported child problem behaviors or competence. Although reporter differences may explain these results, the finding that parenting behaviors are not associated with teacher-rated levels of competence (assessed by the Vineland scales) is consistent with Tucker, Brady, Harris, Fraser, and Tribble's (1993) large-scale study of the effects of parent behaviors on the adaptive functioning of African-American and White second graders.

Maternal Support for Education and Child Outcomes

The positive influence of parent support for education on school outcomes for children is well recognized (Grolnick, Benjet, Kurowski, & Apostoleris, 1997; McLoyd, 1998). However, the influence of this support for school entry success for the children of adolescent mothers has not been studied. In the videotaped interactions in the New York study, the majority of the adolescent mothers spent a great deal of time actively teaching their preschoolers how to use the toys provided (nesting cups, a drop box with a square, circle, and triangle). Although the quality of these teaching interactions varied from playful to instructive to intrusive (Raver & Leadbeater, 1995), the mothers' desire for their children's competence in these activities was apparent in all but the most passive interactions.

TABLE 10.2

Zero-Order Correlations of Child Problem Behaviors at 12, 20, 36, and 72 Months Postpartum and Maternal Sensitivity and Insensitivity at 12, 20, and 72 Months Postpartum

Variable	1	2	3	4	5	6	7	8	9	10	11	12	13
Child Problem Behaviors													
1. Video ratings: 12 months[a]													
2. Video ratings: 20 months[b]	.06												
3. Mother report: 36 months[c]	.04	.21^t											
4. Mother report: 72 months[d]	.43***	.13	.48***										
5. Teacher report: 72 months[e]	.21*	−.02	−.01	.21*									
Overall Behavior Competence													
6. Teacher report: 72 months[f]	−.21*	−.10	−.34**	−.38***	−.35***								
Maternal Parenting Behaviors													
7. Sensitivity: 12 months	−.51***	−.09	−.00	−.13	−.09	−.02							

continued on next page

TABLE 10.2 (continued)

Variable	1	2	3	4	5	6	7	8	9	10	11	12	13
8. Insensitivity: 12 months	.64***	.05	.04	.22*	.09	-.13	-.82***						
9. Sensitivity: 20 months	-.06	-.32**	-.17	-.10	-.04	.21^t	.30**	-.28**					
10. Insensitivity: 20 months	.04	.34***	.26*	.17^t	-.11	-.14	-.17^t	.22*	-.76***				
11. Sensitivity: 72 months	-.02	-.06	.04	-.09	-.11	.12	.10	.12	.22*	-.10			
12. Insensitivity: 72 months	.05	.02	-.09	.13	.15^t	.02	-.23*	-.01	-.17^t	.15	-.72***		
13. Educational involvement: 72 months	-.25*	.22^t	-.12	-.17^t	-.18^t	.22*	.23*	-.35**	.15	-.12	.02	-.11	
14. Educational goals: 72 months	-.12	-.08	.07	-.11	.03	-.16^t	.26**	-.16^t	.06	.04	.01	-.06	.14

Note. [a] $n = 98$. [b] $n = 82$. [c] $n = 73$. [d] $n = 92$. [e] $n = 79$. [f] $n = 76$.
$^t p < .10$. * $p < .05$. ** $p < .01$. *** $p < .001$.

Ratings of the mothers' direct educational involvement in their child's school activities from the 6-year follow-up interview data were summed on a 6-point scale indicating that the mothers: (1) *helped with homework;* (2) *read to their children;* (3) *volunteered for school activities;* (4) *attended parent–teacher meetings;* (5) *expressed concerns about their child's schooling;* or (6) *expressed a positive valuing of schooling.* The mothers' educational goals for their child's future were coded from the mothers' response to this question: If you had three wishes for your child that would be true when he/she is 20, what would they be? Responses were rated on a 3-point scale indicating: (0) *no educational goals were expressed;* (1) *graduating from high school was important;* and (2) *goals included going to college.*

The mothers' involvement in their child's education was significantly associated with teacher ratings of overall child competence at 6 years of age ($r = .22$) and also tended to be associated with lower levels of child problem behaviors at this age. As shown in Table 10.2, mothers whose children showed more videotaped problem behaviors at 12 and 20 months were less involved in their children's educational activities at the 6-year follow- up. The maternal sensitivity and insensitivity ratings at 12 months were also related to the mothers' school involvement. Patterns of involvement may well be influenced by maternal efficacy established through the success of early parent-child interactions (Raver & Leadbeater, 1999). The mothers' educational goals for their children were also not significantly related to mother or teacher reports of problem behaviors or competence. It is possible that the mothers' goals for their children and their own educational achievement will have a greater impact on their children's educational outcomes than on the success of their entry into school. Global indicators of the mothers' modeling of education, including her highest grade achieved by the 6-year follow-up interview, were generally not related to the children's competence (with the exception of communication skills; $r = .22, p < .05$) or problem behaviors.

Maternal Depressive Symptoms and Child Outcomes

The association between poverty and risk for depression, particularly for single women with young children, has been well established in psychiatric epidemiology (see by Belle, 1990). Research with high-risk adult samples has also demonstrated associations between parental psychological distress and children's socioemotional development (Cole & Zahn-Waxler, 1992; Gelfand & Teti, 1990; McLoyd, 1990). Maternal depressive symptoms are associated with more punitive, inconsistent, and/or unresponsive adult mother–child interactions (Field, 1992; Gelfand & Teti, 1990; Lyons-Ruth, Connell, Grunebaum, & Botein, 1990). Moreover, these effects may be reciprocal with higher levels of child problems predicting more subsequent depressive symptoms in mothers (Hammen, Burge, & Stansbury, 1990).

In previous reports from the New York study, maternal depressive symptoms predicted more noncontingent (conflicted) responses in mother–toddler play interactions when the children were 20 months old. Conflicted mother–toddler interactions are characterized by (a) maternal attempts to control her child's behaviors that are more verbally harsh, insistent, angry, or demanding than limit-setting attempts or requests for cooperation; and (b) child responses that include vocal (crying, shrieking, yelling) or physical (throwing toys, hitting, kicking) protests. These conflicted interaction patterns were not related to maternal reports of child behavioral problems at 3 years of age (Leadbeater, Bishop, & Raver, 1996). However, the compounding effects of maternal depressive symptoms, plus high levels of conflicted mother–toddler interactions at 20 months, did predict higher levels of problem behaviors in these children at 3 years of age.

Longitudinal findings from the New York study (Bishop et al., 1998; Leadbeater & Bishop, 1994) have also demonstrated the long-term negative effects of maternal depressive symptoms on child outcomes. Maternal depressive symptoms assessed three times in the first year postpartum predicted maternal (but not teacher) reports of child behavior problems at child age 6 to 7 years, even after accounting for concurrent levels of maternal depressive symptoms and the stability of child behavior problems assessed at child age 28 to 36 months (Bishop et al., 1998).

As shown previously in Table 10.1, not living with the grandmother in the first year postpartum, more stressful life events, more housing moves, and number of children in the family also predicted greater risks for children's problem behaviors, reported by the mothers at 3 and 6 years postpartum. Maternal depressive symptoms can also affect child problem behaviors indirectly by contributing to increases in stressful life events. In previous studies, depressive symptoms at delivery predicted increases in stressful life events at the end of the first year, as well as poorer school outcomes for the mothers at 1 and 3 years (Leadbeater & Linares, 1992; see chap. 3). The risk processes that come together to affect child outcomes become evident in the cycling of maternal depressive symptoms and stressful life events. In addition, the correlations in Table 10.1 show that maternal depressive symptoms and levels of stressful life events reported by the mothers at 6 years postpartum were also associated with teacher reports of more problem behaviors and less competent behaviors in the children at school entry. This suggests that long-term consequences for children's school success may be set in motion by the negative cycle of maternal depressive symptoms and stress.

THE INFLUENCE OF THE GRANDMOTHER'S INVOLVEMENT ON MOTHER AND CHILD OUTCOMES

Data from the U.S. Bureau of the Census (1990) indicate dramatic increases (44% over the past decade) in the number of children residing in homes with grandparents (Fuller-Thomson, Minkler, & Driver, 1997; Pearson, Hunter, Cook, Ialongo, & Kellam, 1997). Twelve percent of African-American, 5.8% of Hispanic, and 3.6% of White children lived with grandparents in 1990. Coresidence was most frequent among urban residents. Two thirds of these grandparents lived in homes where at least one parent was also present. Many reasons have been suggested for this increasing presence of grandparents, including not only the generally longer and healthier lives of seniors, but also increases in health problems among child-bearing-age women that limit their ability to parent (e.g., AIDS, substance abuse, and asthma), increases in single parenting created by divorce and unwed parenting, increases in poverty in families with children, and decreases in afford-able housing.

Previous research has documented that a mother-grandmother headed house-hold is the most prevalent household arrangement for adolescent mothers (Caldwell, Antonucci, Jackson, Wolford, & Osofsky, 1997), particularly among younger, never-married adolescent mothers with fewer children (Black & Nitz, 1996; Trent & Harlan, 1994) and African Americans (Pearson et al., 1997; Trent & Harlan, 1994). These multigenerational, female-headed households are also more common among inner-city families (Trent & Harlan, 1994). This may reflect at-tempts by both the adolescent mother and the grandmother to overcome the limited housing options and economic hardships associated with inner-city poverty. Over-crowding and financial burdens may hamper the ability of extended families to house young mothers with more than one child.

As noted in chapter 2, the majority (72%) of mothers in the New York study lived with their own mothers during the first postpartum year. By the 6-year fol-low-up, this number had declined to 22% (with the majority of mothers living alone with their children or with a male partner). Fifty- seven (61.9%) of the grand-mothers in the New York study provided some day care for their grandchildren during their preschool years.

The parenting skills and competence of these grandmothers have not been the focus of much research on the effects of extended family support on the adoles-cent mothers' and their children's outcomes. However, popular opinion and even legislation are based on the assumption that these grandmothers are more com-petent parents and that they can provide financial, housing, parenting, and child-care support. Nevertheless, research findings do not predict uniformly positive outcomes for adolescent mothers or their children when grandmothers are involved.

In cross-sectional analyses of 1980 U.S. Census data for adolescent mothers 15 to 19 years of age, living with extended family was associated with lower school dropout rates, less reliance on public assistance, and greater likelihood of being in school or the labor force (Trent & Harlan, 1994). These findings are similar to other cross-sectional research showing that grandmothers' support can enhance adolescent mothers' economic status, residential stability, child-care responsibili-ties, parenting skills, educational achievement, and psychological well-being (see review in Way & Leadbeater, 1999).

However, the relationship between grandmothers' involvement and adoles-cent mothers' outcomes are less consistently positive in longitudinal analyses (Cramer & McDonald, 1996; Rhodes, Ebert, & Meyers, 1994). Many adoles-cents who appear to benefit from the grandmothers' involvement were better off and more motivated for educational success before they became pregnant (Lead-beater, 1996). Previous findings from the New York study (Leadbeater, 1996; chap. 4, this volume) show that long-term residence with grandmothers did not contribute to the mothers' school outcomes at 3 or 6 years postpartum, after controlling for school performance prior to delivery. However, adolescent mothers who returned to school, after dropping out for a period, reported more emotional support from their families. Child-care assistance from grandmothers was more likely for adolescent mothers who were at grade level when their first child was born, but was not associated with grade completed by the 3-year follow-up. Grandmothers who value education and who have witnessed their daughters' educational success before an unintended pregnancy may be more invested in helping their daughters maintain the positive trajectories previously established (McLoyd & Hernandes-Joszefowicz, 1996; see also chap. 3, this volume). Moreover, coresiding grandmothers may be those who are more able to care for their daughters, whereas grandmothers' illnesses, addictions, or absence may have taken its toll on their daughters' school attendance or achievement before they became pregnant.

Higher perceived emotional support from grandmothers was associated with the mothers' greater satisfaction with financial status, living arrangements, and overall life experiences at 8 months postpartum (Unger & Wandersman, 1988) and predicted fewer depressive symptoms at 12 months postpartum (Leadbeater & Linares, 1992). In a 2-year longitudinal study, Cooley and Unger (1991) found that child-care assistance from grandmothers enhanced school outcomes for adolescent mothers. However, for older adolescent mothers, greater length of coresidence with their mothers and higher levels of family support predicted poorer maternal warmth and responsiveness to their children (Black & Nitz, 1996; Chase-Lansdale et al., 1994; Oyserman, Radin, & Saltz, 1994; Shapiro & Mangelsdorf, 1994; Spieker & Bensley, 1994; Unger & Cooley, 1992). For these older mothers, coresiding with the grandmothers may also reflect continuing problems the adolescent mothers are having with relationships, health, housing, or social supports.

However, the effects of coresidence with grandmothers and family support on young adolescent mothers' parenting styles appear to be positive (Chase-Lansdale et al., 1994; Shapiro & Mangelsdorf, 1994). Younger adolescents may be more willing to defer to the wisdom of their own mothers, whereas older adolescents may be more likely to believe their mothers are interfering with their parenting authority.

Longitudinal findings from the New York study show that long-term residence with and more perceived emotional support from the grandmothers in the first year postpartum were associated with poorer educational outcomes for the adolescent mothers by the 6-year follow-up (see Way & Leadbeater, 1999; chap. 4, this volume). Qualitative analyses of the interview data suggest that these findings were related to the grandmothers' availability, educational expectations, and strictness. Grandmothers who lived with the adolescent mothers in the first year postpartum and who were perceived to be highly emotionally supportive were the most lenient, had lower expectations concerning education, and sometimes encouraged the young mother to stay at home. In contrast, grandmothers who were perceived as demanding or offering little emotional support were described as extremely strict and disappointed in the pregnancy. These grandmothers often did not live with the adolescent mothers in the first year postpartum. These more demanding grandmothers also encouraged (or forced) the adolescent mothers' self-reliance directly or indirectly (when the grandmothers' absence or influence was perceived as a negative role model to be resisted).

Why Some Mothers Did Not Live With the Grandmothers

Mothers in the New York study cited a range of reasons for not living with their mothers, including the grandmothers' histories of abuse, drug addictions, mental or physical disabilities, imprisonment, and moves out of New York. Continued coresidence can also create overcrowded living arrangements and add to the grandmothers' financial strains. Conflicted relationships between the grandmothers and the adolescent mothers and their children affect coresidence and co-parenting (Apfel & Seitz, 1991; Davis & Rhodes, 1994; Davis, Rhodes, & Hamilton-Leaks, 1997; Oyserman et al., 1994; Rhodes, Ebert, & Meyers, 1993). In the New York study, poorer quality of relationship with the grandmothers predicted higher levels of maternal-reported child problem behaviors (see Table 10.1). Apfel and Seitz (1991) identified four models of mother–daughter parenting relationships in African-American, inner-city families. Relationship differences were characterized by varying levels of cooperative alliances, divisions of labor, shared recreation, and respect. It is likely that these differences also influence the possibilities for co-parenting and co-residency. The presence of a grandfather in the home may have positive effects on adolescent mothers' parenting, operating through the grandfathers' ability to alleviate economic strain (Davis et al., 1997) or by increasing maternal nurturance toward the infant (Oyserman et al., 1994).

Beyond mandating residence with an adult for mothers under age 18 (PR&WOA of 1996), debates and policy initiatives for adolescent mothers rarely address their housing concerns. Adolescent mothers who cannot live with their own extended family face extremely limited access to housing due to multiple levels of housing discrimination that disfavor minorities, adolescents, single mother-headed households, families with young children, jobless individuals, and low-income earners. Moreover, housing instability can have negative effects for both mother and child outcomes.

Housing Stability and Child Outcomes

The location and stability of housing determines access to educational and job opportunities and a range of amenities. As Wekerle (1997) pointed out:

> The ability to pay affects housing choice, location and tenure; the segmented labor market means that women who are predominately low paid, in part-time employment, and have low earning compared with men, experience disadvantages in the housing market. (p. 177)

Multiple moves create disruptions in young mothers' school or work pursuits and their children's child-care arrangements.

For many mothers in the New York study, considerable and continuous effort was required to secure and maintain a stable residence. On average, these mothers lived in 3.5 residences ($SD = 2.4$) over the 6-year period; 17% moved more than six times. Living with the grandmothers also did not guarantee stability. Mothers who did not live with their own mothers in the first year postpartum moved only slightly more often than those who did live with grandmothers in the first year postpartum ($M = 3.8$, $SD = 2.8$; and $M = 3.4$, $SD = 2.2$, respectively).

Why Did the Adolescent Mothers Move So Often?

As shown in Table 10.3, older mothers moved less often. Adolescent mothers who reported less acceptance from their own mothers moved more frequently. By the 6-year follow-up, housing moves also tended to be more frequent when the grandmothers had experienced more physical health problems (including diabetes, heart disease, disabilities from injuries, etc.). The number of children born to the adolescent mothers was not significantly related to the number of moves made by the adolescent mothers.

Abuse by a partner precipitated moves for many mothers. Eighty percent of mothers who had experienced abusive relationships with their male partners moved more than two times by the 6-year follow-up, compared with 45% of mothers who had not experienced abusive relationships ($\chi^2 = 10.4$, $p = .001$; see also chap. 9).

Not surprisingly, multiple moves by the adolescent mother by the 6-year follow-up was negatively associated with children's early school competence. For children who moved more, teachers reported lower socialization skills ($r = -.26$). Their mothers also reported significantly more child problem behaviors at 3 and 6 years ($r = .25$ and $r = .21$, respectively; see Table 10.1).

DIFFERENCES IN CHILD-CARE EXPERIENCES OF THE CHILDREN OF ADOLESCENT MOTHERS

The effects of living with the grandmother on child outcomes may also operate through the grandmothers' participation in child care. Relatives, most often grandmothers, are the preferred, and most frequently used, day-care providers for poor single mothers of children under the age of 5 (Fuller, Holloway, Rambaud, & Eggers-Pierola, 1996; Hofferth & Wissoker, 1991; Sonenstein & Wolf, 1991; U.S. Bureau of the Census, 1990; Wolf & Sonenstein, 1991). Child care by relatives creates many advantages, including increasing the flexibility of time in care and coverage for child illnesses, enhancing the perceived security for the child, maintaining cultural or ethnic consistency in childrearing values, and minimizing costs of care (Spencer, Blumenthal, & Richards, 1997).

Little research, however, has addressed the correlates and consequences of grandmothers' involvement in child-care support for adolescent mothers. Younger

TABLE 10.3

Prospective (Year 1) Predictors and Concurrent Correlates of Number of Housing Moves by Mothers by the 6-Year Follow-up

Step Variable	Total Number of Moves		
	Beta	R^2	R^2 Change
Prospective			
1. Mother's age	$-.17^t$	...	...
On welfare	$-.10$	.04	...
2. Depressive symptoms	.07	.09	.05
3. Grandmother acceptance	$-.28*$	.15	.06
4. Stressful life events	.01	...	...
Repeat pregnancies	.02	.15	.00
	$F(6, 83) = 2.36*$		
Concurrent			
1. Mother's age	$-.21*$	...	...
On welfare	.01	.04	...
2. Depressive symptoms	.04	.05	.01
3. Grandmother acceptance	$-.44***$	...	...
Grandmother mental health	$-.07$	...	...
Grandmother physical health	$-.19^t$	.26	.21
4. Stressful life events	$-.01$	...	...
Number of children	.07	.27	.01
	$F(8, 79) = 3.63***$		

$^t p < .10.$ $*p < .05.$ $**p < .01.$ $***p < .001.$

age of the adolescent mother, coresidence with the grandmother, previous school success and current attendance, and better quality mother–daughter relationships may increase grandmothers' involvement in day care (Voran & Phillips, 1993), whereas factors that diminish grandmothers' availability, such as poor health or her own employment demands, may decrease her involvement in child care. The grandmothers' own success at work may make her a good role model for her daughter, but leave her unavailable to provide child-care support.

Low-income families' child-care choices are constrained by both income and location. Results of research based on nationally representative data show that ethnicity is also related to the type and quality of care that poor children receive (Voran & Phillips, 1993). White children were less likely than African-American or Hispanic children to be in nonregulated care provider homes: 12% of White children, 37.5% of African-American children, and 53% of Latino children were receiving care in nonregulated relative homes. Forty-three percent of children from very low-income homes received care in nonregulated relatives' homes, compared with only 9% of children from moderate income homes (Kontos et al., 1997).

In the New York study, 57 (61.9%) of the children received care from their grandmothers in the first 60 months of life (for a mean of 18.15, $SD = 20.25$), 49 (53.3%) received out-of-home care with a sitter or relative who was not the grand-mother (for a mean of 13.92 months, $SD = 16.83$), and 47 (51.1%) attended a child-care center or preschool (for a mean of 8.34 months, $SD = 11.36$). For the 47 children who had some center-care experience, the average age of entry into care was 41.2 months of age ($SD = 11.7$ months), possibly reflecting the availability of center care, the preference for relative care for preverbal children, or the mothers' increasing income.

In the New York study, we examined the predictors of amount of each type of child-care utilized (mother only, mother and grandmother, out of home, or center care) during the child's first 5 years of life for mothers who differed in welfare sta-tus (yes or no), grade attained at school, residence with the grandmothers (yes or no), quality of family support and stressful life events, and repeat pregnancies (yes or no) at 1 year postpartum (see Table 10.4).

The mothers of children who experienced more mother-only care were more likely to report experiencing more stressful life events, but were less likely to have a repeat pregnancy in the first year postpartum (see Table 10.4). The mothers of children who received more mother and grandmother care were more likely to live with the grandmothers, reported more family support, and were more likely to have a repeat pregnancy during the first postpartum year. The mothers of children experiencing more out-of-home care were more likely to not live with the grand-mothers, reported receiving lower quality family support, and experienced more stressful life events during the first year postpartum. Center-based care experience was not significantly associated with any maternal variables assessed possibly due to the low levels of use.

At the 6-year follow-up, mothers who were receiving welfare had used more mother-only care and less out-of-home care than mothers not on welfare (see Table 10.5). In contrast, mothers who were working at the 6-year follow-up were signifi-

TABLE 10.4

Prospective (Year 1) Predictors of Child-Care Types Utilized in the Child's First 5 Years of Life

| | Child Care Utilized | | | | | | | | | | | |
| | Mother Only | | | Mother and Grandmother | | | Out of Home | | | Center | | |
Step Variable	Beta	R^2	R^2 Change	Beta	R^2	R^2 Change	Beta	R^2	R^2 Change	Beta	R^2	R^2 Change
1. On welfare	.04	...	...	.08	...	...	-.11	...	...	-.02	...	...
Last grade	-.10	.00	...	.14	.01	...	-.03	.03	...	-.06	.00	...
2. Living with grandmother	-.06	...	...	.25*	...	...	-.23*	...	...	-.05	...	...
Quality of family support	-.06	.07	.07	.26*	.16	.15	-.28*	.09	.06	.08	.01	.01
3. Stressful life events	.29*	...	...	-.05	...	...	-.27*	...	...	.03	...	...
Repeat pregnancy	-.24*	.16	.09	.28**	.23	.07	-.10	.15	.06	.03	.01	.00
Multivariate F (6, 80)	2.52*			3.98**			2.32*			0.15		

†$p < .10$. *$p < .05$. **$p < .01$. ***$p < .001$.

161

TABLE 10.5

Mean Number of Months of Child Care Utilized in the Child's First 5 Years of Life by Mothers on Welfare (or Not) or Working (or Not) at 6 Years Postpartum

Child Care Utilized	On Welfare		Working	
	Yes ($N = 64$)	No ($N = 29$)	Yes ($N = 34$)	No ($N = 59$)
1. Mother only	20.98	12.38[t]	15.85	19.71
	(22.68)	(14.69)	(17.66)	(22.48)
2. Mother and grandmother	17.67	19.21	15.82	19.49
	(20.12)	(20.84)	(20.45)	(20.18)
3. Out of home	11.98	18.21[t]	18.62	11.22*
	(16.47)	(17.10)	(17.87)	(15.72)
4. Center	8.13	8.83	8.47	8.27
	(11.79)	(11.93)	(12.09)	(11.02)
Multivariate F (1, 91)	1.21		1.18	

[t]$p < .10$. *$p < .05$. **$p < .01$. ***$p < .001$.

cantly more likely to have used out-of- home care for their children during the first 5 years postpartum. Groups did not differ in their use of mother and grandmother care or center-based care.

EFFECTS OF CHILD-CARE EXPERIENCES ON CHILD OUTCOMES

Good quality center care or early childhood education programs can aid mothers without family support for child care who want to enter the labor force. However, out-of-home care can also increase stresses of work for women due to costs as well as limitations on hours of availability, restrictions on the age of children served, concerns about safety of child care, staff turnovers, and problems with transportation.

Studies of single women receiving child-care subsidies while attending employment programs or exiting welfare, under the 1988 Family Support Act, show that assistance with out-of-home day care is not easily accessed, costly, and restricted by narrow eligibility requirements (Meyers, 1995). Meyers found that few single mothers who were engaged in school, work, or training received child-care assistance. Only 25% had full subsidy for their youngest child and 6% had partial subsidy; 19% paid the full cost of day care themselves. Subsidies were even less frequent among mothers who worked (regularly or part time): Only 9% received a full subsidy, 6% a partial subsidy, and 37% paid the full amount for child care. The majority of mothers in the Meyers study were unaware of the child-care benefits for which they might be eligible.

Sonenstein and Wolf (1991) found that the percent of single mothers paying for child care also differed widely by the type of child care used. In-home relative care was paid for by only 18% of mothers, 42% paid for out-of-home relative care, 62% paid for family day care, 39% paid for group care (centers, schools, Head Start, etc.), and 30% paid for sitters (nonrelated individuals). The durability (or length of episodes of child care) also differed widely by type used: Care by nonrelatives (out-of-home care) was the least enduring type of care and in-home care by a relative was the most enduring, possibly reflecting the low costs, convenience, and flexibility of these arrangements.

In one of the few studies of adolescent mothers' utilization of child care, Kisker and Silverberg (1991) compared the types and costs of child care utilized by mothers enrolled in a demonstration program designed to promote self-sufficiency with the care used by nonparticipant controls. The majority of the children in both groups were under 3 years of age. Relative care was most common (including 35% of participants and 25% of controls), followed by nonrelative care (10% vs. 5%, respectively). Center-based care was least frequently used by both groups (5% vs. 2%, respectively).

This distribution reflected the costs and availability of infant and toddler care, as well as the teens' belief that strangers could not be trusted to take care of their nonverbal children. Costs of paid care averaged from $36 to $44 a week for control and participant mothers, respectively. The reliability of child-care arrangements was problematic. One in five mothers in both the participant and control group reported having to adjust their schedule or miss work due to child-care problems. Fifty-percent of the participant and control mothers who were not involved in school, job training, or work activities cited child care as the primary reason.

Research supports the advantages of center-based care experiences for the development of child cognitive and social competence (Clarke-Stewart, 1991; Kontos, Hsu, & Dunn, 1994), although these findings are moderated by differences across settings, such as levels of the providers' training and quality of their interactions with the children. Data from a nationally representative survey of child-care centers and site visits to five centers show that the quality of care available to low-income families was highly variable. Compared with child-care services provided to upper class families, services for lower income families tended to be lower in teacher sensitivity and harshness (Phillips, Voran, Kisker, Howes, & Whitebook, 1994).

In the New York study, the number of months spent in center-based care was significantly related to teacher reports of better overall competence, communication ability, and daily living skills (independence) in the children (see Table 10.6). In contrast, months of care by the adolescent mother in the first 5 years postpartum was significantly associated with less teacher- reported child communicative competence ($r = -.27$). Mother-only care also tended to be related to higher levels of teacher-reported child problem behaviors, whereas center-care experience was associated with fewer teacher-reported problem behaviors.

In a recent study, however, the National Institute of Child Health and Human Development Early Child Care Research Network (1998) evaluated the longitudinal effects of child-care quantity, quality, stability, type, and age of entry on children's self-control, compliance, and problem behaviors at 24 and 36 months of age for a large, demographically diverse sample of children. The findings suggest that: (a) maternal psychological distress and mothering behaviors were stronger predictors of child outcomes than child-care differences; (b) early, extensive, and continuous care was not related to problematic child behavior; and (c) of the child-care variables, quality of care was the most consistent predictor of child functioning although it explained little of the variance in child outcomes.

One of the few studies to investigate the effects of day-care use among adolescent mothers focused on adolescent mothers enrolled in the New Chance Program (Fink, 1995). This program aimed to increase the mothers' educational activities and job skills training. The children of program mothers were more likely to have attended a day-care center or preschool and were in nonrelative care for longer periods than the control group children. They also experienced more different child-care arrangements than control children. The quality of center care accessed through this program was rated as generally good (Fink, 1995). However, mothers in the New Chance Program were more likely than control group mothers to report parenting-related stress, higher levels of aggravation in relation to their children, and more behavior problems in their children compared with control group mothers. Consistent with the New York study, these findings are particularly characteristic of program mothers who were at risk for depression at baseline (Quint, Bos, & Polit, 1997). Research on the effects of day-care experiences on outcomes for the children of adolescent mothers is clearly needed.

This chapter paints a picture of parenting by adolescent mothers that extends well beyond stereotypes of these mothers as isolated children parenting children. The children of adolescent mothers are rarely cared for exclusively by these young

TABLE 10.6

Correlations of Types of Child Care Utilized in the Child's First 5 Years of Life and Teacher-Reported Child Behavior Competence at 6 Years and Mother- and Teacher-Reported Problem Behaviors at 3 and 6 Years of Age

	Behavior Competence				Problem Behaviors		
	Overall	Communication	Daily Living	Socialization	Mother Report (36 months)	Mother Report (72 months)	Teacher Report (72 months)
Child Care Utilized							
1. Mother-only[a]	$-.15^t$	$-.27^{**}$	$-.10$	$-.05$	$-.14$	$.05$	$.16^t$
2. Grandmother[b]	$.06$	$.05$	$.04$	$.05$	$.12$	$.01$	$-.10$
3. Out-of-Home care[c]	$-.02$	$.11$	$-.08$	$-.04$	$-.01$	$-.04$	$.06$
4. Center-care[d]	$.19^*$	$.20^*$	$.25^*$	$.07$	$.10$	$-.03$	$-.17^t$

Note. [a]$n = 55$. [b]$n = 57$. [c]$n = 49$. [d]$n = 47$.

$^t p < .10$. $^* p < .05$. $^{**} p < .01$.

women. Outcomes for these children are affected by the contexts of their young mothers' lives, the involvement of their grandmothers, and their day-care experiences. Mothers' age at the birth of their children can be seen as a marker of parenting risks, but these risks stem from several sources. Maternal characteristics (like depression and school involvement), quality of the adolescent mothers' relationships with her own mother, and adverse circumstances in the contexts in which these families live (including stressful life events and residential instability) all affect child behavioral outcomes in the New York study. Although levels of child problem behaviors are influenced predominately by maternal and family factors, child competence for entry into school is also affected by events that occur outside the family. Teacher ratings of child competence for school entry were positively related to maternal involvement in school activities, center-based day-care experiences, lower levels of mother-reported stressful life events, and greater residential stability. All of these can be influenced by policy decisions, as is discussed in the final chapter of this book.

Building a Rock to Stand On: Policies That Enhance Competence for the Transition to Early Adulthood

Past program and policy solutions to the social costs of adolescent parenting have focused on the obvious corrective: If the problem is out-of-wedlock births, then programs and policies directed at reducing these births are needed. However, the many program and policy efforts directed at limiting sexual activity and births to teens have had only marginal effects—generally attributed to increases in condom use by adolescents in the wake of the safe sex education that has followed the AIDS epidemic (e.g., Child Trends, 1997; Franklin, Grant, Corcoran, Miller, & Bultman, 1997). The availability of abstinence education funds has increased, but there is no evidence supporting the effectiveness of these programs in reducing the sexual activity of youth. The fact remains that each year approximately half a million children are born to adolescents from a wide variety of backgrounds (Alan Guttmacher Institute, 1994). Women already disadvantaged by minority status and poverty are disproportionately likely to become pregnant and likely to suffer negative consequences from adolescent childbearing.

There is little argument that early childbearing poses a significant challenge to the adaptive transitions of adolescents to early adulthood. Nevertheless, the New York study reveals that how young women adapt to this challenge depends on the resources and other risks they encounter. Our data demonstrate the considerable diversity in their education, work, relationships, and housing outcomes. They also demonstrate the interrelationships among these outcomes. Having a child as an adolescent is a turning point in a trajectory that connects their past experiences with poverty, family support, and school and anticipates what are perceived to be their future opportunities. It rests on the stability of the rock these women have stood on and the futures they can build for themselves on this foundation. This study also places the problems of adolescent mothers in the neighborhood and educational contexts that have structured and continue to structure their development. The comprehensive picture of their lives that is presented in this study reveals the need for more integrated, flexible, multitargeted solutions to the obstacles that impede the adaptive transitions to early adulthood for some adolescent mothers.

A great deal has been written about the need for research and welfare reform policies that can contribute to ending long-term dependency (e.g., see reviews by Aaronson & Hartmann, 1996; Zaslow, Tout, Smith, & Moore, 1998), but little of this has focused specifically on particular solutions that could be directed at adolescent women who are at the stage of life when acquiring the means for independence is a central developmental task. In fact, for adolescent mothers, deficit models of policy and programming that are directed at "children having children" have prevailed (Beshavrov & Gardiner, 1996; Luker, 1996). If adolescent mothers are "children," they have children's needs for care, supervision, protection, tough love, and sanctions to promote responsibility.

At what age do adolescent mothers stop being children having children? Should nonparenting adolescents who are financially dependent on welfare also be considered children (e.g., in determining the age of judicial competence in the eyes of the courts or their capacity for a driver's license)? It would seem to make more sense to focus on the developmental accomplishments needed for the transition to young adulthood and on efforts to enhance the success of all youth making this transition in adverse circumstances. Refocusing interventions and policymaking on ensuring the long-term success of adolescent mothers and their partners, rather than on their deficit and risk status, could decrease needs for long-term government support. Policy and programming that focus on supporting the normative tasks of adolescent mothers as young adults require a different orientation. As adolescents making the transition to young adulthood, their needs for acquiring the means to become financially independent are paramount. Many of the needed social structures (e.g., educational institutions and job training) are already set up to assist adolescents with these transitions. Obstacles to early adult transitions for the minority of adolescents who are not successful must be addressed. Seeing adolescent mothers as oppositional or irresponsible children fails to account for their motivations, strengths, and resources as adolescents and emerging adults. It also fails to account for the obstacles beyond individual motivations that stand in their way.

Changing program and policy emphases to build on strengths and promote resilience processes in the face of adversity requires reconceptualizing the multidimensional challenges and realities of early childbearing, as well as the possibilities for multilevel solutions. Using Masten and Coatsworth's (1998) definition of *resilience* as "manifested competence in the context of significant challenges to adaptation or development" (p. 205), the majority of women in the New York study indeed manifest competence in some important domains (acquiring economic capital, demonstrating parenting skills, budgeting small incomes, stabilizing relationships). As Masten and Coatsworth also pointed out, what can be understood as competence for a given individual also rests on public visions of "reasonable success with major developmental tasks expected for a given age and gender in the context of his or her culture, society and time" (p. 206). As a culture, we share in creating and supporting a vision of reasonable success for inner-city adolescent mothers. You cannot reach for what your culture does not offer.

There is a fair amount of consensus in the 1990s among adolescent mothers, service providers, legislators, and policymakers that the developmental tasks of late adolescence for women must involve (a) preparing for financial and residential independence and stability, (b) bearing healthy children or postponing childbearing, (c) acquiring good parenting skills, and (d) establishing lasting support networks. Program visions must be expanded to focus on adolescents' strengths and resources for accomplishing these specific developmental tasks during this transitional phase of life. Success of both individuals and policies can be evaluated in the short term against how well they advance these tasks: Are educational and career opportunities improved? Are housing and social support networks stabilized?

Interconnections among housing, educational resources, employment opportunities and welfare status can support or interfere with the transition to adulthood for adolescent mothers, but these interconnections have not been made explicit. Thinking about policies and programs to support reasonable success in transitions to adulthood requires an analysis of the contextual factors that present significant obstacles to the developmental tasks that characterize this transition. For example, educational failure and rapid subsequent childbearing are major obstacles that create significant challenges to reasonable success in the developmental tasks of adolescence (e.g., Moore et al., 1993). However, if educational failure and repeat pregnancies are considered only as individual deficits, individual-centered solutions that fail to address the broader contextual factors that maintain these outcomes are not addressed. For example, neighborhood biases in educational opportunities for poor families support school failure. These biases originate in regional differences in school funding and socioeconomic differences in the families of children attending that school. There can be little doubt that when poor children of poor parents from the same neighborhood are grouped together in poorly funded schools, this school context offers youth different socialization and educational opportunities than when middle-class children of educated parents are grouped together with their neighbors. It is not surprising that adolescent mothers from disadvantaged contexts are more likely to experience the negative effects of early childbearing. The neighborhood resources that they are born into place them on an unequal foundation with their more affluent peers. Without an infusion of funding and resources into the more disadvantaged schools, social inequities are reproduced.

The diversity in the experiences of the mothers in the New York study demonstrates the need for flexibility in policies and programs for adolescent mothers. One-size-fits-all solutions to address the problems of adolescent childbearing can provide either too much at too great a cost to society or too little at too great a cost to individuals. Policies directed at teenage mothers must be able to take into account and support resources already available to them and build on their strengths. They must also be flexible enough to shore up resources needed to achieve developmental tasks when these resources are exhausted or missing. Our research also suggests that policies that aid adolescent mothers can be derived from broad prevention efforts that influence girls' and women's development at several time points. Strategies that improve career opportunities for girls before a pregnancy occurs, or that address the child-care needs of all working mothers, can also reduce the negative effects of teenage births on the transition to early adulthood.

SUMMARY OF MAJOR FINDINGS
OF THE NEW YORK STUDY

In this chapter, we summarize the major findings of the New York study. Predictors of diversity in outcomes for adolescent mothers and their children are highlighted. What surprises us most about the mothers in the New York study is the considerable diversity in their abilities to meet the challenges of their early adult transitions. Their resilience is evident in the context of high-risk circumstances created not only by too early childbearing, but also by family poverty, domestic and neighborhood violence, parent absences and illnesses, and poor educational opportunities. For some, having a child at an early age provides the motivation for turning toward and rapidly achieving the developmental tasks of early adulthood. For others, early childbearing adds to an already long list of obstacles to their successful adaptation.

The findings of this study are consistent with the growing number of studies of resilience that have identified good relationships with family and male partners, as well as individual efficacy as protective factors for young women growing up in adverse circumstances (Masten & Coastworth, 1998). More important, the processes through which these factors operate to influence the diversity in the early adult transitions of inner-city adolescent mothers are also illuminated in the New York study.

The Mechanisms of Protective Relationships
Go Beyond Emotional Support

The assumption that adolescent mothers' co-residence with their own mothers necessarily enhances outcomes for these young mothers and their children is challenged in this research. The effects of relationships with the grandmothers, in fact, reflect the complexity of parent–adolescent relationships more generally. The nature and effects of family support for an adolescent mother clearly began long before the pregnancy. This support also frequently changed in response to the pregnancy. Long-term residence with grandmothers who provide emotional support but little encouragement for educational achievement may be detrimental to early adult outcomes for adolescent mothers. Moreover, residence with abusive or addicted grandmothers either contributed to the obstacles that overwhelmed mothers with no alternate support or provided the negative role image to be avoided for those with other family support (from fathers, grandmothers, aunts, or sisters).

For the more successful mothers, childhood support took the form of an early life in a strict, disciplined household where educational achievement was clearly valued

—and even insisted on. The pregnancy represented a disruption in the hopes these families held for their daughters and that the daughters held for themselves. In adapting to the pregnancy, the grandmothers supported their daughters' continued education or work, in some cases effectively sharing the care of their grandchildren while the adolescent continued to go to school or began to work. These young women were anxious to redeem themselves in the face of their families' disappointment and prove that they could achieve their goals despite having children.

Marriage or living with a male partner was not a marker of successful adaptation to young adulthood for these adolescent mothers. Indeed, abusive or excessively controlling relationships were frequently reported among the mothers who were struggling most with the adaptation to early adulthood. The mothers' relationships with the child's biological father rarely lasted to the child's sixth birthday as problems with employment, addictions, jail, and other relationships took their toll. Relationships that worked were characterized by prolonged decisions about marriage, mutual respect for autonomy, and egalitarian attitudes toward household chores and child care. Although contributing financially to their child's well-being was only rarely possible (due not only to unemployment but also to welfare restrictions), male partners who were able to care for their children and who provided respect and emotional support for the adolescent mothers enhanced these mothers' early adult transitions. These protective relationships were extremely rare in the lives of the New York study mothers.

Maintaining Efficacy and Optimism in the Contexts of Adversity Depends on a Foundation of Resources

Many of the young mothers in this study became pregnant at a time in their lives when serious disruptions had occurred in their relationships with their families (including the grandmothers becoming addicted to drugs or alcohol; abuse or neglect that disrupted schooling; divorce or separations that undermined the adolescents' supervision; death of a brother, grandmother, or mother). Problems in school also seemed to precipitate the decision to have a child (12 mothers had already dropped out). Although relationships with a boyfriend temporarily filled a gap in their lives, these relationships were typically short lived. Dramatic changes in several of the adolescent mothers' attitudes toward their own futures were catalyzed by the end of (or temporary separation from) their relationships with a boyfriend.

As the young mothers became increasingly aware of their role as the sole provider for their child (and often for themselves as well), the stark reality of their need to become future-oriented and self-sufficient forced those who could to rise to this challenge. The great majority of the mothers in this study wanted to finish high school and work. The young women who were building on a reasonable foundation of prior educational success, access to post-high school education, family support, and their own and their child's good health met this challenge with a strong desire to succeed and considerable optimism about their futures. Their personal optimism depended on an ongoing context that allowed it to be sustained by reasonable success in the adaptation to young adulthood. Mothers who were building on abusive childhood relationships, educational failures, and illnesses, or who were undergoing severe stressful life events (such as domestic violence; traumatic deaths of their children, boyfriends, or relatives; or unstable housing) were more frequently overwhelmed with depressed affect and apathy, and were becoming increasingly powerless to change their lives.

The Negative Cycling of Depression and Life Stress Can Halt Positive Transitions to Young Adulthood

The findings of the New York study repeatedly demonstrated the negative impact on outcomes for both the adolescent mothers and their children of the cycling of depressive symptoms and stressful life events. Although the starting point is often difficult to determine, stressful life events that are associated with depressive symptoms in adolescence can serve to maintain and eventually increase symptoms over time. These symptoms can interfere with cognitive, emotional, and somatic functioning and include sadness, irritability, poor concentration, difficulty getting going, fatigue, work disturbances, and sleep and eating problems. As young women become increasingly overwhelmed by these symptoms, their capacity to take constructive actions to deal with or prevent the stressful life events that they encounter can be markedly reduced. This, in turn, can increase the likelihood that stressful events will persist or re-occur. The toll of this negative cycle on the mothers' educational and work aspirations and on their children's levels of problem behaviors and competence for school entry (rated by their first-grade teachers) was clearly evident in the New York study. Levels of depression were high at several assessment points for the mothers who were the least successful in making the transition to early adulthood. (Problems recovering from posttraumatic stress also interfered with the transition to adulthood for some mothers.) Depression is highly treatable, but most often these symptoms went undiagnosed among the adolescent mothers in the New York study who blame themselves for not getting their lives in order. Without assistance in reducing stress and managing episodes of depression or chronic depressive symptoms, these mothers—those most in need of help— may not benefit from programs designed to increase their economic potential or their children's school readiness.

PROGRAMMING AND POLICIES FOR ADOLESCENT MOTHERS: SUCCESS STORIES AND CREATIVE INNOVATIONS OF THE 1990s

In contrast to the failure of prevention programs to reduce sexual activity in adolescents overall, past reviews have demonstrated that programs designed for adolescent mothers can reduce risks for poor educational outcomes for these mothers (Seitz, 1996) and for poor birth outcomes for their children. Indeed, the once prevalent view that adolescent childbearing is associated with low birthweight infants has been challenged by recent research showing age per se has no effect. Risk factors known to affect birthweight, like smoking, hypertension, alcohol consumption, and a history of spontaneous abortions, are associated with low birthweight and preterm deliveries, but these were more frequent in older women (McCarthy & Hardy, 1993). Programs reporting positive outcomes for adolescent mothers have varied in their particular focus on prenatal care, educational outcomes, case management, or parenting skills. Essential features of programs that have shown positive effects on the health of infants of adolescent mothers or on educational outcomes for these mothers are summarized in Table 11.1. Comprehensive programs that offer more than one service in a single location may also increase the likelihood that young parents will have access to them (Klerman & Horwitz, 1992). However, our data suggest that adolescent mothers may benefit from specific services tailored to their needs, rather then all needing comprehensive services.

Building on the early reviews, we examined program evaluations published in the 1990s, including only reports with adequate subject numbers and comparison group data (see Table 11.2). The results demonstrate the effectiveness of several program approaches for increasing prenatal care, enhancing infant health, for improving educational outcomes, and reducing repeat pregnancy in adolescent mothers compared with controls not exposed to these interventions. Effective programs have also been variously located in schools, health clinics, community services, and social services and have frequently included outreach and home visiting services. The majority focus on providing services to individual adolescent mothers. However, some also offered extended services to families and partners of adolescent mothers. A few have begun to address adolescent mothers' needs for mental health services and stable support networks (Cherniss & Herzog, 1996; Hanson, 1992). The success records of these programs suggest that negative outcomes for adolescent mothers and their children are indeed preventable.

Despite the apparent ability of programs to affect the reasonable educational successes of adolescent mothers and the health of their children, programs are not universally available and their funding is rarely stable. Moreover, our findings indicate that gains may be undermined by problems many young mothers have in limiting fertility, moving permanently from welfare to earning a living wage, obtaining stable housing, accessing reliable child care, coping with their own child's illnesses, or accessing responsible, economically stable father involvement. Klerman and Horwitz (1992) were pessimistic in their forecasts for the creation of adequate services for adolescent mothers. They concluded their review of these programs saying that, "Even though programs are expanding in number, scope, and sophistication, the problems faced by the adolescents involved appear to be outstripping them" (p. 312). Services are frequently fragmented or hard to access. Time limits create arbitrary cutoffs that can come into effect before program benefits are stabilized (Seitz, 1996). Many programs are directed at single problems like welfare dependence or prenatal care, but integration across services is lacking.

Innovative Programming for Adolescent Mothers and Their Partners

Innovative programming efforts for adolescent mothers and their partners have also been initiated most frequently by those in frontline services. Several pro-

TABLE 11.1
Essential Features of Programs for Adolescent Mothers

Program	Focus	Program Goals	Service Providers
Prenatal/child health programs	• prenatal and infant health • parenting skills development	• postpone repeat pregnancies • prevent high school dropout • reduce adverse maternal and infant physical health outcomes • increase understanding of child development and effective parenting	• pediatricians, nurse practitioners, and social workers • home visits from health professionals or paraprofessional mentors
Education-centered programs	• post-delivery services to promote healthy maternal and child development • welfare sanctions for program noncompliance may be included	• improve high school retention/graduation or GED completion • improve employment skills • promote self-sufficiency • promote healthy maternal and child development	• social service workers • public educators • child service providers included in two-generation programs

Case-management programs	• assessment, outreach, advocacy, case planning, monitoring, clinical intervention, coordination of community services, follow-up • may include adoption counseling	• improve maternal mental health • improve parenting skills • provide concrete services such as assistance locating housing, child care, or welfare	• social service workers • health care providers
Family-support programs	• maternal life and parenting skills • quality of family and child's father support	• postpone repeat pregnancies • improve life and parenting skills • improve quality of family support • improve the father–child relationship	• social service workers • public educators • health professionals

175

TABLE 11.2

Summary of Program Evaluations

Program/Locus/Authors	n/Ethnicity	Program Mandate	Setting/Delivery Methods	Data Source/Dates	Outcomes
McCabe School Program (New Haven) Seitz & Apfel (1993)	Treatment n = 52 (> 7 wks postnatal intervention) Control n = 50 (≤ 7 wks postnatal intervention) 100% African American	• prevent rapid repeat pregnancies • improve high school/GED graduation • reduce welfare	School-based Prenatal/Child-Health Program	• hospital records • school records • at 18 months and 6 years postpartum (1979–1980)	Repeat Pregnancy: Treatment 53% vs. Control 77% High School/GED graduation: Treatment 9% vs. Control 30%
Learning, Earning, & Parenting Program (LEAP) (Ohio Statewide) Bloom, Fellerath, Long, & Wood (1994)	Enrolled in School: Treatment 1 n = 1,917 Control 1 n = 355 68.6% African American, 28% White, 2.2% Hispanic Not in school: Treatment 2 n = 1,562 Control 2 n = 317 42.3% African American, 52.6% White, 3.8% Hispanic	• improve high school retention • improve employment • reduce welfare	Statewide school- and social-service-based Multicomponent Program (Case-Management and Education-Centered grant adjustment)	• program case files • school records • statewide GED testing data • state welfare case files (1989–1991)	Continuous School Attenders: Treatment 1 61.3% vs. Control 1 51.1% School Returners: Treatment 2 46.8% vs. Control 2 33.4% Treatment effect greater for young mothers with one child

Program	Sample	Goals	Type	Evaluation	Results
Albany Community Service Project (New York) Carlson, Abagnale, & Flatow (1993)	Treatment $n = 291$ 73% African American, 21% White, 4% Hispanic Control $n = 19,500$ (New York State statistics)	• prevent repeat pregnancies • improve high school retention • provide preventive prenatal care	Statewide community-based Case-Management Program	• comparison of program statistics with national pregnancy rate and NY state school retention rate (1990–1991)	Repeat Pregnancy: Treatment 3% vs. Control 11% High School Retention: Treatment 85% vs. Control 66%
New Chance Demonstration (Bronx, Detroit, Harlem, Lexington, Philadelphia, Pittsburgh & Portland) Zaslow & Eldred (1998)	Treatment $n = 184$ Control $n = 106$ 84.1% African American, 15.9% White	• postpone repeat pregnancies • improve parenting skills, child development, and exposure to high-quality day care • improve high school/GED retention/graduation • improve employment • reduce welfare	Social-service- and community-based Education-Centered Program	• participant interviews and observational assessments at 18 and 42 months postpartum • maternal and teacher child behavior and academic ratings at 42 months (1989–1991)	At 18 months: Regularly Contracepting: Treatment 40% vs. Control 53.1% Regular Child-Care Provider: Treatment 94.6% vs. Control 83% Day Care Attended: Treatment 64.1% vs. Control 30.3%

continued on next page

TABLE 11.2 (continued)

Program/Locus/ Authors	n/Ethnicity	Program Mandate	Setting/Delivery Methods	Data Source/Dates	Outcome
Resource Mothers for Pregnant Teens Project (RMP) (South Carolina counties) Rogers, Peoples-Sheps, & Suchindran (1996)	Treatment n = 1,901 77% African American, 23% White Control 1 n = 4,613 (other counties) 54.6% African American, 45.4% White Control 2 n = 712 (same counties) 70.9% African American, 29.1% White	• promote healthy pregnancies with early and regular prenatal care • reduce risk factors associated with pregnancy • reduce low birthweight and preterm birth infants	Home- and community-based Prenatal/Child Health Mentor Program	• program case files • Department of Health and Environmental Control data • birth certificates (1986–1989)	Initiated Prenatal Care at 1–3 Months: Treatment 45.3% vs. Control 1 40.9% vs. Control 2 40% Received Adequate Prenatal Care: Treatment 35.6% vs. Control 1 31.1% Preterm Births: (unmarried teens) Treatment 17% vs. Control 1 33%
Living for The Young Family (LYFE) (New York) Finkel & Thompson (1997)	Treatment n = 154 Control n = 52	• prevent repeat pregnancies • improve high school retention/graduation • help locate infant daycare • improve maternal coping	School- and social-service-based Education-Centered Program	• program case files • participant interviews • schools records (1987–1992)	Repeat Pregnancy: Treatment < Control High School Graduation: Treatment > Control

178

Program	Sample	Goals	Program Type	Data Sources	Outcomes
Teenage Parent Demonstration Project (TPD) (Chicago, Newark, & Camden) Maynard & Rangarajan (1994)	Treatment $n = 1,721$ Control $n = 1,691$ 75.6% African American, 6.9% White, 16.5% Hispanic	• postpone repeat pregnancies • improve employment • reduce welfare	Social-service-based Multicomponent Program (Case-Management and Education-Centered)	• program case files • participant surveys at 23 months (1987–1991)	Carried Pregnancy to Term: Treatment > Control
Health Care Program for Adolescent Mothers & Infants (Eastern United States) O'Sullivan & Jacobsen (1992)	Treatment $n = 120$ Control $n = 123$ 100% African American	• prevent repeat pregnancies • improve high school retention • increase well-baby clinic attendance and infant immunizations • reduce emergency room use for routine infant care	Clinic- and social-service-based Prenatal/Child-Health Program	• participant interviews at 6 and 18 months postpartum • school records • hospital records • city health district records	Repeat Pregnancy: Treatment 12% vs. Control 28% Attended Well-Baby Clinic: Treatment 40% vs. Control 18% Immunizations: Treatment 33% vs. Control 18%

continued on next page

TABLE 11.2 (continued)

Program/Locus/ Authors	n/Ethnicity	Program Mandate	Setting/Delivery Methods	Data Source/Dates	Outcomes
Elmira Home-Visitation Study (Appalachian region of New York State) Olds et al. (1997, 1998)	Treatment n = 216 Control n = 184 11% African American	• reduce repeat pregnancies • improve prenatal and postnatal infant care • reduce child abuse/neglect, developmental delays and behavioral problems • reduce welfare • improve maternal development	Home- and clinic-based Prenatal/Child-Health Home-Visiting Program	• participant interviews and nurse assessments at 24, 36, 46, and 48 months and 15 years postpartum • child testing at 36 and 48 months and 15 years postpartum and interviews at 15 years • pediatric and hospital records • state Child Protective Service records • NYS Division of Criminal Justice Services records (1977; 15-yr follow-up)	Repeat Pregnancy: Treatment < Control Months Between 1st and 2nd Birth: Treatment 65 vs. Control 37 % of Preterm Births (teens who smoked): Treatment 75% < Control Child Abuse/Neglect: Treatment < Control Months Receiving Welfare: Treatment 60 vs. Control 90 Maternal Substance Abuse Behavior Impairments and Arrests: Treatment < Control

Program	Sample	Goals	Measures	Findings
Memphis Home-Visiting Trial (Memphis) Kitzman et al. (1997); Olds et al. (1998)	Prenatal Phase: Treatment 1 $n = 458$ Control $n = 681$ Postnatal Phase: Treatment 2 $n = 228$ Control $n = 515$ 92% African American	• reduce pregnancy-induced hypertension • reduce repeat pregnancies • reduce low birthweight and preterm birth infants • reduce child injuries/ingestions and behavioral problems • improve child immunizations and mental development • improve maternal development	Home- and clinic-based Prenatal/Child-Health Home-Visiting Program • participant interviews at 28 and 36 weeks prenatal and at 6, 12, and 24 months postpartum • nurse assessments at 6, 12, and 24 months • obstetrical and hospital records • Tennessee Department of Human Services records	Prenatal: Pregnancy-Induced Hypertension: Treatment 1 13% vs. Control 1 20% Postnatal: Repeat Pregnancy: Treatment 2 36% vs. Control 2 47% Child Injuries/ Ingestions Needing Health Care: Treatment 2 < Control 2 Days Child Hospitalized for Injuries: Treatment 2 .03 vs. Control 2 .16

continued on next page

TABLE 11.2 (continued)

Program/Locus/ Authors	n/Ethnicity	Program Mandate	Setting/Delivery Methods	Data Source/Dates	Outcomes
Teenage Pregnancy & Parenting Project (TAPP) (San Francisco) Hanson (1992)	Treatment 1 (child's father included as formal client) Treatment 2 (child's father included as informal client) Control (child's father not included as client) N = 1,513	For adolescent mothers: • improve high school retention/graduation • reduce welfare • improve contraceptive use	School- and social-service-based Multicomponent Program (Case-Management and Family Support)	• program case files at birth, 6, and 12 months postpartum • Archive on Adolescent Pregnancy & Pregnancy Prevention (1981–1987)	At 6 months: High School Graduation: Treatment 1 22.73% vs. Treatment 2 9.34% vs. Control 4.96% Receiving Welfare: Treatment 1 36.36% vs. Treatment 2 43.70% vs. Control 68.42% Contraceptive Use: Treatment 1 and 2 > 90% vs. Control 68%
Teenage Pregnancy & Parenting Program (TAPP) (DeKalb County, Georgia) Fischer (1997)	Treatment n = 311 (school-based) Control n = 230 (clinic-based) 93% African American	• prevent repeat pregnancies • improve high school retention/graduation • improve employment • promote healthy pregnancies and parenting skills • completion of program goals	School- and clinic-based Multicomponent Program (Case-Management and Family-Support)	• program case files (school setting 1992–1994; clinic setting 1990–1992)	Repeat Pregnancy: Treatment 10% vs. Control 3% High School Retention/ Graduation: Treatment 84% vs. Control 50% Employment: Treatment 31% vs. Control 18% Program Goals Completed: Treatment 54% vs. Control 13%

Program/Citation	Sample	Goals	Intervention Type	Data Sources	Results
Chance to Grow Project (Dayton area) Donnelly & Davis-Berman (1994)	Treatment *n* = 161 53% White, 47% Non-White Control *n* = 87 70% White, 30% Non-White	• postpone repeat pregnancies • improve high school retention • improve employment • improve parenting and decision-making skills • provide adoption counseling	Clinic-based Multicomponent Program (Case-Management and Family-Support)	• program files at birth and 6, 12, and 24 months postpartum (1987–1993)	6 Months: Repeat Pregnancy: Treatment 8% vs. Control 19% Employment: Treatment 39% vs. Control 24% At 24 Months: High School Retention: Treatment 80% vs. Control 58% Adoption Rate: Treatment 43% vs. Control 0% Sexually Active: Treatment 57% vs. Control 75%
Home-Based Family Therapy Cherniss & Herzog (1996)	Treatment *n* = 58 (family therapy) Control *n* = 58 (individual therapy) 56% African American, 17% White, 27% Hispanic	• reduce welfare • improve quality of family support • improve adolescent mothers' quality of parenting	Home-based Multicomponent Program (Case-Management and Family-Support Therapy)	• participant self-reports • family self-reports • therapist assessments • at birth, 12, and 24 months postpartum	Receiving Welfare: Treatment < Control Family Support: Treatment > Control Adolescent Mothers' Quality of Parenting: Treatment > Control

continued on next page

Table 11.2 (continued)

Program/Locus/ Authors	n/Ethnicity	Program Mandate	Setting/Delivery Methods	Data Source/Dates	Outcomes
Ounce of Prevention Fund (OPF) Parents Too Soon Project (Illinois) Ruch-Ross, Jones, & Musick (1992)	Treatment n = 1,004 (OPF) 51.3% African American, 41.8% White, 6.9% Hispanic Control n = 790 (NLSY) 33.8% African American, 46.8% White, 19.4% Hispanic	• postpone repeat pregnancies • improve high school retention/graduation • reduce welfare • improve parenting skills • improve healthy child development	Home- and community-based Multicomponent program (Prenatal/Child-Health Home-Visiting and Peer-Support)	• program case files at 12 months postpartum • Data archive on adolescent pregnancy (OPF 1985–1987; NLSY 1979–1982)	Repeat Pregnancy: Treatment 10.7% vs. Control 14.8% High School Retention: Treatment 47.3% vs. Control 11.8% High School Graduation: Treatment 22.1% vs. Control 34.8% Receiving Welfare: Treatment 68.3% vs. Control 20.4%

grams have been piloted that focus on empowering young men and women to create work and housing opportunities for themselves, increase their social support and mentoring networks, and improve their self-esteem (e.g., Koniak-Griffin, 1994). Primary prevention programs have also developed innovative strategies that range from educating young adolescents about the financial costs of early parenting to drawing youth into making connections that matter with their communities (e.g., Allen, Philliber, Herrling, & Kuperminc, 1997). Although evaluations of these innovative programs are often limited by their newness, the small numbers of youth served, and the absence of adequate comparison groups, their impact on the young adult transitions of adolescent mothers is potentially enhanced by their efforts to build on competence and enhance resources available in the neighborhoods where they seek housing, education, child care, and jobs.

SUPPORTING THE TRANSITION TO EARLY ADULTHOOD: IMPLICATIONS FOR POLICY

This section discusses specific policy initiatives for adolescent mothers in the context of supporting their transitions to young adulthood. We review current initiatives in the light of this study's findings. We go on to suggest concrete policies that would address obstacles to adolescent mothers' success in becoming financially independent and in acquiring stable housing and social supports. Specifically, we address approaches to limiting fertility, reevaluating child support, fostering father involvement, supporting early adult transitions to work, addressing child-care needs, stabilizing housing, and promoting the physical and mental health of adolescent mothers and their children.

Many approaches are described. This is not to suggest that only costly, comprehensive programs can be effective for inner-city teen mothers. On the contrary, our research on the diversity of their outcomes suggests that targeted interventions that are responsive to the specific short-term needs of most adolescent mothers, as they make the transition to young adulthood, would be effective in removing obstacles that threaten to derail resilience in many of these young women. Our discussion of policy initiatives is intended to highlight the many potential points of intervention that could enhance the development of these young women—not only immediately after they become adolescent mothers, but before.

Limiting Fertility

Reducing out-of-wedlock births is the target of federal bonuses for the fiscal year 1999 to 2000, which will reward the five states that show greatest decreases in illegitimacy and abortion rates (Gillespie & Schellhas, 1994; PR&WOA of 1996). Despite the success of programmatic efforts in limiting subsequent births to adolescent mothers, recent efforts appear to be directed at sanctioning individuals rather than supporting program success. Policies that advocate family caps deny welfare benefits to children born to mothers already on welfare in an effort to control what is seen as irresponsible, promiscuous sexuality and refusals to work among these women (PR&WOA of 1996). Yet sanctions like family caps on welfare benefits are likely to be unsuccessful without taking into consideration factors beyond popular beliefs about women's sexual behaviors, including culturally based attitudes toward birth control and abortion and gender equity in sexuality and parenting.

Many of the mothers in the New York study, as elsewhere (e.g., Luker, 1996), voiced lack of knowledge about birth control, fears about abortions, and family disapproval of abortions as reasons why they had the baby. However, these women's ability to limit their fertility is not only driven by their knowledge of and access to effective birth control or abortion. Life course choices for the New York study women also figured into their decisions to have a second child. Mothers attending school had substantially fewer pregnancies than those who dropped out. Mothers who had one child were more likely to have graduated from high school and be working at the 6-year follow-up. Some women in the New York study acted on their belief that having all the children that they planned to have at about the same time (when they were home anyway with one) would free them to pursue work options when these children went to school. However, few understood the currently limited options and supports open to them as adult students. Few knew what they would need to reenter the educational system, and few anticipated how stresses related to having a second child to care for would affect the costs of returning to school. Programs that focus on teenage parents do not address the needs of women with school-age children who could take advantage of school-based training programs that operate on school schedules.

Domestic violence and childhood sexual abuse, educational and career aspirations and opportunities, depressed affect, and nonegalitarian gender role attitudes also have an impact on decisions to use birth control effectively, have abortions, or bear children. Policies addressing these problems are relevant to efforts to limit unwanted pregnancies in teens. Sex education programs must provide information with discussions of gender roles.

Our data also suggest that there is clearly a need to address issues of gender equity with respect to women and men's roles—not only for birth control, but also for responsible parenting. The belief that mothers' child-care roles were obligatory, whereas fathers' roles were optional, was widely held by the New York study mothers. Their beliefs that birth control and responsibility for children born out of wedlock are primarily women's concerns were also consistently reinforced because their partners could not assume responsibility for their children due to unemployment, imprisonment, domestic violence, drug use, or promiscuity. Infidelity and promiscuity were also among the major reasons for the relationships ending and for fathers withdrawing their involvement. Efforts to support more than one child with differing mothers create overwhelming difficulties for these young fathers. The financial demands of supporting more than one child frequently cannot be met, forcing them to painfully choose which child they will support.

Policy Implications: Birth Control

- Education and policy that guide young men toward responsible parenting not only by mandating child-support payments (as we discuss next), but also through enlisting their actions in preventing pregnancies, limiting partners, and avoiding early childbearing are urgently needed. Fathering children is too often seen as a right of manhood rather than as a responsibility of fatherhood. There is little doubt that responsibility for fatherhood must start in gender equity in attitudes toward the responsible use of birth control, respect for women's autonomy, and intolerance of sexual harassment. One 12th-grade student put it:

The percentage of teen-aged girls who have been raped has risen dramatically and yet no one has educated them on their sexual rights.... no teacher talks about rape and the link with alcohol and nobody [in my Career and Personal Planning class] has ever told me that I am more likely to be raped by a boyfriend than a stranger in a dark alley.... Sexual harassment occurs daily in most high schools yet no one recognizes it as a crime and tries to prevent it. I believe the only way to prevent sexual harassment in school is to educate the minds of the future. (Sidhu, 1999, p. D2)

- Abstinence programs are unlikely to decrease sexual activity in adolescents who are already sexually active. Ample research has demonstrated that increasing use of contraception, as well as access to education and work opportunities, can reduce the incidence of early parenting and its negative effects.
- Direct education and counseling about birth control options is needed for adolescents having abortions and for adolescents who bear children. It must elicit and be sensitive to these women's beliefs (sometimes mistaken, but firmly held) about the morality and acceptability to male partners, risks, and side effects of different birth control methods.
- Inexpensive access to birth control needs to be improved. Frequent visits to hospital or community-based family planning or health clinics that have long waiting lines will not be made by young mothers with young children. Appointments that interfere with education or work schedules cannot be kept. Alternative distribution methods are needed (e.g., through school health clinics, local drug stores, welfare and food stamp distributors, health professionals conducting well-child visits and immunization clinics). Phone contacts and home-visiting services by paraprofessionals to monitor side effects of and compliance/difficulties with birth control methods could reduce the need for face-to-face follow-up visits with health professionals, particularly for women at low risk for side effects.
- Education programs, health insurance, welfare, child care, and family leave policies must promote gender equity in access to and responsibility for birth control, child support, and childrearing.

- Education about birth control needs to be made more public. In a society that barrages children with TV, movie, and advertising messages showing explicit sexual behaviors, taboos against discussing birth control methods, and restrictions on advertising birth control contribute to the perception that the use of birth control constitutes deviant behavior for adolescents, whereas sexual activity is normative.

Beyond Child Support: Fostering the Capacity for Nurturant Fathering

Policy planning for unwed fathers with young infants and children has focused on paternity identification to enforce child support mandates. However, as described later, policies that are designed to promote responsible fatherhood in divorced fathers can create disincentives for never-married fathers of the children of mothers receiving public assistance (Bernard, 1998). These are not deadbeat dads; they are at best dads in training.

Rhetoric concerning mandated paternity identification as a condition for welfare benefits for adolescent mothers suggests that either their desires to protect their partners from financial responsibility or their limited future perspective fuels a reluctance to name their child's fathers at the birth of their child. Discussing factors that might interfere with establishing paternity, Levin-Epstein (1996) asked "How can the state best communicate with a teenager about the life-long advantages to the teen and her child of establishing paternity and child support when teens typically have little orientation to the future?" (p. 60). Although this is a popular belief, there is little evidence that lack of a future perspective characterizes the majority of adolescents' thinking.

Indeed, thinking about future possibilities is among the cognitive advances of early adolescence (Keating, 1990). Several mothers in this study contrast the differences between living day to day without much hope of positive changes or building a rock for the future. Discouragement in the face of overwhelming obstacles rather than limitations in cognition due to immaturity is the likely cause of present-oriented thinking among some adolescent mothers. For many young women, the reality is that their relationships with drug-addicted, unemployed, jailed, abusive, or promiscuous men have no future. We might better ask: How can poor adolescent mothers best communicate to the state the conditions of their lives that make establishing paternity an inadequate approach to the problems in these relationships and their ability to care for their children?

Under the PR&WOA of 1996, requirements for unwed minor fathers are vague and merely suggest they fulfill "community work obligations" or take "parenting or money management classes after school" (Levin-Epstein, 1996, p. 62). No incentives are directed at the creation of the means for greater participation of these young fathers in their children's economic support. Strategies that promote the establishment of paternity and the formation and maintenance of two-parent families are encouraged, but are not specified. States are given the option of making parents of noncustodial fathers who are minors financially responsible for their offspring.

Studies estimate that less than a third of the fathers of adolescent mothers' children are under 18 (Landry & Darroch- Forrest, 1995; Lindberg, Sonenstein, Ku, & Martinez, 1997), whereas 19% are 6 or more years older than these mothers (Alan Guttmacher Institute, 1994). In the New York study, the biological fathers were 3 years older than the mothers on average. In contrast to the mothers, who are thought of as children having children at age 18, the fathers of these children are considered adults at 18. Restrictions under the PR&WOA of 1996 create disadvantages for these families. When they are receiving welfare benefits, they are subject to the loss of child-support payments. As a condition of eligibility for Temporary Assistance for Needy Families (TANF), which is the replacement for AFDC, unwed mothers are required to cooperate in the establishment of paternity, but they must assign child-support rights to the state. This means the state, not the family, collects the child-support payments established through court proceedings. On average, court-ordered support represents 28% of the fathers' income. These payback programs were designed to reimburse the state for benefits given to the family when deadbeat dads avoided their responsibilities following marriage breakdowns. With AFDC, the first $50 collected was allowed to pass through to the family. With the new legislation, there is no requirement that any amount of child support be passed through to families. As a result of these policies, there is no observable association between the amount of child support given by biological fathers and family income for adolescent mothers receiving welfare. By limiting the potential economic benefit of these child support payments to families formed by young, unwed parents, this legislation not only guarantees the stability of poverty in their lives, but also undermines the financial benefits of remaining in a relationship. Mothers who remain involved with their child's biological father lose child support income to the state. When the biological father stays involved, TANF becomes a loan that must be repaid. In contrast, mothers who form new relationships with men who are not related to their child can receive economic support from these men that cannot be garnished to reimburse state coffers.

Establishing paternity with fathers who are unable to be positively involved in their children's lives or add to their economic well-being, and who are unlikely to become involved in the future, can become merely another bureaucratic hoop that is unlikely to have any positive effect on income or welfare use among adolescent mothers.

The mothers in the New York study were keenly aware of the multiple risks and economic disadvantages that can be part of marriage or cohabitation with their children's fathers. They reported dignity and self-respect in becoming able to support their children themselves, even if it meant budgeting meager welfare incomes. Leaving abusive or otherwise negative relationships motivated several mothers to take control of their futures. Our research and that of others (see Garfinkel & McLanahan, 1997; Leadbeater, Way, & Raden, 1996) also shows that involvement of nonresidential fathers is not uniformly positive for their children. It can be detrimental if it increases conflict between the custodial and non custodial parents or increases their exposure to domestic violence, drugs, or criminal activities.

This is a choice point for policymakers. Funds spent on identifying noncustodial, unwed fathers and setting up procedures for garnishing their intermittent or nonexistent child support could be spent on programs that enhance their long-term ability to support their families economically or that enhance children's incomes directly. Dollar levels for assets that can be accumulated and earned income ceilings for welfare recipients must be raised to move families above the poverty level. If establishing paternity provided some benefit to young fathers in terms of education, training, access to their children when in jail, couples counseling, family income, or their children's actual income levels, voluntary establishment of paternity would also be more likely.

Policy Implications: Nurturant Fathering

- Changes are needed in the rhetoric that surrounds these young families. Adolescent mothers are not "children having children" or "unwed mothers." Similarly, the fathers of these children are not "deadbeat dads." The status of these young families might better be understood as couples with young children. Many adolescent mothers are not single parents.
- Child-support payments from noncustodial, unwed fathers of families on TANF with children under the age of 3 should be exempt from state payback requirements. The entire child-support payments should be passed through to these families—to make benefits of the relationship visible and support transitions to work.
- Income supplements should be provided for children whose fathers cannot provide for them by reason of illness, disability, imprisonment, unemployment, and so on while the fathers are engaged in education or job training programs, again making clear the financial advantages of maintaining connections between children and their fathers.
- Mothers' and fathers' work should be rewarded by allowing for direct increases in family income up to levels that are set substantially higher than what can be gained on TANF alone.
- The availability of and eligibility for job training and education should be increased for the biological fathers of children under 3 in families receiving TANF.
- Women should be exempt from establishing paternity when the pregnancy was due to rape or when the involvement imposes risk to the child's well-being through abuse, domestic violence, drug addiction, or exposure to criminal behaviors.
- In-kind support from unemployed fathers (including child care and contributions of food, clothing, transportation, housing, etc.) should be credited as child support to promote involvement.
- Community- and church-based family preparation courses and parenting education must focus on equity in relationships. Relationship building and conflict resolution counseling needs to be made available for adolescent couples at the time of the first birth.

- In the event of breakdowns in the couples' relationship, the biological fathers' access to and positive relationships with their children need to be supported.

Beyond Welfare: Supporting the Transition to Earning a Living Wage

Welfare assistance programs for adolescent mothers must be particularly tailored for them or they run the risk of derailing their efforts to gain social capital and lift themselves out of poverty. As adolescents, these young mothers are not the long-term welfare recipients who are addressed in the federal legislation. However, they are at risk of becoming welfare dependent if their transitions to young adulthood are not supported.

Policy debates concerning the relative advantages of building human capital among welfare recipients or mandating their rapid entry into jobs have recently resolved in favor of the latter (Zaslow & Eldred, 1998). Such policies could negatively affect adolescent mothers' transitions to early adulthood if their particular circumstances are not considered. For mothers under 18 without high school graduation diplomas, school attendance and residence with an adult is mandatory. For mothers who are at their ideal age for grade, high school graduation is typically at age 18. For mothers under the age of 20, school attendance can be counted under the PR&WOA of 1996 toward states' work participation rates (up to an overall limit of 20% of the states' caseload). Women over 20 must work after receiving benefits for 24 months. This policy is particularly damaging for the most resilient of adolescent mothers who could begin and complete a 4-year college degree in their early 20s with extended support. In the best-case scenario, an 18-year-old adolescent mother receiving TANF who has graduated on time from high school and enters a full-time, 4-year college program immediately could finish a college or bachelor's degree by age 22 and move into a higher paying job that could end welfare dependence. However, this scenario also collapses if any factor in the age-benefits equation changes. For example, if a mother is a year behind her ideal grade for her age and does not graduate from high school until she is 19, she can only finish 2 years of a college program by age 22, when work requirements would begin; if a mother remains home for 12 months to care for her infant, she loses an equivalent amount for educational pursuits. If an 18-year-old high school graduate returns to school at age 23 when her child is in school, she may have no remaining assistance for education.

At the delivery of their first child, the mothers in the New York study were 17 years old on average and most were from families that received welfare. Women from families on welfare were more likely to have experienced a year or more delay in their grade placement and had achieved fewer years of schooling than those not on welfare. In other words, mothers who were most in need of assistance would not be able to use the assistance to gain the educational capital that would allow them to enter higher income categories. As it stands, the PR&WOA of 1996 builds in restraints that impede access to education and work opportunities for adolescent mothers.

As we have seen for most of the adolescent mothers in the New York study, welfare dependency was not due to a lack of work motivation or a purposeful decision to have multiple children on welfare. Continued adherence to these simplistic beliefs about the causes of women's welfare dependency prevents establishing policies directed at enhancing the success of their transitions to financial independence as young adults. Our findings show that adolescent childbearing was but one of many obstacles to financial independence for poor young women. Pre-pregnancy school history remained the strongest predictor of school outcomes for the mothers in the New York study 6 years after their first birth. Depression, stressful life events, health problems, repeat pregnancies, Hispanic ethnicity, and lack of family support for education also influenced educational outcomes for the adolescent mothers in the New York study. The interview data also suggest that overlapping disadvantages, including lack of family support and opportunities for education and career development, chronic illnesses (HIV, asthma, depression, etc.), physical illness or behavioral problems among the children, involvement in abusive or restrictive relationships with men, and lack of or fears about day care, also contributed to poor school outcomes in these mothers.

The New York study is limited in its focus on adolescent mothers and their families' support for education. The quality of career education in the schools that they attended was not assessed. Most of the young mothers in the New York study wanted to work after their children were in school, but many aspired to low-income jobs because these seemed to be the only jobs within reach. Education about a full range of career options, with onsite experiences, needs to start in the early school years for poor girls (Brooks & Buckner, 1996; De Leon, 1996). Most of the mothers in the New York study did not come from families with steady or higher income work, nor did they have family models of women with higher paying careers to enhance their own career aspirations. Yet working will not be optional for these young women; even those who live with a partner will not escape poverty without two incomes.

Creative solutions to education and job training need to be supported for inner-city families living in neighborhoods with high rates of unemployment. Financial support, participatory learner-centered training, ongoing technical assistance, mentoring and establishing networking mechanisms, appropriate credit services, marketing assistance, and cooperation of welfare programs to permit asset building were all needed to promote the success of low-income entrepreneurs funded by the MS Foundation for Women (Wadia, 1997). Innovative models of women who run businesses (coffee shops, thrift stores, etc.) that provide onsite, subsidized training for a year are beginning to emerge and have the potential to ease the transition to work for some women.

Policy Implications: Education

- Steps must be taken to improve the motivation of inner-city youth to remain in school and improve their access to secondary education and skilled career choices. Dropout rates for all adolescents exceeded 50% in many of the neighborhoods where the mothers in the New York study lived.

- Special initiatives are particularly needed to prevent early school failure and increase career aspirations among girls from poor families (e.g., through preventing early school failure among girls from poor families through early follow-up of absences, mentoring [advisor/advisee] programs, remediation, special programs for parenting adolescents, mental health services for abused girls, and family involvement programs).
- Cooperative and apprenticeship career development programs must be instituted for middle school girls to help them to reach beyond low-paying jobs by increasing their knowledge of and exposure to jobs with potentials for higher wage earnings and advancement.
- Long-term cooperative programs that allow for both continued education and paid employment across several years of the early adult transition would aid young families that must spread their time resources between gaining education and earning enough to support their children.
- The mothers of adolescent mothers need to be involved in career development programs aimed at their daughters to increase their support. Girls often miss school to care for younger family members or family emergencies. Savings for children's education must be tax deductible and exempt from asset calculations for low-income families.
- State educational resources need to be redistributed to compensate for the greater needs of inner-city school children. School readiness and social skills training programs, smaller student–teacher ratios, career options training, work-apprenticeship programs, cooperative programs, library and computer resources, as well as mental and physical health services are needed to offset disadvantages of poor children. Although wealthier school districts can increase school resources and services through such means as volunteer work (primarily supplied by at-home mothers) and fundraisers directed at parents, poor working families cannot make these contributions. This removes an important avenue of informal support and funding for schools in poorer neighborhoods. Tax incentives could be promoted for individuals and businesses to invest in Registered Educational Savings Plans for the education of youth from schools in poor neighborhoods (e.g., The New York City: I Have A Dream Project promised each fifth grader a 4-year scholarship when they entered college).

Policy Implications: Work

- Many employers cannot afford to employ and train young mothers who may need flexible time schedules, personal days off for child care and illnesses, day-care assistance, and so on. In high unemployment labor markets, economic incentives to compensate employers that hire and train young adults are needed.
- Reducing stresses associated with work for parents (particularly through accessible day care, flexible scheduling, personal days for child illnesses, etc.) is imperative for stability of their labor market engagement.

- Commuting to jobs creates costs in transportation, time, and child care that can be excessive for poor families. To our knowledge, no study has evaluated the effects of differences in the availability (e.g., time of day scheduled) and accessibility (e.g., distance traveled) of job opportunities, child care, and educational programs for adolescent parents on their successful transitions to work.
- Incentives (through training and financial support) of small business endeavors initiated by adolescent mothers, particularly those with long-term growth prospects, are needed. (Some mothers in the New York study informally offered hair dressing, child care, bakery, and computer services, but unstable income from these endeavors threaten the stability of their AFDC and Medicaid.) Longer term provision of health insurance and training allowances are needed to support enterprises begun by poor women.

Child Care

In the New York study and elsewhere (Presser, 1989), relative care was by far the preferred mode of care for children under the age of 3. Concerns about the safety of preverbal children in day-care centers were widespread. The choice of relative care for children over 3 was income dependent and used more frequently by young mothers who were employed. Yet characteristics of home environments that foster school readiness and health of young children are limited for families on welfare (Zill et al., 1997).

Overall, the preference of relative care and disadvantages of out-of-home care for adolescent mothers creates a dilemma for policymakers. What advantages would be gained by increasing day-care stipends to adolescent mothers if they generally prefer relative care that is convenient, low or no cost, and perceived to be safer for nonverbal children? Generalizations from what works for some mothers to what should be policy for all mothers are short sighted.

The teenage mothers who lack support from their families were often at risk for noninvolvement in job-related activities in the New York study. Policies for child care cannot be driven by fantasies about what families should be able to do to support adolescent mothers and their children. For mothers without access to relative care, child-care costs may average 23% of a single mothers' income (Cherlin, 1997) and can force the choice between work or nonwork in favor of the latter. State reluctance to get involved in child care for the children of adolescent mothers for fear of enticing those with support from grandmothers is misplaced. These informal day-care relationships depend on the quality of these mother–daughter relationships, the durability of the grandmothers' availability as a volunteer caregiver, and the family's beliefs about the safety of out-of-home care for preverbal children. The preponderance of evidence also suggests that experiences of center-based care of good quality may indeed improve poor children's competence to enter school.

Policy Implications: Child Care

- Mothers on welfare who are caring for their own children and want to return to school or jobs would benefit from community-based, part-time GED programs with onsite day care.
- Programs that pay relatives to care for preverbal children should be continued.
- Community-based day-care centers must acknowledge and be sensitive to these women's beliefs that they cannot trust strangers with their children. Procedures and standards for ensuring children's safety and parents' ability to monitor their children's care (e.g., encouraging drop-in visits by parents or a designated relative) need to be in place and visible in all public centers.

Housing

Debates and policy initiatives for adolescent mothers have rarely addressed their housing problems beyond mandating residence with an adult for mothers under age 18. Adolescent mothers face extremely limited access to housing due to multiple levels of housing discrimination that disfavor minorities, adolescents, single mother-headed households, families with young children, jobless individuals, and low-income earners. As Wekerle (1997) argued,

> The ability to pay affects housing choice, location and tenure; the segmented labor market means that women who are predominately low paid, in part-time employment, and have low earning compared with men, experience disadvantages in the housing market. (p. 177)

For many of the New York mothers, considerable and continuous effort was needed to secure and maintain a stable residence. On average, mothers lived in 3.5 residences over the 6-year period—17.2% moved six or more times. Income versus expense equations for adolescent mothers determine work versus welfare options. Housing represents the biggest monthly expense for these mothers, with rents routinely exceeding their total welfare benefits (Children's Defense Fund, 1995). In addition, saving the necessary security deposit for living independently is an arduous or impossible task for most of these young women, and accruing these savings can result in reductions in welfare benefits. Housing is also a problem of income security. Wage interruptions as these young women went on and off welfare and in and out of low-income jobs also affected their ability to pay housing costs, putting them at risk for evictions.

Access to low-cost housing or rent-proportioned-to-income housing can determine whether women are able to secure stable, safe residences. In the New York study, conflicts with family members, extreme overcrowding, domestic violence, and long waits for housing sent adolescent mothers and their children into shelters, thereby raising the ranks of homelessness. Unstable housing disrupted many aspects of the adolescent mothers' lives. When moves were the result of evictions, fires, family illnesses or violence, and crises in relationships, having a safe place to live took priority over schooling, job searches, or making child-care arrangements.

Several of the adolescent mothers in the New York study expressed the desire to relocate out of inner-city neighborhoods to pursue job opportunities, provide a safer environment for their children, or escape abusive partners, but they could not save the money needed for a move. Some would benefit from incentives to move to areas where they would be more likely to get work. Having relatives in the new site who offered support as well as direct assistance in job finding would help stabilize these moves. Subsidized relocation costs would be needed for these mothers.

The adolescent mothers in the New York study and their mothers were concentrated in substandard housing by limited incomes. Their children attended neighborhood schools with few resources and other children also from poor families. Commitments to education, career aspirations, and possible futures are envisioned in these limiting early experiences with peers. These experiences form the basis for adolescents' efforts to prepare themselves for young adulthood. The intergenerational cycle of poverty is re-created by the stability of these contextual factors. The need for stable housing for poor women is acute.

Policy Implications: Housing

- Increased access of young mothers to low-cost housing in mixed-income neighborhoods would go a long way in improving their access to other resources and breaking the cycle of poverty for their children.
- Stabilizing income security for adolescent mothers and allowing credit for housing expenses and savings directed at securing stable housing is essential to increase their capacity to benefit from education or job training programs.
- Incentives for alternative, shared, or cooperative housing (e.g., with sisters and friends) would be more successful in supporting mothers who cannot afford housing, rather than regulations that deny welfare to teen mothers who do not live with their own mothers or another adult.
- Women-initiated and women-managed housing projects have been developed in some areas. These offer alternate models of housing that include more than shelter. These projects work to enhance available supports by providing counseling, early childhood education centers, and child care (Wekerle, 1997).

Health and Illnesses

Health problems contributed directly or indirectly to negative outcomes for several of the mothers in the New York study. Programming and policy debates have addressed the needs for prenatal care of adolescent mothers to reduce obstetrical complications and improve infant health. Beliefs that good prenatal care could reduce poor birth outcomes for the children of adolescent mothers fueled the expansion of Medicaid in 1980 (Hughes & Runyan, 1995). The success of prenatal care programs in improving outcomes for the children of adolescent mothers has been documented (McCarthy & Hardy, 1993). Efforts to improve infant nutrition through Women, Infants, and Children (WIC) food supplement programs and increased childhood immunizations have also shown considerable success in reaching needy children. Public education campaigns to prevent fetal alcohol, sudden infant death, and shaken baby syndromes are also reaching audiences of teenagers.

Nevertheless, the singular focus on health concerns that impact infants and children has overshadowed concerns about maternal health problems. Investments in these mothers' health problems essentially stop at delivery. The absence of secondary prevention and treatment programs that address stresses related to the chronic physical and mental health problems of adolescent mothers is particularly stark. Despite that accidents (often drug or alcohol related), homicides, and suicides are the leading causes of deaths in adolescents, secondary prevention efforts and mental health treatments that could address these problems are generally not available for youth. Domestic violence is the leading cause of physical injury to women (Davis & Smith, 1995), and programs to assist women to leave violent relationships are needed.

Stresses associated with illnesses frequently overwhelmed the mothers' efforts to return to school or work by creating obstacles to employment and day care. Employers are unwilling and often unable to take on health costs of chronically ill mothers or their children, or to subsidize the mothers' days off. Grandmothers who were ill could not provide child care or residential and financial support to adolescent mothers and their children. Several grandmothers in the New York study had died (of cancer or heart problems) or were drug involved.

Mental health problems that affected outcomes for both the adolescent mothers and their children are almost completely neglected in current policy debates and program efforts. Yet our research also pointed repeatedly to the negative effects of psychological distress on outcomes for adolescent mothers and their children. Depressive symptoms contributed to increases in stressful life events for these mothers and to increases in problem behaviors for their children. In the New York study, only mothers who were suicidal had received brief treatment for mental health problems. Treatment for severe trauma, childhood physical and sexual abuse or neglect, domestic violence, or depression was brief or nonexistent. One mother was receiving treatment for a long-standing drug addiction 6 years after her first child was born and only after her three children had been placed in foster care. Domestic violence also interferes with early adult transitions—not only through the physical injuries inflicted, but by restricting women's efforts to become self-sustaining, undermining self-efficacy, and increasing the likelihood of days lost at work (Davis & Smith, 1995). In the New York study, apart from police intervention (often repeated) and the treatment of physical injuries, few mothers sought or received any kind of help to deal with abusive partners. Reasons for leaving abusive relationships included hoping to protect themselves and their children, gaining control over their own resources, having family that could offer support to them, and an intolerance to being hit even once. Mothers who remained in these relationships lacked the emotional and physical resources that would allow them to leave. Childhood histories of physical and sexual abuse, overwhelming depression, financial dependency, and isolation from family are known obstacles to leaving these relationships.

Policy Implications: Health

- Mental health problems, particularly depression, must become the focus of major public health education and treatment efforts for adolescent mothers.
- Expanding Medicaid and insurance coverage for mental health problems could result in better school and employment outcomes for adolescent mothers and fewer problem behaviors in their children.
- Frontline workers (e.g., nurses, pediatric specialists, pediatricians) must be trained to diagnose, treat, or refer, if necessary, moderate depression in the mothers of children whom they see for preventive well-child care. An integrated family approach to both mental and physical health care is needed to reduce the negative effects of domestic violence and mental health problems for adolescent mothers and their children.
- Supplemental health insurance for poor working families with chronic health problems is needed to ease employers' burdens of providing flexible work schedules for these families and to reduce the effects of this disability on work.
- Policies that support programming to stop domestic violence would also aid the early adult transitions of adolescent mothers and the healthy development of their children. It is possible that one of the mechanisms underlying the effectiveness of home-visiting programs for adolescent mothers is to reduce the isolation of those experiencing domestic violence, although more restrictive partners could also prevent these visits. Training of police officers to deal effectively with domestic violence and initiate care for child witnesses to violence is essential.
- Treatments for child and sexual abuse must recognize that negative effects of these experiences can emerge in adolescence, when sexuality and desires for intimate partnerships come to bear on life decisions. Counseling services to adolescent mothers and adolescents undergoing abortions need to treat the sequelae of abuse for affected young women.
- Public education campaigns against domestic violence need to address early markers of abusive relationships (threats, intimidation, jealousy, controlling behaviors) and effective resistance strategies for teens (e.g., see "Love Doesn't Have to Hurt Teens" published by the American Psychological Association, 1998). Effective elementary school campaigns have addressed issues such as not talking to strangers and respecting *private parts*. Public media and education campaigns against gender inequities in relationships and intimate violence need to be extended to high school students.

Overall, the bottom-line message of this study for reform of policies for adolescent mothers must be regarded as hopeful. There is considerable diversity in outcomes, even for poor inner-city minority group adolescent mothers. At the birth of their first child, most are highly motivated to improve their own and their children's lives. In the 6 years after the birth of their first child, there are clearly many targets and times for effective interventions that can set the course for adaptive, independent adult functioning. Investments in these young women's transitions to adulthood may pay off in future gains for these young women and their children. Real reform is needed to rethink how to support the early adult transitions of adolescent mothers.

Appendix A:
Description of Measures

᷄

MEASURES

Questionnaire Data

Risk Variables

Occupational Commitment.   Occupational commitment was coded from mothers' responses to open-ended questions that explored current work aspirations: "Would you like to be working?" "At what?" "What would your ideal job be say in 5 years?" "How do you plan to achieve your goals?" "Have you begun to work toward these goals?" These were coded for work aspirations as 0 (*no choice elicited*), 1 (*gives a vague choice or several possible choices*), or 2 (*gives a clear statement of work aspirations*); has plans for achieving goals as 0 (*no*) or 1 (*yes*); and is currently pursing goals as 0 (*no*) or 1 (*yes*). Scores were summed to give a score for overall occupational commitment, with high scores reflecting a clear choice with plans for achieving that goal as well as active pursuit of it. Agreement on codes for two coders for a third of the interviews was 79% for choice, 85% for having plans, and 89% for active pursuit.

Plans to Seek Postsecondary Education.   Plans to seek postsecondary education was coded as 0 (*no*) or 1 (*yes*) from mothers' responses to questions about their plans for achieving their career goals. Agreement for two coders for a third of the interviews was 89%.

Delayed Grade Placement.   Being "over-age" for grade level, a correlate of eventual school dropout (Hahn, Danzberger, & Lefkowitz, 1987), was calculated as the discrepancy score between the mother's last grade completed and her ideal grade placement if she had entered Grade 1 by age 6 and had not been retained subsequently (Foltz, Klerman, & Jekel, 1972). High school graduation or attainment of a GED was set as the highest ideal level of achievement because only five of the mothers had some postsecondary education by Time 5.

Demographic Variables.   Information on several demographic variables, including mother's age at first birth, ethnicity, receipt of AFDC, number of months the teen mother had lived with her own mother or the person who raised her during the first year postpartum, and child gender, was obtained from maternal reports during the first year postpartum and at Time 6.

Depressive Symptoms.   The Beck Depression Inventory (BDI; Beck, 1967) is a widely used, 21-item questionnaire that assesses cognitive, behavioral, affective, and somatic symptoms of depression. Weighted response categories were scored from 0 to 3 for each of the 21 items and summed to yield a single score. The inventory has been shown to have good internal consistency and stability in nonclinical populations (Beck, Steer, & Garbin, 1988), as well as good sensitivity and specificity to discriminate depressed and nondepressed adolescents on the basis of structured clinical interviews (Barrerra & Garrison-Jones, 1988; Beck, Carlson, Russell, & Brownfield, 1987). Its psychometric properties have been established for minority adolescents (Leadbeater & Linares, 1992).

Life Stress.   Life stresses were assessed using the Life Events Scale (Egeland, Breitenbucher, & Rosenberg, 1980), which is a structured interview that investigates occurrence of and circumstances surrounding 44 events common to low-income primiparous women. For example, frequently reported events included unemployment for themselves or someone they were dependent on, school problems, moves, inadequate housing, chronic illnesses in immediate family, deaths of family members or close friends, involvement in physical fights, changes in social life, problems with relatives, and unstable relations with boyfriends. Minor modifications were made to make items relevant to adolescent mothers. The interview format includes examples reflecting degrees of disruption resulting from the event. Higher scores (on a scale of 0–3) reflect greater disruption due to the greater frequency or longer duration of the event, closeness of the relationships involved, or consequences of the event. To ensure that the ratings reflected the mother's perceived degree of stress, she was also asked to rate how stressful the event was for her on a scale of 1 to 10. Total scores were moderately stable at 1, 6, and 12 months postpartum ($r = .43–.52$).

Self-Critical and Interpersonal Vulnerability.   The 66-item Depressive Experiences Questionnaire for Adolescents (DEQ–A) was developed for participants ranging from early (age 12) through late adolescence (Blatt et al., 1992) and was based on the widely used adult Depressive Experiences Questionnaire. Three factor scores are consistently identified in data with adults, college students, and adolescents. They are Dependency (or interpersonal vulnerabilities), including items such as "Without the support of others who are close to me, I would be helpless" and "You have to work hard to get other people to love you"; Self-criticism, including items such as "If I fail to live up to expectations, I feel unworthy" and "Other people expect a lot of me"; and Efficacy (e.g., "I have many strengths and abilities"). The efficacy factor is not used here.

Responses are given on a Likert-type scale ranging from 1 (*strongly disagree*) to 7 (*strongly agree*). The construct validity and psychometric properties of the Interpersonal and Self-Criticism scales of the Adult Depressive Experiences Questionnaire have been supported (Zuroff, Moskowitz, Wielgus, Powers, & Franko, 1983; Zuroff, Quinlan, & Blatt, 1990). The reliability and validity of these factors for the DEQ–A have also been documented among high school samples ranging from lower to upper middle socioeconomic status (Blatt et al., 1992; Blatt, Hart, Quinlan, Leadbeater, & Auerbach, 1993; Luthar & Blatt, 1995).

Social Support Variables

Child-Care Assistance.   As an assessment of concrete support provided by the maternal or paternal grandmothers or from the person who raised the adolescent mother, child-care assistance was determined from a questionnaire administered at the 12-month assessment. Provision of regular child-care assistance was coded from a timeline chart as 0 ("No, grandmother does not help or helps very rarely") or 1 ("Yes, grandmother shares in the child's care").

Child's Father's Involvement.   The father's support of the child was coded from the mother's descriptions of the child's relationship with the father from the interview data as 1 (*little or no contact*), 2 (*sees child but does not have a good relationship*), or 3 (*sees child frequently and has a close relationship*). Descriptions of the father's relationship to the mother were coded as 1 (*little or no contact*), 2 (*neutral relationship*), or 3 (*sees frequently in a warm, emotionally supportive relationship*). Agreements for two coders for one third of the interviews were 95% for relationship with the child and 89% for relationship with the mother.

Child's Father's Noninvolvement.   Reasons for noninvolvement with the child's father were coded as 0 (*no problems mentioned*), 1 (*immature, irresponsible, seeing other women*), 2 (*excessively macho, restrictive, or physically abusive*), 3 (*involved in selling or using drugs*), 4 (*in prison*), or 5 (*dead*). All categories mentioned were noted. However, scores analyzed reflect the highest category given, reasoning that the problems overlapped (i.e., prison terms and violent deaths were often for drug-related reasons), and those at higher levels reflected greater likelihood that fathers were unavailable. Agreement between two coders was 84%.

Perceived Social Support.   The Perceived Social Support from Family (PSSFA) and Perceived Social Support from Friends (PSSFR) scales (Procidano & Heller, 1983) were used as a measure of the perceived quality of emotional support received. Although many social support measures are available, this one has the advantage of focusing specifically on the quality of emotional relations to family and friends (Tardy, 1985). Reported internal consistencies are high ($\alpha = .90$ for PSSFA and .88 for PSSFR), as is test–retest reliability ($r = .80$; Tardy, 1985). In our sample, internal consistencies were also high ($\alpha = .90–.91$). For both PSSFA and

PSSFR, scores from each of the three assessments during the first year postpartum were averaged.

At Time 6, a more extensive assessment of social support and frequency of contact with each network member was obtained using the Norbeck Social Support Questionnaire (NSSQ; Norbeck, Lindsey, & Carrieri, 1981). On a 5-point Likert-type scale, mothers rated the supportiveness and frequency of contact with each network member. Ratings were summed for each network member. Overall scores for family support consist of totals of ratings for the adolescent's mother, father, and any other older relatives. Overall scores for friends' support consist of totals of ratings for all peers (i.e., people not more than 3 years older or younger than the adolescent mother). Previous research has demonstrated the reliability and validity of the NSSQ (Norbeck et al., 1981; Norbeck, Lindsey, & Carrieri, 1983).

Quality of Grandmother–Daughter Relationships.   The quality of the relationships were assessed using the maternal subscale of the Mother–Father–Peer Scales (Epstein, 1983). This scale assesses whether mothers agree or disagree on a 5-point Likert-type scale with statements reflecting childhood experiences of acceptance versus rejection (e.g., "When I was a child my mother enjoyed being with me") and encouragement of independence versus overprotection (e.g., "When I was a child my mother encouraged me to do things for myself"). Concurrent correlations with current family support (PSSFA) were high (r = .58–.63 for acceptance and r = .52–.61 for encouragement of independence). A shorter version of the measure was used previously with adolescent mothers and has high reliability (Crockenberg, 1987). Alphas of .81 for acceptance and .88 for independence scales are reported by Epstein (1983).

Residence With the Grandmother.   Residence with the grandmother (i.e., the adolescent mother's mother) was established at each assessment from self-reports on a timeline chart. At Times 3 and 6, a code of 1 was given if the adolescent mother lived with her own mother and 0 if she did not.

Romantic Partners' Support.   The mothers' descriptions of relationships with men other than their children's fathers were coded as 1 (*no relationship*), 2 (*seeing someone in a conflicted or neutral relationship*), or 3 (*sees frequently in a warm, emotionally supportive relationship*). Agreement between two coders for one third of the interviews was 95%.

Outcome Variables

Child Outcomes.   Information on birthweight and gestational age was recorded from medical records. Temperament was rated by mothers at child age 6 months on the Perception of Baby Temperament Instrument (Pederson, Zaslow, Cain, Anderson, & Thomas, 1980). The Bayley Scales of Infant Development (Bayley, 1969) provided scores for the child's mental development index (MDI) and physical development index (PDI). Language development was evaluated on the Sequenced Inventory of Communication Development (SICD; Hendrick, Prather, & Tobin, 1984), which yields scores representing deviations from age norms for both receptive and expressive communication. The SICD is significantly correlated with the Peabody Picture Vocabulary Test (Hendrick et al., 1984).

Mothers' reports of child behavior problems were obtained using the CBCL/2-3 (Achenbach, 1992) at Time 5 and the CBCL/4-18 (Achenbach, 1991) at Time 6. The CBCL/4-18 is a 112-item checklist that has been used extensively in studies of low-income children from many ethnic backgrounds. The measures yield scores for internalizing and externalizing behaviors as well as total problems. Subscale scores can also be computed to reflect levels of withdrawn, somatic complaints; anxious/depressed, social problems; thought problems; attention problems; aggressive behaviors; and delinquent behaviors. Consistent with Achenbach's (1991) findings, associations between internalizing and externalizing problems were moderately high for this sample (rs = .62 at Time 5 and .43 at Time 6). As a result, we focused our analyses on predictors of Total Problem Behaviors scores, although exploratory findings for subscales are reported in Footnote 1.

Teachers' reports of child behavior problems were obtained using the TRF of the CBCL (Achenbach, 1991). It is essentially parallel in content to the CBCL/4-18. Additional items are included to tap school-specific behaviors related to anxiety (e.g., overconforms, afraid of mistakes), social problems (e.g., cries, feels unloved), aggressive behaviors (e.g., defiant, disturbs others), and attention problems (e.g., difficulty with following directions, fails to finish work). As with the CBCL/4-18, scores for internalizing and externalizing behavior problems were moderately correlated (r = .46).

Teacher reports of child adaptive behaviors were obtained using the Classroom Edition of the Vineland Adaptive Behavior Scales (Sparrow et al., 1984) at Time 6. The Adaptive Behavior Scales, Classroom Edition assessment was standardized for children ages 3 to 13 years and includes three subscales to reflect: (a) Communication Skills (what the individual understands, says, reads, and writes); (b) Daily Living Skills (personal care, household tasks, use of phone, etc.); and (c) Socialization Skills (interpersonal relationships, use of play and leisure time, responsibility, and sensitivity in coping skills). These subscales were moderately intercorrelated in the New York sample (rs = .55 – .77). Total Adaptive Behavior Composite scores were also used in the analyses. Both reliability (Holden, 1984) and validity (Sparrow & Cicchetti, 1985) have been established for the Vineland Adaptive Behavior Scales.

Maternal Sensitivity.   Sensitivity was coded using the CARE-INDEX (Crittenden, 1981). Using videotaped free-play interactions of the mothers and infants, seven aspects of maternal behavior were coded: facial expression, vocal expression, position and body contact, expression of affection, pacing of turns, control, and developmental appropriateness of choice of activity.

Mothers were classified as "high" in sensitivity if they scored 1 standard deviation above the mean, "moderate" in sensitivity if they scored within 1 standard deviation above or below the mean, and "low" in sensitivity if they scored at least 1 standard deviation below the mean. We then analyzed the reciprocity of bidding sequences (i.e., each time the mother offered a new toy to her child, a bid, the child's response to this bid, and the mother's subsequent reaction to this response) and duration of joint attention by gender and sensitivity level for each age group.

Interactive Behaviors.   Mother and toddler play interactions were videotaped and rated as contingent responses or negative interactive behaviors. Ratings of contingent responses were coded as the proportion of interactive bidding sequences that were reciprocal (Raver & Leadbeater, 1995). The child's response was coded as either "accepts" or "does not accept", and the maternal reaction was coded as either "persists" or "does not persist." When a bid was followed by a child accept and a maternal persist, the bid sequence was coded as a "reciprocal bid sequence." The frequency of bid sequences that met these criteria were reported as a proportion of the total frequency of maternal bids. Reliability ($\kappa = .76$) calculated as agreement for two coders' ratings of 10 randomly selected tapes across the four categories of maternal sequences was good (Fleiss, 1981).

The negative interactive behaviors were rated according to a coding system described by Kochanska, Kuczynski, Radke-Yarrow, and Welsh (1987). These videotaped behaviors were coded as "maternal verbal harshness" (i.e., mother's attempts to influence her child's behaviors in ways that were affectively more harsh, insistent, angry, or demanding than mere limit-setting attempts or requests for cooperation) and "child vocal or physical protests" (i.e., dysregulated vocal or physical expressions of negative emotions, including whining, shrieking, screaming, crying, yelling, and throwing toys, hitting, or kicking). Two coders independently rated 20 videotapes for these mother and child conflict behaviors. Reliability for two coders was computed as agreement on the presence or absence of the target behavior in each 1-second interval of the 10-minute continuously rated episode. Cohen's kappas were good for maternal verbal harshness ($\kappa = .68$) and for child vocal and physical protests ($\kappa = .76$; Fleiss, 1981). Maternal verbal harshness and child verbal and physical protests were summed to yield a score for the total frequency of dyadic "conflict."

Repeat Pregnancies.   Repeat pregnancies and their outcomes were based on self-reports at Times 3 and 5. At Time 3, these reports were also verified through a search of medical records available for 61% of the subjects (Linares et al., 1991). Agreement between the medical records and self-reports was high (95%; $\kappa = .91$) at that time.

School Outcomes.   School outcome groups were determined from the adolescent mothers' responses to questions about type of school enrolled in, when last attended, last grade completed, and current grade level at Times 1, 2, 3, and 5. The criterion for in-school status was defined as current school attendance (not merely school enrollment) or attendance in the last marking period if interviewed during the summer months. The sample was divided into four groups: *Continuous Attenders/Graduates* were 28 (33.3%) mothers who attended school through the pregnancy and at Times 1, 2, 3, and 5, or had graduated from high school or GED program (67.9% of attenders). *School Returners* were 16 (19%) mothers who were not in school during the pregnancy or at Times 1, 2, or 3, but who reported returning or graduating by Time 5. *Before-pregnancy dropouts* were 10 (12%) mothers who had dropped out before the pregnancy and were not attending school at Times 1, 2, 3, or 5. *After-pregnancy dropouts* were 30 (35.7%) mothers who had dropped out of school during the pregnancy or by Times 1, 2, or 3 and had not returned by Time 5.

Educational Attainment.   Educational attainment was assessed from a questionnaire and a semistructured interview with the mothers at Time 6. The questionnaire asked the mother to indicate the last grade in school or year in col lege she had completed. The qualitative interview included a similar question (i.e., "How far have you gotten in your schooling?"). The mothers' responses were consistent across methods and time of assessment.

Appendix B:
Interview for
Ethnographic Data

TIME 6: INTERVIEW FOR MOTHERS

1. What stands out for you in your life just now? What kinds of things have been important?
2. What things have happened in your life that have been particularly difficult to deal with lately? What has been particularly enjoyable for you lately?
3. Tell me something about what your life is like right now:
    a. What do you care about? What kinds of things do you think about a lot?
    b. What do you worry most about?
    c. What do you enjoy?
    d. What do you usually do during the day? At night?
    PROBES: What's a typical day like for you? What did you do yesterday—when did you wake up, then what ...?

Future

4. What would you like to see happen in your future? What are you most afraid of happening in your future?
    a. What would you like to be able to say about yourself in the future? In 5 years? Why?
5. You said you were (weren't) working or in school;
    > If YES: Do you like your job or school program? What do and don't you like?
    > If NO: Would you like to be working? or in school?
6. What would be the ideal job for you? What kind of work would you like to be doing in 5 years?

a. What appeals to you about being a _____?
b. How do you plan to achieve your goals?
c. What do you think might make it or has made it difficult to do this?
d. What has helped you or might help you reach your goals?

Self

7. How would you describe yourself to yourself? If you tell yourself who you really are, what would you say?
    INTERVIEWER: For each adjective ask: What do you mean by _____?
8. What do you like/dislike about yourself? Why?
9. Is the way you see yourself now different from the way you saw yourself in the past? What led to the changes?
10. What does being a woman mean to you? Has what it means to be a woman changed for you?

Parenting

11. How would you describe yourself as a parent?
    INTERVIEWER: For each adjective ask: What do you mean by _____?
    What are your best qualities? Your worst qualities?
12. What do you think are the best things about being a mother?
13. What do you think are the worst things about being a mother?

Relationships

Closest Person

14. When you look around and see who is there for you, who is the person that you feel closest to? Why?
15. How would you describe her or him?
    INTERVIEWER: For each adjective ask: What do you mean by [rule]?
16. How would you describe this relationship? What do you particularly like/dislike about this relationship?
17. What would you like to change about the relationship? Why?
18. Is there anyone else with whom you feel particularly close?
    (If YES: SAME PROBING QUESTIONS AS ABOVE)

Mother

19. How would you describe your mother?
    INTERVIEWER: For each adjective ask: What do you mean by [rule]?
20. How would you describe your relationship with your mother? What do you like/dislike about your relationship with her?
21. What would you like to change about the relationship? Why?

22. Is the way you see your mother now different from the way you saw her in the past? What led to the changes?

23. How helpful has your mother been to you since you've had the baby? What does she help with?

24. In what ways are you like your mother? How are you different? Do you ever find yourself behaving like your mother when you are with (BABY'S NAME)? In what ways? A lot of mothers say to us, "I'm not going to do what my mother did when she was bringing me up. Is there anything you'd like to do differently?

Father

25. Do you have any contact with your father? Have you had a father figure in your life so far who is not your biological father (e.g., a stepfather who raised you)?
    INTERVIEWER: If YES to either question, then ask the following (if yes to both, then only ask these questions about the biological father):

26. How would you describe your father (or "father figure")?
    INTERVIEWER: For each adjective ask: What do you mean by [rule]?

27. What would you like to change about the relationship? Why?

28. How would you describe your relationship with your father? What do you like/dislike about this relationship?

29. Is the way you see your father now different from the way you saw him in the past? What led to the changes?

30. How helpful has your father been to you since you've had the baby? What does he help with?

31. In what ways are you like your father? How are you different? Do you ever find yourself behaving like your father when you are with (BABY'S NAME)? In what ways?

Child (First Child Only)

32. What is your child like? How would you describe (CHILD'S NAME)?
    INTERVIEWER: For each adjective ask: What do you mean by [rule]?

33. How would you describe your relationship with your child? What do you mean by ?

34. Is the way you see your (CHILD'S NAME) now different from the way you saw her/him in the past? What led to the changes?
    PROBE: How is it for you now that your child is older?

35. Does (CHILD'S NAME) remind you of anybody in the family? Who? What about her or him reminds you of (FAMILY MEMBER)?

36. Do you have any fears or worries about your child now or for when she/he grows up?

37. If you had three wishes for your child that would be true when she/he is 20 what would you wish for? When your child grows up, what would you like her/him to be?

Child's Father

38. Are you still involved with the child's father?
    If YES: How often do you see him?
    If NO: Do you know what he is doing these days?
39. How would you describe (CHILD'S FATHER'S NAME)?
    INTERVIEWER: For each adjective ask: What do you mean by [rule]?
40. What is your relationship like? What do you like/dislike about this relationship?
41. What would you like to see change in this relationship? Why?
42. Is the way you see your child's father now different from the way you saw him in the past? What led to the changes?
43. What is his relationship with the child like? What do they do together? How often does he see the child?

Boyfriend

44. Are you in a romantic relationship just now?
    If YES: How would you describe him?
    If NO: Why not?
    INTERVIEWER: For each adjective ask: What do you mean by [rule]?
45. How would you describe your relationship with this person? What do you like/dislike?
46. What would you like to change about this relationship?
47. What do you look for in guys these days? As you look back, have things changed in what you look for? What does love mean to you? What does commitment mean?

Friends (Ask Following Questions for Each Best Friend)

48. Do you have a close or best friend(s)?
    If YES: How would you describe this friend? What do you mean by [rule]?
    If NO: Why do you think you don't have close or best friends? Would you like to have such friends? What makes it difficult for you to have such friends?
49. How would you describe the relationship? What do you like/dislike about the relationship?
50. What would you like to change about this relationship? Why?
51. What do you do together? How often do you see this friend? Has she/he been helpful with your child? How has he/she been helpful?
52. How long have you been close with this friend? How has this friendship changed over the years? Why has it changed?
53. How have your friendships in general changed over the years? Why have they changed or not changed?

Other Relationships

54. Looking back over the time since (BABY'S NAME) was born, has there been anyone else who has been really important for you (family or any others)?
INTERVIEWER: For each relationship ask: How would you describe _____? How would you describe the relationship? How and why is the relationship important to you? How has this relationship changed over the years?

Religion

55. Do you consider yourself religious?
If YES: How has being religious affected you?
If NO: Do you think religion has played any part in your life at all? How?

Conclusions

56. What would you like to change most from the way things are now?
57. Tell me about your neighborhood you live in. What is it like? What do you like/dislike about your neighborhood? Do you feel safe?
58. Is there anything else I should know about you?
59. What kinds of services have been helpful for you since your first child was born? Why? What has not been helpful? What do you think we should do to help young mothers to do well in their lives?
60. Do you have any questions that you would like to ask me?

References

Aaronson, S., & Hartmann, H. (1996). Reform, not rhetoric: A critique of welfare policy and charting new directions. *American Journal of Orthopsychiatry, 66,* 583–598.

Abma, J. C., Chandra, A., Mosher, W. D., Peterson, L., & Piccinino, L. (1997). Fertility, family planning, and women's health: New data from the 1995 National Survey of Family Growth. National Center for Health Statistics. *Vital Health Statistics, 23.*

Achenbach, T. M. (1991). *Integrative guide for the 1991 CBCL/4-18, YSR, and TRF profiles.* Burlington, VT: University of Vermont, Department of Psychiatry.

Achenbach, T. M. (1992). *Manual for the Child Behavior Checklist/2-3 and 1992 Profile.* Burlington: University of Vermont, Department of Psychiatry.

Adams, G., Pittman, K., & O'Brien, R. (1993). Adolescent and young adult fathers: Problems and solutions. In A. Lawson & D. Rhodes (Eds.), *The politics of pregnancy* (pp. 216–237). New Haven, CT: Yale University Press.

Aguilar, R. J., & Nightingale, N. N. (1994). The impact of specific battering experiences on the self-esteem of abused women. *Journal of Family Violence, 9*(1), 35–45.

Alan Guttmacher Institute. (1976). *11 million teenagers: What can be done about the epidemic of adolescent pregnancies in the United States?* New York: Author.

Alan Guttmacher Institute. (1994). *Sex and America's teenagers.* New York: Author.

Alexander, K., Entwisle, D., & Thompson, M. (1987). School performance, status relations, and the structure of sentiment: Bringing the teacher back in. *American Sociological Review, 52,* 665–682.

Allen, J. P., Philliber, S., Herrling, S., & Kuperminc, G. P. (1997). Preventing teen pregnancy and academic failure: Experimental evaluation of a developmentally based approach. *Child Development, 68*(4), 729–742.

Alpern, L., & Lyons-Ruth, K. (1993). Preschool children at social risk: Chronicity and timing of maternal depressive symptoms and child behavior problems at school and at home. *Development and Psychopathology, 5,* 371–388.

American Psychological Association. (1998). *Love doesn't have to hurt teens.* Washington, DC: Author.

Apfel, N. H., & Seitz, V. (1991). Four models of adolescent mother–grandmother relationships in black inner-city families. *Family Relations, 40,* 421–429.

Arias, I., Samios, M., & O'Leary, K. D. (1987). Prevalence and correlates of physical aggression during courtship. *Journal of Interpersonal Violence, 2*(1), 82–90.

Astone, N. M. (1993). Are adolescent mothers just single mothers? *Journal of Research on Adolescence, 3,* 353–371.

211

Baldwin, A. L., Baldwin, C. P., Kasser, T., Zax, M., Sameroff A., & Seifer, R. (1993). Contextual risk and resiliency during late adolescence. *Development and Psychopathology, 5*(4), 741–761.

Bane, M. J. (1986). Household composition and poverty. In S. H. Danziger & D. H. Weinberg (Eds.), *Fighting poverty: What works and what doesn't* (pp. 209–231). Cambridge, MA: Harvard University Press.

Baranowski, M. D., Schilmoeller, G. L., & Higgins, B. S. (1990). Parenting attitudes of adolescent and older mothers. *Adolescence, 25,* 781–790.

Barrerra, M., & Garrison-Jones, C. (1988). Properties of the Beck Depression Inventory as a screening instrument for adolescent depression. *Journal of Abnormal Child Psychology, 16,* 263–273.

Battle, L. S. (1995). Teenage mothers' narratives of self: An examination of risking the future. *Advances in Nursing Science, 17,* 22–36.

Bayley, N. (1969). *Manual for the Bayley Scales of Infant Development.* New York: Psychological Corporation.

Beck, A. (1967). *Depression: Causes and treatment.* Philadelphia: University of Pennsylvania Press.

Beck, A., Steer, R., & Garbin, M. (1988). Psychometric properties of BDI: 25 years of evaluation. *Clinical Psychology Review, 8,* 77–100.

Beck, D. C., Carlson, G. A., Russell, A. T., & Brownfield, F. E. (1987). The use of depression rating instruments in developmentally and educationally delayed adolescents. *Journal of the American Academy of Child and Adolescent Psychiatry, 26,* 97–100.

Belle, D. (1990). Poverty and women's mental health. *American Psychologist, 45,* 385–389.

Bernard, S. (1998). Responsible fatherhood and welfare: How states can use the new law to help children. *Children and Welfare Reform* (Issue Brief 4). New York: National Center for Children in Poverty.

Besharov, D. J., & Gardiner, K. N. (1996). Paternalism and welfare reform. *Public Interest, Winter,* 1–15.

Bishop, S. J., Leadbeater, B. J., & Way, N. (1998). *First year postpartum depressive symptoms in African-American and Puerto Rican adolescent mothers predict child behavior problems six years later.* Manuscript submitted for publication.

Black, M. M., & Nitz, K. (1996). Grandmother co-residence, parenting, and child development among low income, urban teen mothers. *Journal of Adolescent Health, 18,* 218–226.

Blatt, S. J., Hart, B., Quinlan, D. M., Leadbeater, B. J., & Auerbach, J. (1993). The relationship between dependent and self-critical depression and problem behavior in adolescents. *Journal of Youth and Adolescence, 22,* 253–269.

Blatt, S. J., & Homann, E. (1992). Parent–child interaction in the etiology of dependent and self-critical depression. *Clinical Psychology Review, 12,* 47–91.

Blatt, S. J., Schaffer, C. E., Bers, S., & Quinlan, D. M. (1992). Psychometric properties of the Depressive Experiences Questionnaire for adolescents. *Journal of Personality Assessment, 59*(1), 82–98.

Bloom, D., Fellerath, V., Long, D., & Wood, R. G. (1994). Ohio boosts attendance among teen parents: LEAP aims to increase the graduation rate. *Public Welfare, 52,* 18–30.

Bonvillain, N. (1995). *Women and men: Cultural constructs of gender.* Englewood Cliffs, NJ: Prentice-Hall.

Boyer, D., & Fine, D. (1992). Sexual abuse as a factor in adolescent pregnancy and child maltreatment. *Family Planning Perspectives, 24,* 4–11.

Brooks, M. G., & Buckner, J. C. (1996). Work and welfare: Job histories, barriers to employment, and predictors of work among low-income single mothers. *American Journal of Orthopsychiatry, 66,* 526–537.

Brooks-Gunn, J., & Furstenberg, F. F. (1986). The children of adolescent mothers: Physical, academic and psychological outcomes. *Developmental Review, 6,* 224–251.

Bullock, L., & McFarlane, J. (1988). A program to prevent battering of pregnant students. *Response, 11*(1), 18–19.

Burbridge, L. C. (1995). Policy implications of a decline in marriage among African Americans. In M. B. Tucker & C. Mitchell-Kernan (Eds.), *The decline in marriage among African Americans: Causes, consequences, and policy implications* (pp. 323–344). New York: Russell Sage.

Burton, L. M., Dilworth-Anderson, P., & Merriweather-de Vries, C. (1995). Context and surrogate parenting among contemporary grandparents. *Marriage and Family Review, 20*, 349–366.

Caldwell, C. H., Antonucci, T. C., Jackson, J. S., Wolford, M. L., & Osofsky, J. D. (1997). Perceptions of parental support and depressive symptomatology among Black and White adolescent mothers. *Journal of Emotional and Behavioral Disorders, 5*, 173–183.

Camp, B. W. (1996). Adolescent mothers and their children: Changes in maternal characteristics and child development and behavioral outcome at school. *Journal of Developmental & Behavioral Pediatrics, 17*, 162–169.

Campbell, J. (1986). Nursing assessment for risk of homicide with battered women. *Advances in Nursing Science, 8*(4), 36–51.

Campbell, J. (1989). Women's response to sexual abuse in intimate relationships. *Women's Health Care International, 10*, 335–346.

Campbell, J., Poland, M., Waller, J., & Ager, J. (1992). Correlates of battering during pregnancy. *Research in Nursing and Health, 15*, 219–226.

Campbell, S. B., Ewing, L. J., Breaux, A. M., & Szumowski, E. K. (1986). Parent-referred problem three-year-olds: Follow-up at school entry. *Journal of Child Psychology and Psychiatry, 27*, 473–488.

Campbell, S. B., Pierce, E. W., Moore, G., & Marakovitz, S. (1996). Boys' externalizing problems at elementary school age: Pathways from early behavior problems, maternal control, and family stress. *Development and Psychopathology, 8*(4), 701–719.

Carlson, B. E., Abagnale, S., & Flatow, E. (1993). Services for at-risk pregnant and parenting teenagers: A consortium approach. *Families in Society: The Journal of Contemporary Human Services, 74*, 375–380.

Cate, R. M., Henton, J. M., Koval, J., Christopher, F. S., & Lloyd, S. (1982). Premarital abuse: A social psychological perspective. *Journal of Family Issues, 3*, 79–91.

Chase-Lansdale, P. L., Brooks-Gunn, J., & Paikoff, R. (1992). Research and programs for adolescent mothers: Missing links and future promises. *American Behavioral Scientist, 35*, 290–312.

Chase-Lansdale, P. L., Brooks-Gunn, J., & Zamsky, E. S. (1994). Young African-American multigenerational families in poverty: Quality of mothering and grandmothering. *Child Development, 65*, 373–393.

Chase-Lansdale, P. L., & Vinovskis, M. A. (1987). Should we discourage teenage marriage? *The Public Interest, 87*, 23–27.

Cherlin, A. J. (1997). Policy issues of child care. In P. L. Chase-Lansdale & J. Brooks-Gunn (Eds.), *Escape from poverty: What makes a difference for children?* (pp. 121–137). Cambridge, New York: Cambridge University Press.

Cherniss, C., & Herzog, E. (1996). Impact of home-based family therapy on maternal and child outcomes in disadvantaged adolescent mothers. *Family Relations, 45*, 72–79.

Child Trends. (1997). *Facts at a glance.* Washington, DC: Author.

Child Trends. (1999). *Facts at a glance.* Washington, DC: Author.

Children's Defense Fund. (1993). *The state of America's children, yearbook 1993.* Washington, D.C.: Author.

Children's Defense Fund. (1995). *The state of America's children, yearbook 1995.* Washington, DC: Author.

Children's Defense Fund. (1996). *The state of America's children, yearbook 1996.* Washington, DC: Author.

Cicchetti, D., & Garmezy, N. (1993). Prospects and promises in the study of resilience. *Development and Psychopathology, 5*(4), 497–502.

Cicchetti, D., Rogosch, F. A., Lynch, M., & Holt, K. D. (1993). Resilience in maltreated children: Processes leading to adaptive outcome. *Development and Psychopathology, 5*(4), 629–647.

Clarke-Stewart, K. (1991). A home is not a school: The effects of child care on children's development. *Journal of Social Issues, 47,* 105–123.

Cole, P., & Zahn-Waxler, C. (1992). Emotional dysregulation in disruptive behavior disorders. In D. Cicchetti & S. L. Toth (Eds.), *Developmental perspectives on depression.* Rochester, NY: University of Rochester Press.

Collins, A., & Aber, J. L. (1997). How welfare reform can help or hurt children. *Children and Welfare Reform* (Issue Brief No. 1). New York: National Center for Children in Poverty.

Cooley, M. L., & Unger, D. G. (1991). The role of family support in determining developmental outcomes in children of teen mothers. *Child Psychiatry and Human Development, 21*(3), 217–234.

Cramer, J. C., & McDonald, K. B. (1996). Kin support and family stress: Two sides to early childbearing and support networks. *Human Organization, 55*(2), 160–169.

Crittenden, P. M. (1981). Abusing, neglecting, problematic, and adequate dyads: Differentiating by patterns of interaction. *Merrill-Palmer Quarterly, 27,* 1–18.

Crockenberg, S. (1987). Predictors and correlates of anger toward and punitive control of toddlers by adolescent mothers. *Child Development, 58,* 964–975.

Culp, R. E., Appelbaum, M. I., Osofsky, J. D., & Levy, J. A. (1988). Adolescent and older mothers: Comparison between prenatal maternal variables and newborn interaction measures. *Infant Behavior and Development, 11,* 353–362.

Danziger, S. K. (1995). Effect of employment on marriage: Commentary. In M. B. Tucker & C. Mitchell-Kernan (Eds.), *The decline in marriage among African Americans: Causes, consequences, and policy implications* (pp. 96–101). New York: Russell Sage.

Darabi, K., Graham, E., Namerow, P., Philliber, S., & Varga, P. (1984). The effect of maternal age on the well-being of children. *Journal of Marriage and the Family, 46,* 933–936.

Davis, A. A., & Rhodes, J. E. (1994). African-American teenage mothers and their mothers: An analysis of supportive and problematic interactions. *Journal of Community Psychology, 22,* 12–20.

Davis, A. A., Rhodes, J. E., & Hamilton-Leaks, J. (1997). When both parents may be a source of support and problems: An analysis of pregnant and parenting female African-American adolescents' relationships with their mothers and fathers. *Journal of Research on Adolescence, 7,* 331–348.

Davis, R. C., & Smith, B. (1995). Domestic violence reforms: Empty promises or fulfilled expectations? *Crime and Delinquency, 41,* 541–552.

De Leon, B. (1996). Career development of Hispanic adolescent girls. In B. J. Leadbeater & N. Way (Eds.), *Urban girls: Resisting stereotypes, creating identities* (pp. 380–398). New York: New York University Press.

Dishion, T. J., French, D. C., & Patterson, G. R. (1995). The development and ecology of antisocial behavior. In C. Cicchetti & D. J. Cohen (Eds.), *Developmental psychopathology: Vol. 2. Risk, disorder, and adaptation* (pp. 421–471). New York: Wiley.

Donnelly, B. W., & Davis-Berman, J. (1994). A review of the Chance to Grow Project: A care project for pregnant and parenting adolescents. *Child and Adolescent Social Work Journal, 11*(6), 493–506.

Donovan, P. (1995). *The politics of blame: Family planning, abortion and the poor.* New York: Alan Guttmacher Institute.

Douglas, M. A. (1987). The battered woman syndrome. In D. J. Sonkin (Ed.), *Domestic violence on trial: Psychological and legal dimensions of family violence* (pp. 34–54). New York: Springer.

Downey, G., & Feldman, S. I. (1996). Implications of rejection sensitivity for intimate relationships. *Journal of Personality and Social Psychology, 70*(6), 1327–1343.

Dubow, E. F., & Luster, T. (1990). Adjustment of children born to teenage mothers: The contribution of risk and protective factors. *Journal of Marriage and the Family, 52,* 393–404.

Dutton, D., & Painter, S. (1993). The battered woman syndrome: Effects of severity and intermittency of abuse. *American Journal of Orthopsychiatry, 63*(4), 614–622.

East, P. L., & Felice, M. E. (1996). *Adolescent pregnancy and parenting: Findings from a racially diverse sample.* Mahwah, NJ: Lawrence Erlbaum Associates.

Edlin, K., & Jencks, C. (1992). Reforming welfare. In C. Jencks (Ed.), *Rethinking social policy: Race, poverty, and the underclass* (pp. 205–275). Cambridge, MA: Harvard University Press.

Edlin, K., & Lein, L. (1996). *Making ends meet: How single mothers survive welfare and low-wage work.* New York: Russell Sage.

Egeland, B., Breitenbucher, M., & Rosenburg, D. (1980). Prospective study of the significance of life stress in the etiology of child abuse. *Journal of Consulting and Clinical Psychology, 48,* 195–205.

Egeland, B., Kalkoske, M., Gottesman, N., & Erickson, M. F. (1990). Preschool behavior problems: Stability and factors accounting for change. *Journal of Child Psychology and Psychiatry, 31,* 891–909.

Egeland, B., Pianta, R., & Ogawa, J. (1996). Early behavior problems: Pathways to mental disorders in adolescence. *Development and Psychopathology, 8,* 735–749.

Epstein, S. (1983). *The Mother–Father–Peer Scale.* Unpublished manuscript, University of Massachusetts at Amherst.

Fagan, J. A., Stewart, D. K., & Hansen, K. V. (1983). Violent men or violent husbands? Background factors and situational correlates. In D. Finkelhor, R. J. Gelles, G. T. Hotaling, & M. A. Straus (Eds.), *The dark side of families: Current family violence research* (pp. 49–67). Beverly Hills, CA: Sage.

Fasick, F. A. (1994). On the "invention" of adolescence. *Journal of Early Adolescence, 14*(1), 6–23.

Field, T. (1992). Infants of depressed mothers. *Development and Psychopathology, 4,* 49–66.

Fine, M. (1988). Sexuality, schooling, and adolescent females: The missing discourse of desire. *Harvard Educational Review, 58,* 29–53.

Fink, B. (1995). Providing quality child care in a comprehensive program for disadvantaged young mothers and their children. *Child Welfare, 24*(6), 1109–1134.

Finkel, M. L., & Thompson, S. (1997). Focus on teenage motherhood: An innovative response to a growing problem. *Early Child Development and Care, 129,* 105–113.

Fischer, R. L. (1997). Evaluating the delivery of a teen pregnancy and parenting program across two settings. *Research on Social Work Practice, 7*(3), 350–369.

Fleiss, J. L. (1981). *Statistical methods for rates and proportions.* New York: Wiley.

Follingstad, D., Rutledge, L., Berg, B., Hause, E., & Polek, D. (1990). The role of emotional abuse in physically abusive relationships. *Journal of Family Violence, 5*(2), 107–119.

Foltz, A. M., Klerman, L., & Jekel, J. F. (1972). Pregnancy and special education: Who stays in school? *American Journal of Public Health, 62,* 1612–1619.

Franklin, C., Grant, D., Corcoran, J., Miller, P. O., & Bultman, L. (1997). Effectiveness of prevention programs for adolescent pregnancy: A meta-analysis. *Journal of Marriage and the Family, 59,* 551–567.

Freeman, E. W., & Rickels, K. (1993). *Early childbearing: Perspectives of black adolescents on pregnancy, abortion, and contraception.* Newbury Park, CA: Sage.

Fuller, B., Holloway, S. D., Rambaud, M., & Eggers-Pierola, C. (1996). How do mothers choose child care? Alternative cultural models in poor neighborhoods. *Sociology of Education, 69,* 83–104.

Fuller-Thomson, E., Minkler, M., & Driver, D. (1997). A profile of grandparents raising grandchildren in the United States. *Gerontologist, 37,* 406–411.

Furstenberg, F. F. (1995). Fathering in the inner city: Paternal participation and public policy. In W. Marsiglio (Ed.), *Fatherhood: Contemporary theory, research, and social policy* (pp. 119–147). Thousand Oaks, CA: Sage.

Furstenberg, F. F., Brooks-Gunn, J., & Morgan, S. P. (1987). *Adolescent mothers in later life.* Cambridge, MA: Cambridge University Press.

Furstenberg, F. F., & Harris, K. M. (1993). When fathers matter/Why fathers matter: The impact of paternal involvement on the offspring of adolescent mothers. In A. Lawson & D. Rhodes (Eds.), *The politics of pregnancy* (pp. 189–209). New Haven, CT: Yale University Press.

Gamache, D. (1991). Domination and control: The social context of dating violence. In B. Levy (Ed.), *Dating violence: Young women in danger.* Seattle: Seal Press.

Garcia-Coll, C. T., Escobar, M., Cebollero, P., & Valcarcel, M. (1989). Adolescent pregnancy and childbearing: Psychosocial consequences during the postpartum period. In C. T. Garcia-Coll & M. de Lourdes Mattei (Eds.), *The psychosocial development of Puerto Rican women* (pp. 84–114). New York: Praeger.

Garfinkel, I., & McLanahan, S. (1997). The effects of child support reform on child well-being. In P. L. Chase-Lindsay & J. Brooks-Gunn (Eds.), *Escape from poverty: What makes a difference for children?* (pp. 211–238). Cambridge, NY: Cambridge University Press.

Garmezy, N., Masten, A. S., & Tellegen, A. (1984). The study of stress and competence in children: A building for developmental psychopathology. *Child Development, 55,* 97–111.

Gelfand, D. M., & Teti, D. M. (1990). The effects of maternal depression on children. *Clinical Psychology Review, 10,* 329–353.

Gillespie, E., & Schellhas, B. (Eds.). (1994). *Contract with America: The bold plan by Representative Newt Gingrich, Representative Dick Armey and the House Republicans to change the nation.* New York: Times Books.

Gore, S., & Eckenrode, J. (1996). Context and processing research on risk and resilience. In R. J. Haggerty, L. R. Sherrod, N. Garmezy, & M. Rutter (Eds.), *Stress, risk, and resilience in children and adolescents: Processes, mechanisms, and interventions* (pp. 19–63). New York: Cambridge University Press.

Grolnick, W. S., Benjet, C., Kurowski, C. O., & Apostoleris, N. H. (1997). Predictors of parent involvement in children's schooling. *Journal of Educational Psychology, 89*(3), 538–548.

Haggstrom, G., Kanouse, D., & Morrison, P. (1986). Accounting for the educational shortfalls of mothers. *Journal of Marriage and the Family, 48,* 175–186.

Hahn, A., Danzberger, J., & Lefkowitz, B. (1987). *Dropouts in America: Enough is known for action.* Washington, DC: Institute for Educational Leadership.

Hammen, C., Burge, D., & Stansbury, K. (1990). The relationship of mother and child variables to child outcomes in a high-risk sample: A causal modeling analysis. *Developmental Psychology, 26,* 24–30.

Handler, J. H. (1995). *The poverty of welfare reform.* New Haven, CT: Yale University Press.

Hanson, S. L. (1992). Involving families in programs for pregnant teens: Consequences for teens and their families. *Family Relations, 41,* 303–311.

Hao, L., & Brinton, M. C. (1997). Productive activities and support systems of single mothers. *American Journal of Sociology, 102*(5), 1305–1344.

Harris, K. M. (1997). *Teen mothers and the revolving welfare door.* Philadelphia, PA: Temple University Press.

Hatchett, S., Veroff, J., & Douvan, E. (1995). Marital instability among Black and White couples in early marriage. In M. B. Tucker & C. Mitchell-Kernan (Eds.), *The decline in marriage among African Americans: Causes, consequences, and policy implications* (pp. 177–218). New York: Russell Sage.

Hayes, C. D. (Ed.). (1987). *National Research Council: Risking the future: Adolescent sexuality, pregnancy and childbearing.* Washington, DC: National Academy Press.

Helton, A., McFarlane, J., & Anderson, E. (1987). Battered and pregnant: A prevalence study. *American Journal of Public Health, 77,* 1337–1339.

Hendrick, D. L., Prather, E. M., & Tobin, A. R. (1984). *Sequenced Inventory of Communication Development: Instruction Manual.* Seattle: University of Washington Press.

Henshaw, S. K. (1997). Teenage abortion and pregnancy statistics by state, 1992. *Family Planning Perspectives, 29,* 115–122.

Henshaw, S. K., Kenney, A. M., Somberg, D., & Van Vort, J. (1989). *Teenage pregnancy in the United States: The scope of the problem and state responses.* New York: Alan Guttmacher Institute.

Henton, J., Cate, R., Koval, J., Lloyd, S., & Christopher, S. (1983). Romance and violence in dating relationships. *Journal of Family Issues, 4,* 467–482.

Heuser, R. L. (1980). *Fertility tables for birth cohorts by color: United States, 1917–1980* (DHEW Publication No. (HRA) 76-1152). Washington, DC: U.S. Department of Health, Education, and Welfare.

Hofferth, S. L., & Wissoker, D. A. (1991). Price, quality, and income in child care choice. *Journal of Human Resources, 27,* 70–111.

Holden, R. H. (1984). *Vineland Adaptive Behavior Scales: Test Critiques* (Vol. 1). Kansas City, MO: Test Corporation of America.

Horwitz, S. M., Klerman, L. V., Kuo, H. S., & Jekel, J. F. (1991). School-age mothers: Predictors of long-term educational and economic outcomes. *Pediatrics, 87*(6), 862–868.

Hubbs-Tait, L., Hughes, K. P., Culp, A. M., Osofsky, J. D., Hann, D. M., Eberhart-Wright, A., & Ware, L. M. (1996). Children of adolescent mothers: Attachment representation, maternal depression, and later behavioral problems. *American Journal of Orthopsychiatry, 66*(3), 416–426.

Hughes, D. C., & Runyan, S. J. (1995). Prenatal care and public policy: Lessons for promoting women's health. *Journal of the American Medical Women's Association, 50,* 156–163.

Jarrett, R. L. (1995). Growing up poor: The family experiences of socially mobile youth in low-income African-American neighborhoods. *Journal of Adolescent Research, 10,* 111–135.

Jessor, R. (1993). Successful adolescent development among youth in high risk settings. *American Psychologist, 48,* 117–127.

Jones, E. F., Forrest, J. P., Goldman, N., Henshaw, S., Lincoln, R., Rosoff, J. I., Westoff, F., & Wulf, D. (1986). *Teenage pregnancy in industrialized countries.* New Haven: Yale University Press.

Keating, D. (1990). Adolescent thinking. In S. Feldman & G. Elliott (Eds.), *At the threshold: The developing adolescent* (pp. 54–89). Cambridge, MA: Harvard University Press.

Ketterlinus, R. D., Henderson, D., & Lamb, M. E. (1991). The effects of maternal age-at-birth on children's cognitive development. *Journal of Research on Adolescence, 1,* 173–188.

Kids Count Data Book: 1991 New York State Kids Count Project [Electronic data file]. (1994). Center for the Study of Social Policy. Albany, NY: Annie E. Casey Foundation. [Producer and Distributor]

Kiecolt, K. J., & Fossett, M. A. (1995). Mate availability and marriage among African Americans: Aggregate- and individual-level analyses. In M. B. Tucker & C. Mitchell-Kernan (Eds.), *The decline in marriage among African Americans: Causes, consequences, and policy implications* (pp. 121–135). New York: Russell Sage.

Kisker, E. E., & Silverberg, M. (1991). Child care utilization by disadvantaged teenage mothers. *Journal of Social Issues, 47,* 159–177.

Kitzman, H., Olds, D. L., Henderson, C. R., Jr., Hanks, C., Cole, R., Tatelbaum, R., McConnochie, K. M., Sidora, K., Luckey, D. W., Shaver, D., Engelhardt, K., James, D., & Barnard, K. (1997). Effects of prenatal and infancy home visitation by nurses on pregnancy outcomes, childhood injuries, and repeated childbearing: A randomized controlled trial. *Journal of the American Medical Association, 278,* 644–652.

Klerman, L. V. (1993). The relationship between adolescent parenthood and inadequate parenting. *Children & Youth Services Review, 15,* 309–320.

Klerman, L. V., & Horwitz, S. M. (1992). Reducing the adverse consequences of adolescent pregnancy and parenting: The role of service programs. *Adolescent Medicine: State of the Art Reviews, 3,* 299–316.

Kochanska, G., Kuczynski, L., Radke-Yarrow, M., & Welsh, J. D. (1987). Resolutions and control episodes between well and affectively ill mothers and their young children. *Journal of Abnormal Child Psychology, 15,* 441–456.

Koenig, M. A., & Zelnik, M. (1982). Repeat pregnancy among metropolitan-area teenagers: 1971–1979. *Family Planning Perspectives, 14,* 341–344.

Koniak-Griffin, D. (1994). Aerobic exercise, psychological well-being, and physical discomforts during adolescent pregnancy. *Research in Nursing and Health, 17,* 253–263.

Kontos, S., Howes, C., Shinn, M., & Galinsky, E. (1997). Children's experiences in family child care and relative care as a function of family income and ethnicity. *Merrill-Palmer Quarterly, 43,* 386–403.

Kontos, S., Hsu, H. C., & Dunn, L. (1994). Children's cognitive and social competence in child care centers and family day-care homes. *Journal of Applied Developmental Psychology, 15,* 387–411.

Lamb, M. E. (Ed.). (1988). *The father's role: Applied perspectives.* New York: Wiley.

Lamb, M. E., & Elster, A. B. (1986). Parental behavior of adolescent mothers and fathers. In A. B. Elster & M. E. Lamb (Eds.), *Adolescent fatherhood* (pp. 89–106). Hillsdale, NJ: Lawrence Erlbaum Associates.

Lancaster, J. B., & Lancaster, C. S. (1987). The watershed change in parental-investment and family-formation strategies in the course of human evolution. In J. B. Lancaster, J. Altmann, A. S. Rossi, & L. R. Sherrod (Eds.), *Parenting across the life span: Biosocial dimensions* (pp. 187–205). New York: Aldine.

Landry, D. J., & Darroch-Forrest, J. (1995). How old are U.S. fathers? *Family Planning Perspectives, 27*(4), 159–161, 165.

Laner, M. R., & Thompson, J. (1982). Abuse and aggression in courting couples. *Deviant Behavior, 3,* 229–244.

Lawson, A., & Rhodes, D. L. (Eds.). (1993). *The politics of pregnancy.* New Haven, CT: Yale University Press.

Leadbeater, B. J. (1996). School outcomes for minority-group adolescent mothers at 28 to 36 months postpartum: A longitudinal follow-up. *Journal of Research on Adolescence, 6*(4), 629–648.

Leadbeater, B. J., & Bishop, S. J. (1994). Predictors of behavior problems in preschool children of inner-city Afro-American and Puerto Rican adolescent mothers. *Child Development, 65,* 638–648.

Leadbeater, B., Bishop, S., & Raver, C. (1996). Quality of mother–toddler interactions, maternal depressive symptoms, and behavior problems in preschoolers of adolescent mothers. *Developmental Psychology, 32,* 280–288.

Leadbeater, B. J., & Linares, O. (1992). Depressive symptoms in Black and Puerto Rican adolescent mothers in the first 3 years postpartum. *Development and Psychopathology, 4,* 451–468.

Leadbeater, B. J., & Way, N. (Eds.). (1996). *Urban girls: Resisting stereotypes, creating identities.* New York: New York University Press.

Leadbeater, B. J., Way, N., & Raden, A. (1996). Why not marry your baby's father? Answers from African-American and Hispanic adolescent mothers. In B. J. Leadbeater & N. Way (Eds.), *Urban girls: Resisting stereotypes, creating identities* (pp. 193–209). New York: New York University Press.

Leadbeater, B. J., & Wilson, G. L. (1993). Flipping their fins for a place to stand: 19th and 20th- century mermaids. *Youth & Society, 24*(4), 466–486.

Lerner, J. A., Inui, T. S., Trupin, E. W., & Douglas, E. (1985). Preschool behavior can predict future psychiatric disorders. *Journal of the American Academy of Child and Adolescent Psychiatry, 24,* 42–48.

Leventhal, J. M., Horwitz, S. M., Rude, C., & Stier, D. M. (1993). Maltreatment of children born to teenage mothers: A comparison between the 1960s and 1980s. *The Journal of Pediatrics, 122,* 314–319.

Levin-Epstein, J. (1996). *Teen parent provisions in the Personal Responsibility and Work Opportunity Reconciliation Act of 1996.* Washington, DC: Center for Law and Social Policy.

Linares, L. O., Leadbeater, B. J., Kato, P. M., & Jaffe, L. (1991). Predicting school outcomes for minority group adolescent mothers: Can subgroups be identified? *Journal of Research on Adolescence, 1,* 379–400.

Lindberg, L. D., Sonenstein, F. L., Ku, L., & Martinez, G. (1997). Age differences betweeen minors who give birth and their adult partners. *Family Planning Perspectives, 29,* 61–67.

Ludtke, M. (1997). *On our own: Unmarried motherhood in America.* New York: Random House.

Luker, K. (1996). *Dubious conceptions.* Cambridge, MA: Harvard University Press.

Luthar, S. S. (1991). Vulnerability and resilience: A study of high-risk adolescents. *Child Development, 62,* 600–616.

Luthar, S. S. (1993). Annotation: Methodological and conceptual issues in research on childhood resilience. *Journal of Child Psychology and Psychiatry and Allied Disciplines, 34*(4), 441–453.

Luthar, S. S., & Blatt, S. J. (1995). Differential vulnerability of dependency and self-criticism among disadvantaged teenagers. *Journal of Research on Adolescence, 5,* 431–449.

Luthar, S. S., Dorenberger, C. H., & Zigler, E. (1993). Resilience is not a unidimensional construct: Insights from a prospective study of inner-city adolescents. *Development and Psychopathology, 5*(4), 703–717.

Lyons-Ruth, K. (1992). Maternal depressive symptoms, disorganized infant–mother attachment relationships and hostile-aggressive behavior in the preschool classroom: A prospective longitudinal view from infancy to age five. In D. Cicchetti & S. L. Toth (Eds.), *Development perspectives on depression* (pp. 173–209). Rochester, NY: University of Rochester Press.

Lyons-Ruth, K., Connell, D. B., Grunebaum, H. U., & Botein, S. (1990). Infants at social risk: Maternal depression and family support services as mediators of infant development and security of attachment. *Child Development, 61,* 85–98.

Marsiglio, W. (1987). Adolescent fathers in the United States: Their initial living arrangements, marital experience, and educational outcomes. *Family Planning Perspectives, 19*(6), 240–251.

Martin, D. (1981). *Battered wives.* San Francisco: Volcano Press.

Martin, S. R., Holsapfels, S., & Baker, P. (1992). Wife abuse: Are we detecting it? *Journal of Women's Health, 1*(1), 77–80.

Masten, A. S. (1994). Resilience in individual development: Successful adaptation despite risk and adversity. In M. C. Wang & E. W. Gordon (Eds.), *Educational resilience in inner-city America: Challenges and prospects* (pp. 3–25). Hillsdale, NJ: Lawrence Erlbaum Associates.

Masten, A. S., & Coatsworth, J. D. (1998). The development of competence in favorable and unfavorable environments: Lessons from research on successful children. *American Psychologist, 53*(2), 205–220.

Mathews, T. J., & Ventura, S. J. (1997). Birth and fertility rates by educational attainment: United States, 1994. *Monthly Vital Statistics Report, 45*(Suppl. 10), 1–20.

Maynard, R. (Ed.). (1997). *Kids having kids: Economic cost and social consequences of teen pregnancy.* Washington, DC: Urban Institute Press.

Maynard, R., & Rangarajan, A. (1994). Contraceptive use and repeat pregnancies among welfare-dependent teenage mothers. *Family Planning Perspectives, 26*(5), 198–205.

McCarthy, J., & Hardy, J. (1993). Age at first birth and birth outcomes. *Journal of Research on Adolescence, 3,* 373–392.

McFarlane, J. (1991). Violence during teen pregnancy: Health consequences for mother and child. In B. Levy (Ed.), *Dating violence: Young women in danger* (pp. 136–141). Seattle: Seal Press.

McLoyd, V. C. (1990). The impact of economic hardship on Black families and children: Psychological distress, parenting, and socioemotional development. *Child Development, 61,* 311–346.

McLoyd, V. C. (1998). Socioeconomic disadvantage and child development. *American Psychologist, 53,* 185–204.

McLoyd, V. C., & Hernandez-Joszefowicz, D. M. (1996). Sizing up the future: Predictors of African-American adolescent females' expectations. In B. J. Leadbeater & N. Way (Eds.), *Urban girls: Resisting stereotypes, creating identities* (pp. 355–379). New York: New York University Press.

Meyers, M. K. (1995). Child day care in welfare reform: Are we targeting too narrowly? *Child Welfare, 24*(6), 1071–1090.

Miller, C. L., Miceli, P. J., Whitman, T. L., & Borkowski, J. G. (1996). Cognitive readiness to parent and intellectual-emotional development in children of adolescent mothers. *Developmental Psychology, 32,* 533–541.

Mitchell, R. E., & Hodsen, C. A. (1983). Coping with domestic violence: Social support and psychological health among battered women. *American Journal of Community Health, 11,* 629–654.

Moore, K. A., Miller, B. C., Glei, D., & Morrison, D. R. (1995). *Adolescent sex, contraception, and childbearing: A review of recent research.* Washington, DC: Child Trends.

Moore, K. A., Myers, D. E., Morrison, D. R., Nord, C. W., Brown, B., & Edmonston, E. (1993). Age at first childbirth and later poverty. *Journal of Research on Adolescence, 3,* 393–422.

Moore, K. A., Nord, C. W., & Peterson, J. L. (1989). Nonvoluntary sexual activity among adolescents. *Family Planning Perspectives, 21,* 110–114.

Moore, K. A., & Snyder, N. O. (1991). Cognitive attainment among firstborn children of adolescent mothers. *American Sociological Review, 56,* 612–624.

Mott, F., & Marsiglio, W. (1985). Early childbearing and completion of high school. *Family Planning Perspectives, 17,* 234–237.

Muslow, M. H., & Murry, V. M. (1996). Parenting on edge: Economically stressed, single, African-American adolescent mothers. *Journal of Family Issues, 17,* 704–721.

Musick, J. S. (1993). *Young, poor and pregnant: The psychology of teenage motherhood.* New Haven, CT: Yale University Press.

Nathanson, C. A. (1991). *Dangerous passage: The social control of sexuality in women's adolescence.* Philadelphia: Temple University Press.

National Center for Children in Poverty. (1990). *Five million children: A statistical profile of our poorest young citizens.* New York: Author.

National Center for Children in Poverty. (1998). *Young children in poverty: A statistical update.* New York: Author.

National Center for Chronic Disease Prevention and Health Promotion, Division of Adolescent and School Health. (1995). Trends in sexual risk behavior among high school students–United States, 1990, 1991, and 1993. *Morbidity and Mortality Weekly Report, 44*(7), 124–125, 130–132.

National Institute of Child Health and Human Development Early Child Care Research Network. (1998). Early child care and self-control, compliance, and problem behavior at twenty-four and thirty-six months. *Child Development, 69,* 875–887.

National Institute of Mental Health Basic Behavioral Science Task Force of the National Advisory Mental Health Council. (1996). *American Psychologist, 51*(1), 22–28.

New York's Dropouts-to-Be: A Grim Class Portrait. (1989, April). *New York Times,* p. B1.

Norbeck, J. S., Lindsey, A. M., & Carrieri, V. L. (1981). The development of an instrument to measure social support. *Nursing Research, 30,* 264–269.

Norbeck, J. S., Lindsey, A. M., & Carrieri, V. L. (1983). Further development of the Norbeck Social Support Questionnaire: Normative data and validity testing. *Nursing Research, 32,* 4–9.

Olds, D. L., Eckenrode, J., Henderson, C. R., Jr., Kitzman, H., Powers, J., Cole, R., Sidora, K., Morris, P., Pettit, L. M., & Luckey, D. (1997). Long-term effects of home visitation on maternal life course and child abuse and neglect: Fifteen-year follow-up of a randomized trial. *Journal of the American Medical Association, 278,* 637–643.

Olds, D., Henderson, C., Jr., Kitzman, H., Eckenrode, J., Cole, R., & Tatelbaum, R. (1998). The promise of home visitation: Results of two randomized trials. *Journal of Community Psychology, 26*(1), 5–21.

Osofsky, J. D., & Eberhart-Wright, A. (1992). Risk and protective factors for parents and infants. In G. Suci & S. Robertson (Eds.), *Human development: Future directions in infant developmental research* (pp. 29–35). New York: Springer/Verlag.

Osofsky, J. D., Hann, D. M., & Peebles, C. (1993). Adolescent parenthood: Risks and opportunities for mothers and infants. In C. H. Zeanah, Jr. (Ed.), *Handbook of infant mental health* (pp. 106–119). New York: Guilford Press.

O'Sullivan, A. L., & Jacobsen, B. S. (1992). A randomized trial of a health care program for first-time adolescent mothers and their infants. *Nursing Research, 41*(4), 210–215.

Oyserman, D., Radin, N., & Saltz, E. (1994). Predictors of nurturant parenting in teen mothers living in three generational families. *Child Psychiatry and Human Development, 24,* 215–230.

Payne, N. (1996, December 10). Policy review: The Journal of American Citizenship. *The Hartford Current,* p. A21.

Pearson, J. L., Hunter, A. G., Cook, J. M., Ialongo, N. S., & Kellam, S. G. (1997). Grandmother involvement in child caregiving in an urban community. *Gerontologist, 37,* 650–657.

Pederson, F. A., Zaslow, M., Cain, R. L., Anderson, B. J., & Thomas, M. (1980). A methodology for assessing parent perception of baby temperament. *JSAS: Catalog of Selected Documents in Psychology, 10,* 1–17.

Personal Responsibility and Work Opportunity Reconciliation Act of 1996 (Public Law 104–193).

Philliber, S. G., & Graham, E. H. (1981). The impact of age of mother on mother–child interaction patterns. *Journal of Marriage and the Family, 10,* 109–115.

Phillips, D. A., Voran, M., Kisker, E. E., Howes, C., & Whitebook, M. (1994). Child care for children in poverty: Opportunity or inequity? *Child Development, 65,* 472–492.

Pianta, R. C., Steinberg, M., & Rollins, K. (1995). The first two years of school: Teacher–child relationships and deflections in children's classroom adjustment. *Development and Psychopathology, 7,* 295–312.

Pianta, R. C., & Walsh, D. J. (1998). Applying the construct of resilience in schools: Cautions from a developmental systems perspective. *School Psychology Review, 27,* 407–417.

Presser, H. B. (1989). Can we make time for children? The economy, work schedules, and child care. *Demography, 26*(4), 523–543.

Procidano, M., & Heller, K. (1983). Measure of perceived social support from friends and family. *American Journal of Psychology, 11,* 1–24.

Quint, J. C., Bos, J. M., & Polit, D. F. (1997). *New chance: Final report on a comprehensive progream for young mothers in poverty and their children.* New York: Manpower Demonstration Research Corporation.

Quinton, D., & Rutter, M. (1988). *Parenting breakdown: The making and breaking of intergenerational links.* Aldershot: Avebury.

Raeff, C. (1994). Viewing adolescent mothers on their own terms: Linking self- conceptualization and adolescent motherhood. *Developmental Review, 14,* 215–244.

Rainey, D. Y., Stevens-Simon, C., & Kaplan, D. W. (1995). Are abused adolescents who report prior sexual abuse at higher risk for pregnancy? *Child Abuse and Neglect, 19,* 1283–1288.

Raver, C. C., & Leadbeater, B. J. (1995). Factors influencing joint attention between socioeconomically disadvantaged adolescent mothers and their infants. In C. Moore & P. Dunham (Eds.), *Joint attention: Its origins and role in development* (pp. 251–271). Hillsdale, NJ: Lawrence Erlbaum Associates.

Raver, C. C., & Leadbeater, B. J. (1999). Mothering under pressure: Environmental, child and dyadic correlates of maternal self-efficacy among low income women. *Journal of Family Psychology, 13*(4), 524–534..

Reis, J. (1988). The comparison of young teenage, older teenage and adult mothers on determinants of parenting. *The Journal of Psychology, 123,* 141–151.

Rhodes, J. E., Ebert, L., & Meyers, A. B. (1993). Sexual victimization in young, pregnant and parenting, African-American women: Psychological and social outcomes. *Violence and Victims, 8*(2), 153–163.

Rhodes, J. E., Ebert, L., & Meyers, A. B. (1994). Social support, relationship problems and the psychological functioning of young African-American mothers. *Journal of Social and Personal Relationships, 11,* 587–599.

Rhodes, J. E., Fischer, K., Ebert, L., & Meyers, A. B. (1993). Patterns of service utilization among pregnant and parenting African-American adolescents. *Psychology of Women Quarterly, 17,* 257–274.

Rogers, M. M., Peoples-Sheps, M. D., & Suchindran, C. (1996). Impact of social support program on teenage prenatal care use and pregnancy outcomes. *Journal of Adolescent Health, 19*(2), 132–140.

Rose, S. L., Rose, S. A., & Feldman, J. F. (1989). Stability of behavior problems in very young children. *Development and Psychopathology, 1,* 5–19.

Ruch-Ross, H. S., Jones, E. D., & Musick, J. S. (1992). Comparing outcomes in a statewide program for adolescent mothers with outcomes in a national sample. *Family Planning Perspectives, 24,* 66–71, 96.

Russell, D. (1986). *The secret trauma: Incest in the lives of girls and women.* New York: Basic Books.

Rutter, M. (1979). Protective factors in children's responses to stress and disadvantage. In M. W. Kent & J. E. Rolfe (Eds.), *Primary prevention of psychopathology: Vol. 3. Social competence in children* (pp. 49–74). Hanover, NH: University Press of New England.

Rutter, M., & Rutter, M. (1993). *Developing minds: Challenge and continuity across the life span.* New York: Basic Books.

Salguero, C. (1984). The role of ethnic factors in adolescent pregnancy and motherhood. In M. Sugar (Ed.), *Adolescent parenthood* (pp. 75–98). New York: Spectrum.

Sampson, R. J. (1995). Unemployment and imbalanced sex ratios: Race specific consequences for family structure and crime. In M. B. Tucker & C. Mitchell-Kernan (Eds.), *The decline in marriage among African Americans: Causes, consequences, and policy implications* (pp. 229–254). New York: Russell Sage.

Sander, J. H., & Rosen, J. L. (1987). Teenage fathers: Working with the neglected partner in adolescent childbearing. *Family Planning Perspectives, 19,* 107–110.

Schellenbach, C. J., Whitman, T. L., & Borkowski, J. G. (1992). Toward an integrative model of adolescent parenting. *Human Development, 35,* 81–99.

Schenkel, S., & Marcia, J. E. (1972). Attitudes toward premarital intercourse in determining ego identity status in college women. *Journal of Personality, 40,* 472–482.

Schoen, R. (1995). The widening gap between black and white marriage rates: Context and implications. In M. B. Tucker & C. Mitchell-Kernan (Eds.), *The decline in marriage among African Americans: Causes, consequences, and policy implications* (pp. 103–116). New York: Russell Sage.

Scott-Jones, D. (1991). Adolescent childbearing, risks and resilience. *Education and Urban Society, 24,* 53–64.

Scott-Jones, D., & Turner, S. L. (1990). The impact of adolescent childbearing on educational attainment and income of black females. *Youth and Society, 22,* 35–53.

Seitz, V. (1996). Adolescent pregnancy and parenting. In E. F. Zigler & S. L. Kagan (Eds.), *Children, families, and government: Preparing for the twenty-first century* (pp. 268–287). New York: Cambridge University Press.

Seitz, V., & Apfel, N. H. (1993). Adolescent mothers and repeated childbearing: Effects of a school-based intervention program. *American Journal of Orthopsychiatry, 63*(4), 572–581.

Seitz, V., Apfel, N. H., & Rosenbaum, L. K. (1991). Effects of an intervention program for pregnant adolescents: Educational outcomes at 2 years postpartum. *American Journal of* Community Psychology, 19, 911–930.

Shapiro, J. R., & Mangelsdorf, S. C. (1994). The determinants of parenting competence in adolescent mothers. *Journal of Youth & Adolescence, 23,* 621–641.

Shaw, D. S., Owens, E. B., Vondra, J. I., & Keenan, K. (1996). Early risk factors and pathways in the development of early disruptive behavior problems. *Development and Psychopathology, 8,* 679–699.

Sidhu, R. (1999, May 17). Girls poorly prepared for dangers. *The Times Colonist,* Victoria, BC, Canada, p. D2.

Sonenstein, F. L., & Wolf, D. A. (1991). Satisfaction with child care: Perspectives of welfare mothers. *Journal of Social Issues, 47*(2), 15–31.

Spalter-Roth, R., Burr, B., Hartmann, H., & Shaw, L. (1995). *Welfare that works: The working lives of AFDC recipients.* Washington, DC: Institute for Women's Policy Research.

Sparrow, S., Balla, D. A., & Cicchetti, D. V. (1984). *Vineland Adaptive Behavior Behaviors Scales: Interview edition. Survey form manual.* Circle Pines, MN: American Guidance Service.

Sparrow, S., & Cicchetti, D. V. (1985). Diagnostic uses of the Vineland Adaptive Behavior Scales. *Journal of Pediatric Psychology, 10,* 215–225.

Spencer, M. B., Blumenthal, J. B., & Richards, E. (1997). Child care and children of color. In P. L. Chase-Lansdale & J. Brooks-Gunn (Eds.), *Escape from poverty: What makes a difference for children?* (pp. 138–156). New York: Cambridge University Press.

Spieker, S. J., & Bensley, L. (1994). Roles of living arrangements and grandmother social support in adolescent mothering and infant attachment. *Developmental Psychology, 30*(1), 102–111.

Spieker, S. J., Bensley, L., McMahon, R. J., Fung, H., & Ossiander, E. (1996). Sexual abuse as a factor in child maltreatment by adolescent mothers of preschool aged children. *Development and Psychopathology, 8*(3), 497–509.

Stacey, W., & Shupe, A. (1983). *The family secret.* Boston: Beacon.

Strauss, A. (1987). *Qualitative analysis for social scientists.* New York: Cambridge University Press.

Strawn, J. (1992). The states and the poor: Child poverty rises as the safety net shrinks. *Social Policy Report: Society for Research in Child Development, 6,* 1–19.

Sugar, M. (1993). Adolescent motherhood and development. In M. Sugar (Ed.), *Female adolescent development* (2nd ed., pp. 213–230). New York: Bruner/Mazel.

Sugarman, D., & Hotaling, G. (1989). Dating violence: Prevalence, context, and risk markers. In M. A. Pirog-Good & J. E. Stets (Eds.), *Violence in dating relationships: Emerging social issues* (pp. 3–32). New York: Praeger.

Sullivan, M. L. (1989). Absent fathers in the inner city. *Annuals of the American Academy of Political and Social Science, 501,* 48–58.

Tardy, C. H. (1985). Social support measures. *American Journal of Community Psychology, 13,* 187–202.

Testa, M., & Krogh, M. (1995). The effect of employment on marriage among black males in inner-city Chicago. In M. B. Tucker & C. Mitchell-Kernan (Eds.), *The decline in marriage among African Americans: Causes, consequences, and policy implications* (pp. 59–95). New York: Russell Sage.

Trent, K., & Harlan, S. L. (1994). Teenage mothers in nuclear and extended households: Differences by marital status and race/ethnicity. *Journal of Family Issues, 15,* 309–337.

Tucker, C. B., Brady, B. A., Harris, Y. R., Fraser, K., & Tribble, I. (1993). The association of selected parent behaviors with the adaptive and maladaptive functioning of Black children and White children. *Child Study Journal, 23,* 39–55.

Tucker, M. B., & Mitchell-Kernan, C. (1995). Trends in African-American family formation: A theoretical and statistical overview. In M. B. Tucker & C. Mitchell-Kernan (Eds.), *The decline in marriage among African Americans: Causes, consequences, and policy implications* (pp. 3–26). New York: Russell Sage.

Unger, D. G., & Cooley, M. (1992). Partner and grandmother contact in Black and White teen parent families. *Journal of Adolescent Health, 13,* 546–552.

Unger, D. G., & Wandersman, L. P. (1988). The relation of family and partner support to the adjustment of adolescent mothers. *Child Development, 59,* 1056–1060.

Upchurch, D. M. (1993). Early schooling and childbearing experiences: Implications for postsecondary school attendance. *Journal of Research on Adolescence, 3,* 423–443.

Upchurch, D. M., & McCarthy, J. (1990). The timing of a first birth and high school completion. *American Sociological Review, 55,* 224–243.

U.S. Bureau of the Census. (1990). Who's minding the kids? Child care arrangements: 1986–87. *Current Population Reports* (Series P-70, No. 20). Washington, DC: U.S. Government Printing Office.

U.S. Senate Committee on the Judiciary. (1990). *Ten facts about violence against women.* Washington, DC: U.S. Senate Committee on the Judiciary Hearings on Women and Violence, 78.

Vera, E. M., Reese, E. R., Paikoff, R. L., & Jarrett, R. L. (1996). Contextual factors of sexual risk-taking in urban African-American preadolescent children. In B. J. Leadbeater & N. Way (Eds.), *Urban girls: Resisting stereotypes, creating identities* (pp. 291–304). New York: New York University Press.

Verhlst, F. C., & van der Ende, J. (1992). Six-year stability of parent-reported problem behavior in an epidemiological sample. *Journal of Abnormal Child Psychology, 20,* 595–610.

Voran, M., & Phillips, D. (1993). Correlates of grandmother childcare support to adolescent mothers: Implications for development in two generations of women. *Children and Youth Services Review, 15,* 321–334.

Wadia, A. S. (1997). *Assisting low-income women entrepreneurs: Lessons from the programs of the Ms. Foundation for women.* Ms. Foundation for Women.

Walker, L. (1979). *The battered woman.* New York: Harper & Row.

Wasserman, G. A., Rauh, V. A., Brunelli, S. A., Garcia-Castro, M., & Necos, B. (1990). Psychosocial attributes and life experiences of disadvantaged minority mothers: Age and ethnic variations. *Child Development, 61,* 566–580.

Watson, B. J., Rowe, C. L., & Jones, D. J. (1989). Dispelling myths about teenage pregnancy and male responsibility: A research agenda. *Urban League Review,* (Summer–Winter), 119–127.

Way, N., & Leadbeater, B. J. (1999). Pathways toward educational achievement among African-American and Puerto Rican adolescent mothers: Re-examining the role of social support from families. *Development and Psychopathology, 11,* 349–364.

Way, N., & Stauber, H. (1996). Are "absent fathers" really absent? Urban girls speak out about their fathers. In B. J. Leadbeater & N. Way (Eds.), *Urban girls: Resisting stereotypes, creating identities* (pp. 132–148). New York: New York University Press.

Wekerle, G. R. (1997). The shift to the market: Gender and housing disadvantage. In P. M. Evans & G. R. Wekerle (Eds.), *Women and the Canadian welfare state: Challenges and change* (pp. 170–194). Toronto: University of Toronto Press.

Werner, E. E. (1993). Risk, resilience, and recovery: Perspectives from the Kauai longitudinal study. *Development and Psychopathology, 5*(4), 503–515.

Werner, E. E., & Smith, R. S. (1982). *Vulnerable but invincible: A longitudinal study of resilient children and youth.* New York: McGraw-Hill.

Werner, E. E., & Smith, R. S. (1992). *Overcomimg the odds: High risk children from birth to adulthood.* Ithaca, NY: Cornell University Press.

William T. Grant Foundation. (1988). *The forgotten half: Pathways to success for America's youth and young families.* Washington, DC: Author.

Wilson, K., Vercella, R., Brems, C., Benning, D., & Renfro, N. (1992). Levels of learned helplessness in abused women. *Women and Therapy, 13*(4), 53–67.

Wilson, W. J. (1987). *The truly disadvantaged: The inner city, the underclass, and public policy.* Chicago: University of Chicago Press.

Wilson, W. J. (1995). *Jobless ghettos: The disappearance of work and its effect on urban life.* New York: Knopf.

Wilson, W. J., & Aponte, R. (1987). Urban poverty: A state-of-the-art review of the literature. In W. J. Wilson (Ed.), *The truly disadvantaged: The inner city, the underclass, and public policy* (pp. 165–187). Chicago: University of Chicago Press.

Wolf, D. A., & Sonenstein, F. L. (1991). Child-care use among welfare mothers: A dynamic analysis. *Journal of Family Issues, 12*(4), 519–536.

Wolkind, S. N., Zajicek-Coleman, E., & Ghodsian, M. (1980). Continuities in maternal depression. *International Journal of Family Psychiatry, 1,* 167–182.

Wright, M. O., Masten, A. S., Northwood, A., & Hubbard, J. J. (1997). Long-term effects of massive trauma: Developmental and psychobiological perspectives. In D. Cicchetti & S. L. Toth (Eds.), *Rochester Symposium on Developmental Psychopathology: Vol. 8. The effects of trauma on the developmental process* (pp. 181–225). Rochester, NY: University of Rochester Press.

Yoshikawa, H., & Seidman, E. (1999). Competence among urban adolescents in poverty: Multiple forms, contexts, and developmental processess. In R. Montemayor, G. R. Adams, & R. P. Gullotta (Eds.), *Advances in adolescent development: Vol. 10. Cultural and economic diversity in adolescent development* (pp. 9–42). Thousand Oaks, CA: Sage.

Yoshikawa, H., Seidman, E., Allen, L., Aber, J. L., & Friedman, J. (1997). *Multidimensional profiles of competence among urban adolescents in poverty.* Manuscript in preparation.

Zahn-Waxler, C., Iannotti, R. J., Cummings, E. M., & Denham, S. (1990). Antecedents of problem behaviors in children of depressed mothers. *Development and Psychopathology, 2,* 271–291.

Zaslow, M. J., & Eldred, C. A. (Eds.). (1998). *Parenting behavior in a sample of young mothers in poverty: Results of the New Chance observational study.* New York: Manpower Demonstration Research Corporation.

Zaslow, M. J., Moore, K. A., Morrison, D. R., & Coiro, M. J. (1998). The Family Support Act and children: Potential pathways of influence. *Children and Youth Services Review, 17,* 231–249.

Zaslow, M. J., Tout, K., Smith, S., & Moore, K. (1998). Implications of the 1996 welfare legislation for children: A research perspective. *Society for Research in Child Development: Social Policy Report, 12,* 1–35.

Zelizer, V. A. (1985). *Pricing the priceless child: The changing social value of children.* New York: Basic Books.

Zelnik, M., & Kanter, J. F. (1978). First pregnancies to women aged 15–19: 1976 and 1971. *Family Planning Perspectives, 10,* 11–20.

Zill, N., Moore, K. A., Nord, C. W., & Steif, T. (1991). *Welfare mothers as potential employees: A statistical profile based on national survey data.* Washington, DC: Child Trends.

Zill, N., Moore, K. A., Smith, E. W., Stief, T., & Coiro, M. J. (1997). The life circumstances and development of children in welfare families: A profile based on national survey data. In P. L. Chase-Lindsay & J. Brooks-Gunn (Eds.), *Escape from poverty: What makes a difference for children?* (pp. 38–59). Cambridge, NY: Cambridge University Press.

Zill, N., & Nord, C. W. (1994). *Running in place: How American families are faring in a changing economy and an individualistic society* . Washington, DC: Child Trends.

Zuravin, D. J., & DiBlasio, F. A. (1992). Child-neglecting adolescent mothers: How do they differ from their non-maltreating counterparts? *Journal of Interpersonal Violence, 7,* 471–489.

Zuroff, D. C., Moskowitz, D. S., Wielgus, M. S., Powers, T. A., & Franko, D. L. (1983). Construct validation of the Dependency and Self-Criticism scales of the Depressive Experiences Questionnaire. *Journal of Research in Personality, 17,* 226–241.

Zuroff, D. C., Quinlan, D. M., & Blatt, S. J. (1990). Psychometric properties of the Depressive Experiences Questionnaire. *Journal of Personality Assessment, 55,* 65–72.

Author Index

Subject Index